ENI

Well, I just finished reading *Breaking Hell's Economy*—and I am honestly amazed at the depth I found in this book! In addition to being written in a captivating and masterful way, it is absolutely loaded with insights that will make it well worth the time for anyone who reads this book. For sure, it is a book that will make you think. Chapter after chapter, I found myself saying, This is remarkable! I encourage you to devour it, for it is material that comes from the spirit, mind, and pen of a genuine prophetic voice who speaks soberly, soundly, and profoundly about the days to come and what we as the Church must-believe and do in this season. I am personally excited about Joseph Z's ministry—I believe his is a ministry to pay attention to, both now and in the days to come.

Rick Renner
Author, minister, and broadcaster
Moscow, Russia

Joseph Z covers a very important subject for the body of Christ in this hour. We must live in the light of redemption and the blessing of the Lord. The earth is the Lord's and the fullness thereof, and we are heirs of God and joint heirs with Christ.

Mark Hankins
Mark Hankins Ministries
Markhankins.org

You need to read *Breaking Hell's Economy!* Its profound insights and practical guidance on how to prosper God's way during these unprecedented times are essential reading. Joseph Z is a leading prophetic voice to our generation in government, church, and the marketplace. I have had the great honor of ministering many times alongside Joseph, coast to coast and around the world, as well as being a close personal friend. I have seen him prosper supernaturally while using finances to glorify God in ministry, in business, and in his family. That's why I encourage you to read this book, because when you apply its principles by faith, you'll break hell's economy in your life once and for all and start living in the Lord's abundant financial freedom!

Ashley Terradez
President and founder, Terradez Ministries International and Global Church Family

A fantastic book by author and man of God, Joseph Z. He has certainly done all his homework and handles the scripture with precision. The world and Satan preach a distorted mindset that seeks to imprison us in poverty. *Breaking Hell's Economy* is the truth to break that off a generation of believers, ushering us into a "kingdom of God" mindset to resource the message of the gospel.

I recommend this book to anyone seeking to step deeper into the financial principles of the kingdom of God and to see the curse of poverty broken off of them and their seed.

Jason Anderson
Pastor, Living Word Church
Mesa Arizona

What great hindsight, insight, and foresight Joseph Z has given us through the lens of God's Word concerning our financial covenant.

From the prophets, psalms, proverbs, parables, and numerous references to Scripture, the financial dots are connected for us to understand our past, present, and future position of God's economic plan for us.

True enrichment comes from the blessing of the Lord, with rest and contentment in knowing that it all comes from him.

Proverbs 10:22 TPT

Pastor Gregory Pope
Covenant Church
Douglas, Georgia

Joseph Z is one of the best teachers of the Word I have ever heard! This book is not just truth but revealed knowledge. It's a *now word* for this generation. God is ready to break people free—if you read this with faith, breakthrough will certainly happen in your life!

Ryan Edberg
Conference speaker, author, founder of Kingdom Youth Conference

I have known Joseph for well over 30 years. We have ministered together countless times, and from the beginning of our friendship I have seen Joseph push back the gates of hell and take ground for the kingdom of God. *Breaking Hell's Economy* will provide you with insight and revelation to who you really are in Christ and that you can have God's economy on this side of heaven. Each chapter is powerful, but I especially enjoyed Chapter Three where Joseph wrote, *"Jesus slapped sin and death around, then threw them all out of their own party!"*

Joseph has impacted my life through his teachings and has imparted more revelation to me than anyone I have ever met. Not only is he a great prophet, teacher, and author, he is also a great family man and friend. This book will break the strongholds of lack and poverty off your mind that have been holding you back from your full potential. Get ready to thrive in the last days! I wholeheartedly recommend *Breaking Hell's Economy!* It's a must read!

Joshua Ercoli
President of Souled Out International

This book has stirred me up! I believe *Breaking Hell's Economy* should be required reading for every believer as they navigate the times we are living in. Joseph has a very unique set of prophetic gifts that I really appreciate. It sets him apart and over-qualifies him to write about difficult subjects. Prophets have a deep gift of revelation but at times can be hard for the rest of us to follow. However, Joseph also is a very gifted teacher! He explains deep revelation in a way we can all understand it clearly. He additionally has a healthy and complete revelation of grace, which is not common among many prophets. What Joseph has written is not only informative, but it leaves the reader hopeful for their future.

Ben Diaz
Pastor, Word of Life Church
Mesa, Arizona

From the very first moment I met Joseph, I realized that he was a minister like no other. He carries power and passion with a drive that is fused with compassion. He has a genuine love for God and His people. The ministry that Joseph and Heather have built is one of the most impactful, loving, and excellent I've ever seen. They do everything with excellence and this book is no exception. I know that the revelations in this book will be life changing for you and also everyone around you. These revelations will be the roadmap to achieving godly financial freedom. During the last days, a choice will be presented to the church: "Serve God or serve mammon," and this book gives you heavenly insight, tools, and proof of how choosing to serve God is the best financial decision someone can make. Let the revelations in this book be ammunition against the enemy in this day and age.

Javier Macias
Evangelist, pastor, prophetic voice to generation Z

Joseph, Heather, and Z Ministries have had an impact on my family *way* before I read the words contained in this book. *Breaking Hell's Economy* is a spiritual lifestyle and a mindset, not just a concept. It took me *years* to figure out that God desires His kids to live in spiritual abundance, and a byproduct of that is abundance here in this life! Joseph not only *lives* these words but has the *fruit* to back it up. Get ready to have your spiritual dynamic *lit up* and begin to bear fruit in your life...like our family and ministry has!

Massey Campos
President, Self-Evident Ministries
Assistant Pastor, Revive Church

Wow! After hearing so much of Joseph's teaching for many years I was expecting an excellent literary work, but *Breaking Hell's Economy* is next level. This book will challenge you, test you, possibly offend you at points—at the very least it will provoke you to a change of heart. Prepare for a mindset change as you break through religion's barriers and walk into supernatural abundance. As you go through each chapter and act on what you learn, I believe your mindset will change, limitations will move, and a revelation of your position in the corporate body of Christ will become clearer. You will gain understanding of the blessing versus mammon and powerful insights regarding the true wealth of Jesus. This book will assist in positioning you for the coming wealth transfer and even help you navigate the promised persecution when biblical increase happens in your life.

Joseph is not only a brilliant writer, he has also given us a brilliant message in *Breaking Hell's Economy* that is so needed for this moment in the last days. It has been my honor to be a part of Z Ministries and to have worked with Joseph Z for so many years. I know no other man who has more integrity and who loves the Word of God more than him.

David J. Pollock
CEO of Z Ministries
Developer, consultant, ministry pilot

BREAKING
HELL'S
ECONOMY

YOUR GUIDE TO LAST-DAYS
SUPERNATURAL PROVISION

JOSEPH Z

Harrison House

Shippensburg, PA

Published by Harrison House Publishers
Shippensburg, PA 17257

ISBN 13 TP: 978-1-6803-1944-6

ISBN 13 eBook: 978-1-6803-1945-3

For Worldwide Distribution, Printed in the U.S.A.

4 5 6 7 8 / 26 25 24 23 22

DEDICATION

I would like to dedicate this book to the partners of our ministry. For years, so many wonderful individuals have sensed the call of God to stand with us financially and in prayer. Through the support of these wonderful partners, we have traveled the nations, held conferences, ministered to global leaders, and reached masses of people with the gospel. Partners have stood with us as we stepped out in new media ventures, the building of multiple studios, and even supporting the vision of a small aircraft. Through the support of our partners, we have had the ability to pay our own way when traveling to churches and conferences, requiring nothing for the preaching of the gospel. As a direct result of these precious ones who have aligned with us, we have reached millions through nearly every available means of broadcasting.

Heather and I, our two children Alison and Daniel, as well as our staff and team, wish to honor our partners. We thank each one for their tremendous support that they have shown over these many years. The truths in this book are, in part, filled with a desire to see our partners receive the fullness of what God has made available to them. In the times ahead, I believe those who have stood with us, and continue to do so, will reap supernatural benefits causing them to rise and shine in the middle of dark times. Our partners have been with us through thick and thin; without them this project would not be a reality.

We are honored by their commitment to Jesus and their dedication to the assignment He has given us to accomplish. Together I believe we will fulfill our part in the great commission. From the depth of my heart, thank you, partners.

> *Finally, brethren, pray for us, that the word of the Lord may run swiftly and be glorified, just as it is with you.*
>
> —2 Thessalonians 3:1

In the service of Jesus,
Joseph Z

ACKNOWLEDGEMENTS

My beautiful wife, Heather, and my two adult children, Alison and Daniel. You are my best friends. Thank you for your constant support while writing this book and the many projects like it that you assist me in every day. I love each one of you. You are my world.

My mom, Sherry Gazelka. For the years of prayer and encouragement. Thank you for standing when others could not. I appreciate your gift of discernment and advice. I love you and honor you.

Heather's mom, Betty Eatmon. Your example of being a godly lady, combined with the wisdom you share, has been a tremendous source of strength over the years.

I would like to thank our team, both past and present—we would not be where we are today without this wonderful group of dedicated individuals. Some of you we have access to daily in our offices, while others work from states away and even internationally. Each one of you is a blessing to Heather and I. Your value is beyond words.

A very special thank you to Dave and Robyn Pollock. Thank you for the discussions and research that ultimately became the foundation of this book! I also honor you for what you bring to the table every day—both for our lives personally and for our entire staff and team. When you followed the leading of the Lord to come on board, everything began producing at a whole new level. This ministry would not be where it is without you. We love you and thank you.

Thank you to Jason and Stephanie Chandler! Sometimes I think you have believed in my projects and ministry even more than I do! You are some of the finest friends and co-laborers. Thank you for all the days and sacrifices you have poured out before the Lord to see this vision happen. We would not be in this season without you. We love you and your family. You have gone from one of the largest national crop-harvesting outfits to being harvesters of souls! Thank you for your friendship and your belief.

Josh and Mary Ercoli. Thank you for standing with us through thick and thin for over three decades! "I know you too, Josh." Thank you both for all the encouragement and Holy Spirit companionship you both have brought to our lives. A huge thank you to Mary Ercoli for the hours she spent looking over and adjusting the final edits of this manuscript.

Ashley and Carlie Terradez. You are tremendous friends both on the platform and off. We love you and your family. Thank you for your encouragement toward this project! You guys are gold and the impact you are making around the world is only the beginning. Here's to the next coffee and a walk!

Ryan and Jenny Edberg. You have been such a source of encouragement. We have enjoyed building the kingdom with you for the past two decades. From meetings in northern Minnesota, to the jungles of Jamaica, it has been a wild ride! Thank you for being our friends through some unbelievable journeys. The best is yet to come!

John and Dannah Bretz, for your ever-present and unconditional love and support. Thank you for being there; this project is a result of the endless encouragement you have shown us. We love you and your amazing family!

Mark and Trina Hankins. Your friendship, example, and encouragement have made a great impact on our lives. I get stirred to advance God's economy every time I'm around you. You have been a major source of inspiration for this book. Mark, you really are the OG of camp meetings!

Rick Renner. Your example, teachings, and written work have made a life-altering impact on me for decades. Every time I sit down to write, I am reminded of you and the way God works through you. Thank you for building a legacy of written work that the body of Christ will glean from for generations to come. Parts of this book were possible because of your teaching.

Gene and Teri Bailey, thank you for being a leading voice in this season of prophetic journalism. Your tenacity to tell the truth in a world pretending to be deaf is a high calling. So many of us have benefited from the path you have forged. You both are an inspiration and a wonderful example. Thank you for being our friends!

Holly Eide, for the countless hours of editing and giving this book your undivided attention. Thank you for taking on this project; you are a miracle worker!

Brad Herman, you were instrumental in making this project a reality. Your tremendous team at Harrison House and Destiny Image family have greatly encouraged us in this endeavor. It's a privilege working with such wonderful people—thank you!

Kyle Loffelmacher. You are an agent of God, my friend! Divine appointments follow you everywhere you go! Thank you for your belief and encouragement in this process! Many of the doors and opportunities we have experienced in this season are due to you being led by the Holy Spirit.

Finally, all our friends and supporters, near and far. Thank you for your belief and thank you for standing with us. We love you.

CONTENTS

FOREWORD

J oseph Z has become a valued friend and brother in Christ to me. His wisdom, humility, and insight are rare in these times. Joseph's personal story shows his total commitment to the Lord and integrity of his motives in every aspect of his life. He is an exhorter and a reformer. He's chosen God's way and not the world's. Very few of us have had the opportunity to choose earthly abundance or to live totally relying on our faith in God. We talk a big talk, but many waver when the choice is staring them in the face.

In this book, you'll finally capture the real reason for financial gain. Yes, we need to live free of debt. But the truth is we are in a culture war of biblical proportions and the urgency to change our nation, our cities, our families, and our freedoms is at stake. Read on and discover your "why" and your "place" in this war of the ages. In these pages you will be encouraged by Joseph and catch his inspiring spirit.

As you read, look for the two things that make God rich. The answer might just surprise you!

Gene Bailey
Author and host of *Flashpoint*

PREFACE

I was inspired to write this book as a source of hope and inspiration, drawn directly from the scriptures as well as historical scenarios. My desire is for this prophetic message of hope to ignite revelation within you for what could be. Next to the revelation, I long for the spirit of might to awaken within you. For this generation desperately needs those who will stand up to the darkness rising. The driving force behind every page ahead is a response to the mindset of this generation. Truth, justice, and standing up for what is right are very convoluted topics today. In the church, so many in this upcoming generation have very little grasp, if any, of the Bible. Additionally, there is a culture war we are being dragged into. It is a war over ideals and affects the very souls of our children's children. So many before us fought for a better tomorrow, only to see this present generation walk all over their sacrifice. Responsibility lies at the feet of both a weak church and a permissive society that has allowed the lawless spirit of antichrist to run wild.

Where there is no vision, the people perish: but he that keepeth the law, happy is he.

—Proverbs 29:18, KJV

Fist-shaking or cursing the darkness has never been a productive response when dealing with a brainwashed culture. Add a church that is faint of heart and is only a shadow of what Jesus intended for it to be. The highest response is to point to something magnificent—a future of hope and a seemingly impossible vision of what we could have. I have a desire to remind the people of God where they come from and what *could be,* if they only stand up and take it!

We are living in a time after generals of faith and when many heroes from history are gone and largely remembered no more. I'm reminded of Exodus 1:8 where it speaks of a new king who came into power *who did not know Joseph.* The very people who were rescued and made a strong nation, because of a great man of God, had no memory of him. If we do not know the foundation of a thing, we are destined to disrespect it or disregard it.

I believe this book will reignite what was forgotten or start a fire by a revelation of what could be! *Breaking Hell's Economy* is the result of searching out details from history regarding the life of Jesus, what He did, and why He did it. While uncovering historical evidence about His childhood and the wealth He received, I was moved by the Holy Spirit to look at the possibilities Jesus made available to His church.

Many things have come to light while working on this book, such as the potential of a worldwide, once-in-a-lifetime wealth transfer, but discovering the who, why, and how is the fascinating part.

From the truths and information I lay out in this book, a conviction to accomplish the will of God has risen up in me. A conviction to impact this culture and establish my God-ordained place in this global superpower also known as the body of Christ. I believe much of what is in the pages of this book is a revelation that will be largely "caught" not only taught.

The only way to induce change in people is to give them an encounter they cannot deny and show them a glimpse of a future they want to be a part of. By the end of this book, I pray conviction and a burning sense of purpose begin to rise within you, and that you would begin to stand in what God has prepared for you. Together we can change the world; together as one corporate body we can break hell's economy.

INTRODUCTION

We are in the last of the last days. As the wars and rumors of wars increase, it is vital to know that you are not the first generation to experience world-shaking events, but you might be the last. Preparation is in order. First you must know that throughout history, God has always positioned His people as a light in darkness. Second, the very foundation of provision and thriving in a dark world will be due to understanding what Jesus provided for you. This goes all the way back to His childhood.

There is a special weapon of provision God provides for those who choose Him over the comforts of this life. This applies to those who have left all for the sake of the gospel. This is a weapon that should be greatly considered for the days ahead. It is a promise directly from Jesus that offers sustainability through something as catastrophic as a global economic meltdown, as you'll read!

I am living proof of this principle as before the age of 13, a choice was presented to me. My parents were divorced while I was very young, and my mom served the Lord. Through her faith and the faith of her parents, my life was impacted by encounter after encounter with the

Holy Spirit. This was unacceptable to my father, who wanted a much different path for me.

A day came when a choice was presented: follow Jesus or be part of everything my father had, which included cattle, land, real estate, and a future inheritance with a large financial benefit. My father and his family were very well off. We owned a ranch bordered by a large beautiful river. My father was adamantly against me going to church and openly confessing Jesus was my Savior. The issue was, I had encountered God for real! It was undeniable—to walk away from Jesus for property and provision would have been much like the story of the rich young ruler.

I couldn't deny all the Lord had done in my life leading up to this decision. Upon saying to my father, "I choose to follow Jesus," after a very difficult conversation, we got in the car and left the property. He dropped me off at my mother's house. That was one of the last three times I saw my father before he died.

I share this story with you, dear reader, to let you know that God has taken care of me in unbelievable and supernatural ways since those early days in my life and continuing in my adult years. Anyone who will completely throw themselves onto Jesus, forsaking everything that stands in the way, will have a special place with the Father God. He will make Himself responsible for your life. This can apply in a variety of areas. Whenever you seek first His kingdom and give Him your all, supernatural provision will happen in your life. Also, you will experience an unfair advantage when it comes to accessing God's economy. Make no mistake about it—the Lord your God will watch over you and He will fiercely protect you.

When it comes to all the potential terrors this world will eventually unleash, I must say, in no way do you have to live under a sense of dread. Rather, the pages of this book will offer information that brings peace.

A person with a revelation from God is never at the mercy of a culture gone mad.

Much like manna in the wilderness or water from the rock, it is the supernatural provision of God that will sustain His people. You are called to thrive in the middle of dark days. Elijah had ravens provide for him and Peter basically had a fish pay his taxes. This world's system will crumble and, should Jesus tarry, you will need to know what the Lord has made available for you.

Breaking Hell's Economy is a now word for you to declare war and have victory, not over a location but over a system. Hell's economy is a system designed to steal, kill, and destroy. Jesus referred to this system as "the gates of hell" when speaking to Peter. The "gates of hell" represent (among other things) a system driven by the spirit of the age—a demonic luciferin system.

The apostle John wrote about the power that overcomes this system—our faith! *"Every God-born person conquers the world's ways. The conquering power that brings the world to its knees is our faith"* (1 John 5:4 MSG). The Greek word for "world" is *kosmos*, which means system. Another way of saying it is, "Our faith is the power that brings the world's system to its knees!"

There is a system of darkness in the world. It is Hell's system; its economy is attempting to keep you in a place of fear and compliance with the spirit of the age that fearfully says, "You'll never have enough." Hell's economy is a dependence on self, self-reliance, and this world's system.

Through what you learn in this book, you are going to unleash punishment on the kingdom of darkness. We are going to establish the foundation of why Jesus was wealthy, for what purpose, and what He ultimately did with it. The answer might shock you! Darkness has never been a match for Jesus; it is also no match for you with a revelation of Jesus functioning within you. It is imperative that you as a believer in

Jesus are equipped for the days we are dramatically plunging into. Additionally, by our faith, and if the body of Christ can rise to the occasion, there is a once-in-history, conditional wealth transfer being prepared for these last days. It is a corporate anointing, not for one person but also for the whole body of Christ! By doing your part in this earth, along with the greater body of believers, it is very possible that the greatest financial upset in history could happen.

There are levels you can break Hell's economy in your life—thirty, sixty, and up to a hundredfold. It is my desire for you to walk in such a revelation that you will break out at one hundredfold. You were born for this hour! It's time to advance the gospel of Jesus Christ, causing it to reach every person. You are part of the answer this world is looking for. You are called to shine the light of God into this world. You are anointed to set your loved ones free, and you are destined to *Break Hell's Economy!*

Section 1

LIGHT IN DARKNESS

Chapter One

THE LIGHT IN GOSHEN

Then the Lord said to Moses, "Stretch out your hand toward
heaven, that there may be darkness over the land of Egypt,
darkness which may even be felt." So Moses stretched out
his hand toward heaven, and there was thick darkness
in all the land of Egypt three days. They did not see one
another; nor did anyone rise from his place for three days.
But all the children of Israel had light in their dwellings.

—**Exodus 10:21-23**

In Goshen there was blood on the doorposts repelling the invasive darkness. Today it is the blood of Jesus which repels the system of hell. The darkness we are facing in the coming days will be so great that it very well may once again be felt. This growing darkness is supernatural, palpable, and demonic. It will impact every aspect of society and, should Jesus tarry in His return, every living person will not be able to avoid being impacted by it. Yet the answer always remains the same! Even Isaiah, in chapter 60, speaks of a deep darkness that would cover the earth.

This reference is, among other things, prophetic of what is to come—deep darkness that covers the land. It was darkness that covered the face of the deep in Genesis, and the response by God was light! Darkness has repeatedly been a presence throughout scripture, even to the point

Joshua needed a miracle to stop the enemy from escaping under the cover of darkness.

Joshua spoke to the sun to stand still, once again putting off the darkness. As a result, Joshua was able to finish off the enemy. When Jesus gave up His life on the cross, darkness covered the land; three days later His resurrection followed.

Going to the very first chapter of the Book of John, we can see that Jesus is referred to as the Light of the World. He is the first born among many brethren. This means Christ in us, the hope of glory, truly is a continuation of His light in the world. As He is, so are we in this world! In Matthew 5:14, Jesus, when speaking to the disciples, declared, "You are the light of the world. A city that is set on a hill cannot be hidden." Again, references to light dispelling darkness. First John even refers to God as Light. Not that He has light, but rather that He is Light and there is no trace of darkness in Him.

Whenever you see references to darkness and light in the scriptures, it is often referring to the knowledge or understanding a person is working in. It takes knowledge and understanding to activate revelation! A revelation is knowledge revealed to your spirit and discerned by your renewed mind. Those who walk in the light as He is in the light will have the supernatural ability to radiate in the darkness. This greatly applies to the area of provision. As darkness covers the earth, it cannot and will not be able to alter the promises of God! The words "Never will I leave you; never will I forsake you" are more potent during times of difficulty. In the midst of the dark agenda to steal, kill, and destroy, the light will rise up and darkness will not overcome it.

Darkness That Could Be Felt

Going back to Exodus 10, we notice that it says in verse 21, it was a "darkness which may even be felt." It was black like ink to the point "they did not see one another; nor did anyone rise from...their dwellings." In other words, they were "locked down."

Darkness that could be "felt" as represented in Exodus 10 is evil and supernatural. It would be accompanied by a sense of fear, leaving those under its influence terrified from being unable to see one another. This fearful environment, with limited communication, would create a sense of isolation.

The passage in Exodus also gives insight into how terrible it must have been. The darkness was so present and demobilizing that no one would attempt to rise from their dwellings. Those in Egypt were completely stranded by fear, sitting in one position encompassed by the weighty blackness. What a horrifying experience this must have been for the Egyptians. This narrative that the children of Israel experienced in Egypt is something to consider when looking at our present time. There are parallels to our modern culture. Currently this society's path is leading to the deepest darkness ever experienced since Exodus 10.

Horrid darkness plagued Egypt, not only in the form of a nighttime phenomenon, but it was also far worse. Darkness wasn't only present during the night hours; it was present throughout the day as well. Imagine it—intense blackness, morning, noon, and night! The darkness was present at 1 o'clock in the afternoon, just as black and thick as it was at midnight. There was no escape, no reprieve, nothing but the all-encompassing pitch-black darkness. No natural light could penetrate this veil of torment. It was a spiritual force, demonic, and inescapable.

Many voices from generations before our time have predicted terrible days of darkness and unprecedented evil in the form of global difficulties, ultimately arriving at the Great Tribulation. In many ways, it will be similar in nature to the tangible darkness that covered ancient Egypt, only this darkness will be far more sinister. It will be a darkness that impacts every part of society and, rather than blanketing the land of Egypt, this time it will cover the entire earth. One day this prophetic understanding of tribulation will manifest as a global crisis according to the Book of Revelation. Many believe that during those days it will be impossible for anyone to escape the horrors and darkness of that time. This experience, however, does not have to be the case for you if you have ears to hear it.

LIGHT IN THEIR DWELLINGS

Although the world is willingly and rapidly plunging into modern darkness, there is great hope and answers. The real church of the Lord Jesus Christ will rise to meet this oncoming darkness!

Egypt is a representation of the world and its system. When darkness struck the land and its ungodly culture, Egypt became completely crippled, locked down, and in a state of utter dread.

In Goshen, the experience was very different. The people of God did not experience the same things the Egyptians did. They likely could see the darkness—it is also possible they could sense the heaviness and terror of the Egyptians—but they had God on their side. There was no darkness within the houses of Goshen. At the very end of verse 23 in Exodus 10, we see something thrilling! "But all the children of Israel had light in their dwellings." This was no ordinary light! This Light the people of God possessed was supernatural! It shone in the darkness, in each of the dwellings of the righteous! Reminiscent of the Book of Revelation 21:23, "The city had no need of the sun or of the moon to shine in it, for the glory of God illuminated it. The Lamb is its light." It is this light of God that is present within God's people that dispels all demonic darkness.

As this world plummets further into a darkness scenario, we must embrace the revelation of "the Light in Goshen." This Light was in their personal dwelling. *This light is Jesus.*

> *To them God willed to make known what are the riches of the glory of this mystery among the Gentiles: which is Christ in you, the hope of glory.*
>
> —Colossians 1:27

A Corporate Anointing

> *The Lord loves the gates of Zion More than all the dwellings of Jacob.*
>
> —Psalm 87:2

Long have I believed that the potential for epic biblical prosperity, along with end-time wealth transfer, was never designed for only one individual. Rather, the magnitude of increase that is available lies in the possession of a unified body. On an individual level you can increase wildly. A person or family can certainly experience increase and wealth transfers that are mind blowing. Yet, when understanding the New Testament, God expresses the fullness of Jesus through what the Bible refers to as the body of Christ. As He is in this world, so are we. Not I, but we!

There is a corporate blessing, if understood as unity and oneness together, that actually represents one people/group in Jesus. We then could become the number one financial superpower in the world.

Jesus was the first born among many brethren. He wants His family to increase together. The ultimate idea of increase, and the abundance of the sea being turned toward us, was always about the body of Christ prospering on a corporate level.

Each dwelling has what they need to live, move, and have their being in Jesus. Each dwelling all together makes up the body of Christ. In Goshen, the children of Israel brought a unified light in darkness from their own dwellings!

> *The Lord loves the gates of Zion More than all the dwellings of Jacob.*
>
> —Psalm 87:2

The dwellings of Jacob speak of small individual gatherings—those individualistic groups that are scattered around the world. They praise the Lord; they possess their own culture. Each one is good; each dwelling has their own wonderful uniqueness. It needs to be considered that God desires something more. He wants a corporate body coming together. Notice it says the Lord loves the gates of Zion "more." It isn't that the Lord doesn't love the individual dwellings of Jacob; it's that He knows there is something so much better. Corporate purpose!

God loves when your home radiates His supernatural light. What He loves even more is when you take what you have at home and unite it together with all those around you in a corporate setting. This is how church is supposed to work. Even as churches, there should be a unified purpose and principle to lead the culture and stand as a force to be reckoned with. This is how light in darkness works. This is also how a revelation of God's provision works.

Psalm 133:1 says, "Behold, how good and how pleasant it is for brethren to dwell together in unity!"

A Revelation of the Wealth of Jesus

But seek first the kingdom of God and His righteousness, and all these things shall be added to you.

—Matthew 6:33

Jesus is the light in Goshen, along with all the covenant power that comes along with it. Hebrews 6:9 reads, "But, beloved, we are confident of better things concerning you, yes, things that accompany salvation."

Light additionally represents all that God is, and it is His delight that His servants prosper. For a full understanding of what this means, a person must attain a full understanding of what Jesus provided.

Before anyone can fully receive an end-time wealth transfer or have a hell-breaking experience to its fullness, it must be understood—Jesus personally broke the system of Hell, including its economy. Jesus himself was not "without" in any way; He certainly was not poor. Technically, He was wealthy beyond imagination when you consider His access to all the wealth of heaven.

Jesus was the prototype for you and me. He died on the cross and was resurrected so you would not have to be separated from God eternally. He took physical abuse and poured out His blood so that you might have healing and wholeness. Jesus became poor for your sake, so that through His poverty you might become rich. Knowledge of the wealth of Jesus can become a revelatory game changer; it will give you authority to step forward and unleash a palpable light into the darkness.

Jesus said to Peter, "Upon this rock I will build My church and the gates of hell will not prevail against it." John 1 speaks of the light that came into the world and darkness could not overcome it. Walking in a revelation that Jesus is the Son of God and the Messiah is the actual rock that Jesus was speaking to Peter about. Peter's name was changed from Simon to Rock/Peter as a prophetic example, but Peter himself is not the rock Jesus was referring to. Jesus did not mean that upon Peter the church would solely be built. Rather, He was referencing the revelation Peter attained from God, as you will read in the passage below.

> Simon Peter answered and said, "You are the Christ, the Son of the living God." Jesus answered and said to him, "Blessed are you, Simon Bar-Jonah, for flesh and blood has not revealed this to you, but My Father who is in heaven. And I also say to you that you are Peter, and on this rock I will build My church, and the gates of Hades shall not prevail against it. And I will give you the keys of the kingdom of heaven, and whatever you bind on earth will be bound in heaven, and whatever you loose on earth will be loosed in heaven."
>
> —Matthew 16:16-19

Jesus had just asked the disciples, "Who do people say that the Son of Man is?" Peter answered in verse 16 by saying, "You are the Christ, the Son of the living God." Jesus went on to explain to Peter that flesh and blood had not revealed this to him, but rather the Father in heaven.

This was a direct revelation from God. A revelation of what? That Jesus is the Christ, the Son of the living God. Upon changing Peter's name from Simon to Peter, or the Rock, Jesus added it was "upon this rock" (as if he was gesturing to Himself), a play on words, "that I will build My church."

The rock Jesus is referring to means a foundation piece to build a house upon—in this case the chief cornerstone, the stone the builders rejected. He was saying this is the absolute basic, immovable ground-work to the entire church. That Jesus is the Christ, the Son of God. Not only was the information necessary, but it also had to be a revelation in the form of revealed knowledge to them. It could be said that without this revelation a person is lost and certainly not a part of the church.

The notion that Jesus' comments were entirely directed at Peter has additional hurdles making it not plausible. Such as the many other qualified disciples and apostles who did as much or arguably more to develop the church and the gospel as Peter did. Paul, for example, or John who far outlived Peter would easily fall into the same category as Peter. In one instance, Paul had to confront and rebuke Peter in the sight of them all for compromising his stance on Gentile believers. Peter being corrected by Paul is yet another time we see them as equals. Peter's position was not the foundation of the whole church.

"Upon this rock" is the actual revelatory power that fuels the *ekklesia*, the called-out ones, the light in darkness, and the church of Jesus Christ. A revelation of Jesus is required in defeating the gates of hell. Through revelation, light shines on everything Jesus provided for us. This is an empowerment through knowing that we have been given the right to inherit every covenant blessing all the way back to Abraham. Knowing you have a right to manifest everything Jesus had, both individually and corporately, is sadly the best-kept secret in the history of the church.

John 1:12 says, "But as many as received him, to them gave he power to become sons of God" (KJV). *Sons* is a reference to inheritance. Those who "received Him" identify converts with their "fire insurance" policy intact. Sons are very different; they have full access and privilege to all the Father has.

REVELATION, NOT RELIGION

Sonship is about revelation, not religion. Only through knowing Jesus as a son or daughter can we experience the fullness of who He is and what He has. Sons are disciples of His Word; they are followers of the Lord and united with their brothers and sisters.

Converts are those who have received Him, yet they are drifting through this life operating in a low level of understanding. These individuals most often lack conviction, they lack purpose, and are not functioning in the revelation of Jesus. This is one of the greatest issues in the body of Christ today—converts not knowing what is provided for them and as a result they do not take their place in the corporate body. It is a loss for the body of Christ and a loss for the individual convert who has not developed into sonship.

In the following chapters, we are going to dive into the topic I call the wealth of Jesus, how it relates to you, and what it means for a potential end-time wealth transfer. This all makes more sense when you see it at the corporate level, rather than just the individual level. The "us four and no more" is good for a family and enjoying life, but to make disciples of nations and get the attention of the world, there needs to be an understanding of the corporate picture. It is the *ekklesia*, the corporate body of Christ, that the gates of hell will not prevail against.

UNBELIEVERS SHALL COME TO YOUR LIGHT

> *Therefore do not worry, saying, "What shall we eat?" or "What shall we drink?" or "What shall we wear?" For after all these things the Gentiles seek. For your heavenly Father knows that you need all these things.*
>
> —Matthew 6:31-32

The pages ahead will unveil a deeper understanding of the wealth of Jesus. You will realize that the byproduct of this revelation will act as a powerful magnet, placing a draw on the Gentiles and unbelievers.

Unbelievers do not have the capacity in their own natural ability to grasp who Jesus is. Therefore, we preach the gospel to them and believe for the lights to come on, leading them to repentance and into a relationship with Jesus. What Gentiles or unbelievers can grasp are natural things, material substance that meets their needs, things that bring them comfort and provision.

This is the very thing Jesus is speaking of in the Book of Matthew while instructing believers. Through His instruction, we learn that seeking material substance is the very opposite of what we as believers should be pursuing or worried about. For the believer, Jesus' instructions are to "seek first the kingdom of God and His righteousness, and all these things shall be added to you" (Matt. 6:33). Jesus gave us the plan for provision—it's Him. In Him we have everything that pertains to life and godliness. This really means that in Him we have it all!

On Display

They will be called oaks of righteousness, a planting of the Lord for the display of his splendor.

—Isaiah 61:3, NIV

When we exercise this revelation, we will arrive at a place of corporate display, "a planting of the Lord for the display of His splendor."

The fascinating part of this understanding is that the byproduct of believers who are seeking Jesus' provision is the very thing the Gentiles seek! Unbelievers have it backward—they work for things when Jesus says, "Come to Me, and I will give you rest." Strive for a living and then you can rest is their belief. Do whatever you can to get what you can, put it all in the can, and when you're done sit on your can! This is not the believer's way.

Most people work themselves, literally, to death! They work for their own provision, for things, for fun, and for money. This is the basis of hell's economy—Jesus referred to it as mammon.

> *No one can serve two masters; for either he will hate the one and love the other, or else he will be loyal to the one and despise the other. You cannot serve God and mammon.*
>
> **—Matthew 6:24**

Mammon is man's way of providing for themselves without God—by the sweat of their brow and toiling. Please don't misunderstand what I'm saying; hard work is a very good thing, but when it is implemented out of fear and in the pursuit of things alone, it is driven by mammon. Mammon is really idolatry against God's system. Jesus stood directly against mammon to enforce the amazing lengths God has gone through to give you a better system and economy.

> *A good man leaves an inheritance to his children's children, but the wealth of the sinner is stored up for the righteous.*
>
> **—Proverbs 13:22**

God's economy has an inheritance plan and a surprise wealth hidden away for those who enter His system. We are going to take a deeper look at the foundation of the wealth of Jesus. To know what you have available, you must grasp where Jesus began in His journey and the decisions He made for you and me.

In the next several chapters, we will explore what the wealth of Jesus looked like, what it means, and how it applies to you.

To have the fullness of this revelation and the accompanying yoke-breaking increase active in your life, the wealth of Jesus must be understood.

Chapter Two

WHEN THE WORLD COLLAPSES

So when the money failed in the land of Egypt and in the land of Canaan, all the Egyptians came to Joseph and said, "Give us bread, for why should we die in your presence? For the money has failed."

—Genesis 47:15

The world's system has crashed before—it will crash again.

What if one day you woke up to a world that was no longer a world the way you remember it? What if everything you banked on in the natural world was no longer part of the equation? No more economic security, no more job assurance, everything you thought would be there no longer remained. This was the case during the fall of 1929. In the days leading up to the greatest economic collapse in United States history, everything was going according to plan. After all, it was the Roaring Twenties. Children were in school, people working at their jobs, weddings, sports, and dinner with friends. Things were going very well in that 1920s economy. Some would say it was a booming economy right until the unthinkable happened. In a time span of a very few days, the once vibrant stock market suffered a collapse and would not regain its momentum until years later. Some sources say the Great Depression that followed the collapse lasted up to 25 years.

Very few were prepared for the devastating effects and the crippling economic picture of the United States. The financial devastation was felt around the world. Investors and many others who lost everything in the crash suffered immensely. There are stories of people jumping out of windows and off buildings, falling to their death. All their hope was lost.

My grandfather would speak of those days to me. He himself was a wealthy man, some of which came from knowing how to take steps forward after seeing his family navigate through the crisis. For some, the collapse was absolute dread. Others made the choice to go on living any way they could, making the best of what they had to work with. There were also great amounts of wealth that were made during those days by individuals who were positioned and knew how to use the catastrophe to their advantage. It was the average working person who suffered tremendously. Those who engaged in a hopeless scenario and ended their lives had placed their hope in man's economy. Ultimately, they were victims of Hell's economy.

God brought many people through that Great Depression. Throughout history, He has always been the answer to calamity, and He can take wonderful care of you during times of challenge.

As I said at the beginning of this chapter, the global economy has crashed before; it will crash again. It is only a matter of time. The great news is that when you engage God's economy, you will break Hell's economy off your life, and nothing can break you! You can literally thrive in the middle of the very worst situation Hell's system can throw at you, including another global financial crash—which is imminent.

The global economic story is destined to repeat. It doesn't take a rocket scientist to understand that the world's current economic situation cannot continue the way it is. It won't. There will be a day when it all comes to a halt one way or another. Does this mean all hope is lost and that humanity is done for? Of course not! What it means is that those who have their hopes and dreams all wrapped up in this world's ability to provide will suffer without hope.

You have a choice in the matter right now. You can begin to believe God and step completely into His economy, breaking Hell's economy off your life and future. When you go all in with the Lord, He will not be mocked. He will take responsibility for your needs. Remember, whatever you sow you will reap! Thankfully that doesn't mean only when things are going well. God's economy works all the time. Remember, it was dark in Egypt during the time of Moses, yet it was light in Goshen! This still applies today, tomorrow, and until the end of time.

One amazing real-life example of overcoming in a global economic crisis is found in the story of Joseph, contained in the Book of Genesis. Joseph's story is amazing for a variety of reasons, one of which is the way God used his life during a time of horrific famine that struck the known world. The story is remarkable as Joseph was positioned by God to save his people and the lives of countless others in the process. Joseph's story was filled with difficulty, and through his ability to not faint he was ultimately responsible for one of the greatest recorded wealth transfers in history.

The account of Joseph responding to the famine is listed in Genesis 41.

> *Then the seven years of plenty which were in the land of Egypt ended, and the seven years of famine began to come, as Joseph had said. The famine was in all lands, but in all the land of Egypt there was bread. So when all the land of Egypt was famished, the people cried to Pharaoh for bread. Then Pharaoh said to all the Egyptians, "Go to Joseph; whatever he says to*

you, do." The famine was over all the face of the earth, and
Joseph opened all the storehouses and sold to the Egyptians.
And the famine became severe in the land of Egypt. So all
countries came to Joseph in Egypt to buy grain, because the
famine was severe in all lands.

—**Genesis 41:53-57**

In Genesis 47:13-15, you see a wealth transfer in motion. Joseph gathered up all the money from the people purchasing grain until there was no more money in the land. All the money ended up in Joseph's possession, bringing all the money into the house of Pharaoh.

Now there was no bread in all the land; for the famine was
very severe, so that the land of Egypt and the land of Canaan
languished because of the famine. And Joseph gathered up
all the money that was found in the land of Egypt and in
the land of Canaan, for the grain which they bought; and
Joseph brought the money into Pharaoh's house. So when
the money failed in the land of Egypt and in the land of
Canaan, all the Egyptians came to Joseph and said, "Give
us bread, for why should we die in your presence? For the
money has failed."

—**Genesis 47:13-15**

This was an account of wealth transfer. "When the money failed in the land of Egypt and in the land of Canaan, all the Egyptians came to Joseph." Eventually not only the Egyptians came, but it ultimately was also all the surrounding peoples. Not only did they bring all their money and possessions, but from the severity of the famine, the people at last offered their very lives in exchange for provision. They became slaves to Egypt.

The Priestly Inheritance

It is an interesting side note that during this wealth transfer you see a noble action by Pharaoh. He allowed his priests to keep their lands.

> *Only the land of the priests he did not buy; for the priests had rations allotted to them by Pharaoh, and they ate their rations which Pharaoh gave them; therefore they did not sell their lands.*

> —**Genesis 47:22**

This could have been out of Egyptian superstition, or it could have been from Pharaoh's genuine reverence for his religious culture. However one views it, the point of interest is found in Pharaoh's actions. He did right by priests who were not God's; they were Egyptian priests involved in the dark arts of Egypt. Pharaoh could be likened to the unjust judge in this account. In Luke 18:6, Jesus told the story of an unjust judge who did right by a widow because she would not leave the judge alone. He finally granted her what she wanted due to her persistence. Pharaoh's scenario was different, yet the principle remains—he wanted to do right by his priests. In the world's system, institutionalized religion such as these priests in Egypt is often tolerated, accepted, and held in high regard. A godless world may celebrate institutionalized religion, not knowing God Himself is the real answer. The point being, if an unjust judge or ungodly ruler can take care of those around them—both in a legalistic and provisionary way, out of religious obligation to the system's priestly figures—the great God of heaven, by comparison, is far more capable of taking care of His people.

God had several priests and tribes. A moving comparison in light of Pharaoh providing for his priests is the way God treated the Levites. The Levites, unlike the priests of Pharaoh, would receive no land, while all the other tribes received land as an inheritance. Rather, they were not to receive a physical inheritance. Why? Because God said He Himself would be their inheritance!

> *It shall be, in regard to their inheritance, that I am their inheritance. You shall give them no possession in Israel, for I am their possession.*
>
> —**Ezekiel 44:28**

> *But to the tribe of Levi Moses had given no inheritance; the Lord God of Israel was their inheritance, as He had said to them.*
>
> —**Joshua 13:33**

This is powerful, as there is a special provision for priests—those dedicated unto the word of the Lord. Those who serve in the house of the Lord, dedicating their entire lives to this one thing. God is their ultimate provider; He is the ultimate Father, and He being their inheritance means they had it all! If God is your inheritance, you have it all! In a time of a wealth transfer or famine, those who give their entire lives for the service of God have made God responsible for their inheritance and provision. What a tremendous promise. Priests cannot lose if they stay true to the Lord!

100X

> *If you then, being evil, know how to give good gifts to your children, how much more will your Father who is in heaven give good things to those who ask Him!*
>
> —**Matthew 7:11**

You can be part of this type of inheritance if you are in Jesus Christ. Only your inheritance far surpasses that of the Levites! They inherited God; you have Him living within you and additionally possess a much better covenant with much better promises. You have what He has. Not only so, but you also have covenant rights to what He possesses. There is an additional multiplier in the New Testament for anyone who gives up everything the way the Levites did. Jesus said those who sacrifice specifically for Him and the sake of the gospel will receive a hundredfold of the value compared to what they gave up! You must understand the term *hundredfold*. It is a folding, not a multiplying. If you were to take a piece of paper and fold it in half, you would double it. The math on folding a paper quickly exceeds that of multiplication; it becomes an exponential increase. Some argue if you were to surpass folding a piece of paper 100 times it would quickly become as thick as the universe. What Jesus was saying, to anyone who has given up for His sake and the gospel, was that they will have an exponential return available to them!

> So Jesus answered and said, "Assuredly, I say to you, there is no one who has left house or brothers or sisters or father or mother or wife or children or lands, for My sake and the gospel's, who shall not receive a hundredfold now in this time—houses and brothers and sisters and mothers and children and lands, with persecutions—and in the age to come, eternal life. But many who are first will be last, and the last first."
>
> —Mark 10:29-31

Anything that hinders your relationship to Jesus and what He has called you to do is something you can choose to leave. This applies to those who have left all for the sake of the gospel as well. This, of course, is a weapon that should be greatly considered for the days ahead. It is a sure promise directly from Jesus that offers over-the-top returns. This kind of action would provide sustainability through something as catastrophic as a global economic meltdown! You can live and even bloom through whatever days may come. You are part of a royal priesthood and there is a special blessing for anyone who has given up to go up! Jesus said anyone who would keep his life will lose it, yet anyone who would lose his life will find it. Letting go of the things that hold you back from Jesus and the gospel is a sure way for you to peer into the future with great confidence.

In my own life, before the age of 13, a choice was presented to me. My parents were divorced while I was very young, and my mom served the Lord. Through her faith and the faith of her parents, my life was impacted by encounter after encounter with the Holy Spirit. This was unacceptable to my father, who wanted a much different path for me. A day came when a choice was presented: follow Jesus or be part of everything my father had, which included cattle, land, real estate, and a future inheritance with a large financial benefit. My father and his family were very well off; we owned a ranch bordered by a large beautiful river. My father was adamantly against me going to church and following the call of God on my life. The issue was, I had encountered God for real! It was undeniable. To walk away from Jesus for property and provision would have been much like the story of the rich young ruler. I couldn't deny all the Lord had done in my life leading up to this decision. Upon saying to my father, "I choose to follow Jesus," after a very difficult conversation, we got in the car and left the property. He dropped me off at my mother's house. That was one of the last three times I saw my father before he died.

As sad as this story is, the Lord has been so gracious to me. My wife and children are outstanding, and I never would have met my wife had I not made the decision to follow Jesus all the way. I have also been blessed supernaturally in land and provision that is amazing! Miracle after miracle has happened in my life showing the supernatural protection and increase that truly follows someone who gives up to go up. The promise Jesus gave us is true!

THE EGYPTIAN WEALTH TRANSFER

> *A good man leaves an inheritance to his children's children,*
> *but the wealth of the sinner is stored up for the righteous.*
>
> **—Proverbs 13:22**

In a wealth transfer, it is the wealth of the wicked that is stored up for the righteous. It would seem that a global crisis, famine, or something catastrophic is one way a transfer begins. Transfers do not happen suddenly; they may require years of preparation. Again, this is what generational purpose is: preparation for a moment when God opens a monumental, divine occasion in history such as the children of Israel leaving Egypt. Preparation through obedience on Joseph's part led to financing the exodus. Joseph knew the day would come and gave instructions for what to do with his bones when they departed. Hebrews 11:22 says, "By faith Joseph, when he was dying, made mention of the departure of the children of Israel, and gave instructions concerning his bones."

Joseph stored up the wealth of not only Egypt but everyone who brought their belongings and resources to him. He was saving the generation he lived in while preparing for a future day by the divine guidance of the Lord. This is what would be called generational purpose. Without generational purpose, generational wealth transfer is not likely to happen. Let me explain—without a generation rising to what God has called them to accomplish, such as the case of Israel leaving Egypt to occupy a new land, there is no "why" for a wealth transfer. On the other hand, when a generation rises in its purpose, God will take all the treasures of darkness and have them ready at just the right time. When the exodus happened, it was due to preparation meeting opportunity from a life of obedience on Joseph's part.

THE EXODUS WAS FINANCED

And I will give this people favor in the sight of the Egyptians; and it shall be, when you go, that you shall not go empty-handed. But every woman shall ask of her neighbor, namely, of her who dwells near her house, articles of silver, articles of gold, and clothing; and you shall put them on your sons and on your daughters. So you shall plunder the Egyptians.

—**Exodus 3:21-22**

God said to His people, "You will not go empty-handed." The women went out and asked for their neighbor's belongings! Egypt had been so rocked by the events of the plagues that they didn't have any resistance to the Jews. The women boldly went to their neighbors saying, "I want that, and that, and that too." You would think they would resist, but no, they were in a stupor. The light in Goshen was still with God's people. What the Egyptians had was on layaway for the people of God to pick up. The end of verse 22 is very revealing! God said, "So you shall plunder the Egyptians." The King James Version says, "Thus you shall spoil the Egyptians." In the Hebrew, this literally means to strip them for the purpose of your getaway. That is exactly what they did! They stripped the Egyptians to finance their getaway and journey to establish a whole new nation!

Speak now in the hearing of the people, and let every man ask from his neighbor and every woman from her neighbor, articles of silver and articles of gold.

—Exodus 11:2

Now the children of Israel had done according to the word of Moses, and they had asked from the Egyptians articles of silver, articles of gold, and clothing. And the Lord had given the people favor in the sight of the Egyptians, so that they granted them what they requested. Thus they plundered the Egyptians.

—Exodus 12:35-36

He also brought them out with silver and gold, and there was none feeble among His tribes.

—Psalms 105:37

And also the nation whom they serve I will judge; afterward they shall come out with great possessions.

—Genesis 15:14

The people of God left Egypt with great possessions! When the Egyptians came to their senses, they were furious that they lost their slaves and their great possessions. They asked the question, "Why have we done this?" So, they pursued them.

Now it was told the king of Egypt that the people had fled, and the heart of Pharaoh and his servants was turned against the people; and they said, "Why have we done this, that we have let Israel go from serving us?"

—Exodus 14:5

A point of interest is to see God's provision versus those who trust in horses and chariots.

> *And I have led you forty years in the wilderness. Your clothes have not worn out on you, and your sandals have not worn out on your feet.*

> **—Deuteronomy 29:5**

The favor of God did not let their shoes wear out nor their clothes. Compare this with the way Egypt's chariots began to falter by God's doing! After the wealth transfer, the Lord began messing with the enemy's ability to execute a claw back clause. This caused the soldiers to be disheartened from pursuing the people of God.

> *And He took off their chariot wheels, so that they drove them with difficulty; and the Egyptians said, "Let us flee from the face of Israel, for the Lord fights for them against the Egyptians."*

> **—Exodus 14:25**

The army of Egypt met its end when they pursued the people of God through the Red Sea, thereby closing the chapter on those who meant harm to His people. The wealth transfer was now in the hands of God's people. They were off to a new destination—financed by the wealth of sinners and motivated by generational purpose—a land flowing with milk and honey.

In the chapters ahead, we will look at what a possible *last days* wealth transfer might look like.

Chapter Three

THE FOUNDER OF HELL'S ECONOMY

And I also say to you that you are Peter, and on
this rock I will build My church, and the gates
of Hades shall not prevail against it.

—Matthew 16:18

There is a nefarious agenda at work in this present culture; it has operated in each generation since the birth of the church with one intent and one goal—to steal, kill, and destroy. It must be understood, or even well intending believers will fall prey to its devices. Jesus said it would not prevail against His church, yet His statement implies an effort to prevail against the church.

It is important to understand what Jesus meant when He mentioned "the gates of hell." Let's begin by recognizing that hell itself is a location, like heaven. It is a holding place of torment until it is ultimately thrown into the lake of fire. When Jesus mentions the gates of hell, He is referring to something different—it is not a location; rather, it is a system. Jesus spoke about the gates of hell and the church, saying, "the gates of hell shall not prevail against it." The gates of hell is actually a reference to a society that has surrendered itself to the system of the devil.

Regarding Kingdoms

Hell is part of a kingdom system. The gates of hell in context are speaking about a cultural system ruled by darkness. The kingdom of darkness/gates of hell are a perversion of the kingdom of God. The devil is not original in any way. He pollutes and twists God's ideas and systems to create a sad, convoluted reflection of the glorious original. One of the many things the kingdom of darkness does is lure people into its economy—hell's economy.

An economy based on the kingdom of hell is founded on mammon, selfishness, and is the antithesis to sowing and reaping. The draw to hell's economy is founded on natural logic. It seems right to be selfish. To be all about what you can get from life, for you and your natural desires.

Jesus said in Matthew 6:24, "No one can serve two masters." You cannot serve God and mammon. Mammon and riches are two very different things. Riches in themselves are neutral. Everything in God's kingdom has to do with the heart—the intention for a thing. Mammon is a self-centered, self-providing system that makes your money all about you. Mammon is the number one financial mindset in hell's economy.

There is a thin line in understanding the difference between mammon (the love of money) and God's way of provision. To the carnally minded, prosperity and mammon are the same thing! They cannot tell the difference between the blessing and self-centered getting. This is because they are blinded by the gates of hell. The love of money is also the source of hatred and merciless criticism of believers whom God has prospered. If someone is critical of another's increase in the kingdom of God, hell's economy has them fooled.

LUCIFER'S ARC

Everything has an origin. In the case of all things stealing, killing, and destroying, the origin is found in Lucifer, who ultimately became Satan.

> *Thou art the anointed cherub that covereth; and I have set thee so: thou wast upon the holy mountain of God; thou hast walked up and down in the midst of the stones of fire. Thou wast perfect in thy ways from the day that thou wast created, till **iniquity was found in thee. By the multitude of thy merchandise they have filled the midst of thee with violence**, and thou hast sinned: therefore, I will cast thee as profane out of the mountain of God: and I will destroy thee, O covering cherub, from the midst of the stones of fire. Thine heart was lifted up because of thy beauty, thou hast corrupted thy wisdom by reason of thy brightness: I will cast thee to the ground, I will lay thee before kings, that they may behold thee. Thou hast defiled thy sanctuaries by the multitude of thine iniquities, by the iniquity of thy traffick; therefore will I bring forth a fire from the midst of thee, it shall devour thee, and I will bring thee to ashes upon the earth in the sight of all them that behold thee. All they that know thee among the people shall be astonished at thee: thou shalt be a terror, and never shalt thou be any more.*
>
> —Ezekiel 28:14-19, KJV

The above passage of scripture is the story arc of Lucifer turned Satan, from the days of his radiance to his imminent punishment. There are many fascinating pieces within the journey of this fallen cherub. Certainly, that he was once a beautiful angel and he potentially was the worship leader in heaven, having full access to God's creation. Verse 14 speaks of him walking up and down in the midst of the stones of fire, which is likely a reference to the planets in our solar system. He had access to everything on and around the earth, both in the natural realm and the spirit realm. God created him perfect in all his ways, until the day he decided to indulge iniquity. This was due to jealousy toward God.

Eavesdropping on the Devil

Job 4 gives insight into the devil's contempt for God and the devil's hatred toward mankind. Eliphaz, one of Job's friends, is within earshot of a rhetorical conversation the devil is having with himself, which leads to Eliphaz involuntarily eavesdropping on the moment.

> *Now a word was secretly brought to me, and my ear received a whisper of it. In disquieting thoughts from the visions of the night, when deep sleep falls on men, fear came upon me, and trembling, which made all my bones shake. Then a spirit passed before my face; the hair on my body stood up. It stood still, but I could not discern its appearance. A form was before my eyes; there was silence; then I heard a voice saying: "Can a mortal be more righteous than God? Can a man be more pure than his Maker? If He puts no trust in His servants, if He charges His angels with error, how much more those who dwell in houses of clay, whose foundation is in the dust, who are crushed before a moth? They are broken in pieces from morning till evening; they perish forever, with no one regarding. Does not their own excellence go away? They die, even without wisdom."*

> —Job 4:12-21

To me this sounds like the tantrum of a six-year-old. For Eliphaz, this encounter was a terrifying scenario that included trembling, bones shaking, the hair on his body stood up, and he could identify a formless entity before his eyes until finally a voice spoke. If Eliphaz could have seen past all the theatrics—meaning the fear, darkness, and sense of dread—what is left is a voice that begins to complain to itself! About God, no less! This scenario is a strange moment experienced by Eliphaz as he was eavesdropping on the devil, who was whining and telling himself that he is so much better than humanity.

Eliphaz's encounter gives us insight into Satan's disdain for humanity and contempt for God, which led to an insatiable desire to rule the world. His hatred for mankind comes from the reality that God placed mankind in a higher position than him! We are in the place Lucifer desired to be. He desired that all humanity be under him, in a debased fashion. This same issue involved the economy of the world, some believe before the time of Adam!

Ezekiel 28:16 gives insight as to what the devil was doing in a time frame well before the days we live in: *"By the multitude of thy merchandise they have filled the midst of thee with violence"* (KJV). The Amplified Bible says it this way, "Through *the abundance of your commerce* you were internally filled with lawlessness and violence, and you sinned."

There was a point that the devil had an abundance of commerce on the earth. The full meaning of this is not clear. One thing that we know—it involved what was potentially an ancient global economy on a large scale. The devil has always wanted to dominate mankind, and the best way he could rule over the masses would be to place himself in control of the resources and economy of the entire world. This would make him the authority of men's dealings.

It is a revelation to understand that the devil cannot operate under the anointing or through God's supernatural power of the Holy Spirit.

He cannot function in the blessing; therefore, his substitute is mammon! He has enticed mankind to fall in love with money, which is a simple definition of mammon. Mammon creates a self-reliance that cuts God out of the picture and places self on the throne of your provision. This is the foundation of hell's economy.

Hell's economy was offered to Jesus. It was a shortcut to what He came to accomplish. Remember the story?

Being tempted for forty days by the devil. And in those days He ate nothing, and afterward, when they had ended, He was hungry. And the devil said to Him, "If You are the Son of God, command this stone to become bread." But Jesus answered him, saying, "It is written, 'Man shall not live by bread alone, but by every word of God.'" **Then the devil, taking Him up on a high mountain, showed Him all the kingdoms of the world in a moment of time. And the devil said to Him, "All this authority I will give You, and their glory; for this has been delivered to me, and I give it to whomever I wish. Therefore, if You will worship before me, all will be Yours."** *And Jesus answered and said to him, "Get behind Me, Satan! For it is written, 'You shall worship the Lord your God, and Him only you shall serve.'" Then he brought Him to Jerusalem, set Him on the pinnacle of the temple, and said to Him, "If You are the Son of God, throw Yourself down from here. For it is written: 'He shall give His angels charge over you, to keep you,' and, 'In their hands they shall bear you up, lest you dash your foot against a stone.'" And Jesus answered and said to him, "It has been said, 'You shall not tempt the Lord your God.'" Now when the devil had ended every temptation, he departed from Him until an opportune time.*

—Luke 4:2-13

The devil wasn't lying about what he had; it was indeed given to him. Many times, we read these verses and come away with the understanding that Jesus defeated the devil three times. What the vast majority don't understand is the magnitude of what was happening here. First, we need to recognize that this was indeed a temptation for Jesus. How do we know this? Because that is what the Word of God calls it. He was being tempted for 40 days by the devil. During this time, He didn't eat anything. He was likely feeling weak as His flesh was deprived of food and comfort; Jesus was in a vulnerable position. The devil knew this and waited until the very end of the 40 days to pull out all the stops, as if to say, "Let's just cut to the chase here: I can give You what You came for. Why suffer? I will hand over to You what You are seeking. The exchange is simple, just bow down and worship me."

This was not the first time the devil used this type of ploy. It was a familiar strategy and was used previously with another son of God. The original human son—the first Adam. When the lying serpent deceived Eve, Adam was standing next to her. The devil was able to convince Adam and Eve that God was withholding something from them. As a result, they believed the word of the serpent over the command of the Lord. This resulted in Adam and Eve placing their authority and dominion in the control of Satan. This becomes even clearer in the chapters of Job where we learn that the devil had authority not only to appear before God with the angels, but he also additionally had the authority to do a variety of horrible things to Job. This is because he was now operating in the authority of the first Adam.

Upon his temptation of Jesus, he said in Luke 4:6, "All this *authority* I will give You, and their *glory*; for this has been delivered to me, and I give it to whomever I wish."

- **Authority/Power:** in the original Greek language, this word represents executive power of one's rule, dominion, domain, and jurisdiction.

- **Glory:** in the original Greek and etymologically, *glory* primarily means thought or opinion, especially favorable human opinion, reputation, praise, honor, whether it is true or false honor.

Satan was saying to Jesus, "Not only can I give You complete executive power over every kingdom on earth, but I can also make everyone who is a part of that system praise You and create any desired reputation for You I wish."

The issue at hand was severe, as this was a similar strategy that had worked on the first Adam. It is what gave the devil all his executive authority over creation. Satan had grown comfortable ruling over the majority of mankind. He was unchallenged for hundreds of years, doing as he pleased, manipulating and corrupting men as he saw fit—that is, until this moment. The moment he engaged in tempting this new individual. This latest voice on the scene. Surely this one would be like all the others whom he had pressured and compromised all the way back to the garden.

Over 40 days, he unleashed his best persuasion, his highest level of temptation. He became more and more aware that he was dealing with someone vastly different from the first Adam and all who came afterward. The realization must have set in with a growing horror for Satan, with each failed temptation becoming clearer—he was colliding with someone who was strategically weaponized against him. The prince of this world, for the first time, was encountering a man prepared and fashioned for this very fight. This one was sent to destroy all Satan had established and all he had built for generations. Jesus came to destroy the works of the devil (see 1 John 3:8).

Satan had entered into a confrontation with the last Adam.

The Last Adam

And so it is written, "The first man Adam became a living being." The last Adam became a life-giving spirit.

—1 Corinthians 15:45

Not only was the last Adam a direct Son of God, but He was also God in the flesh—the first born among many brethren, a life-giving spirit. Notice the Bible doesn't refer to Him as the second Adam; no, He is the last Adam. There was no plan B after Him.

Jesus was the last line of defense. He was God's perfect plan developed over hundreds of years to be unleashed on this rebellious, fallen angel at just the right moment. This first engagement with Jesus must have left the devil bewildered and highly concerned. Jesus brought his temptations to a screeching halt by authoritatively declaring, "It is written." This sent the devil back on his heels; he had to go away and strategize when he might find another opportunity to overtake this powerful new foe: "Now when the devil had ended every temptation, he departed from Him until an opportune time" (Luke 4:13).

The devil must have known Jesus was different; he remembered the prophecy God himself spoke in Genesis 3:15, saying, "He will crush your head, and you will strike his heel" (NIV). In Satan's arrogance he decided this was his big opportunity. If Jesus was the one God had prophesied about, then it was time to make a big play—not just for dominion over the earth. This time, for the entire kingdom of God, of heaven, and complete dominance over mankind forever. What an unbelievable thought, that God the Father loved us so much that He gave His only Son, sacrificially, and under the risk of losing Him (as well as us forever) to the temptation of the devil. Imagine what would have happened if Jesus bowed to the devil. It is possible earth, heaven, and the kingdom of

God would all fall under Satan's authority. Satan would have won! We would all be eternally under the dominion of a fallen angel! He would enforce a kingdom of stealing, killing, and destroying. However, this new contender was found without blemish, without weakness, He was perfect. He came and condemned sin in the flesh.

A clearer way of saying this would be to say Jesus condemned sin on its own turf. Jesus slapped sin and death around, then threw them all out of their own party!

Even with all that was riding on the line, Satan quickly discovered he was not dealing with the first Adam; he wasn't dealing with a typical king or corruptible man—far from it. He was dealing with someone he didn't count on; he was dealing with the last Adam, not a mere man. Satan was now confronted with God in the flesh, who had arrived to destroy the works of the devil. Jesus didn't come to consider the devil's offers or negotiate; He came to declare war on the kingdom of darkness!

This realization must have enraged and terrified Satan when he offered Jesus everything He came to accomplish, minus the suffering, rejection, and difficulty that would be necessary for Jesus to endure if He was to reclaim a world that had fallen into the hands of Satan. This was the shortcut; Satan was sure Jesus would take the bait and that He would fall to His knees, rendering everything Satan's. His wicked rule would have become permanent and irrevocable. Thank God that the devil's highest and best temptations were no match for the Son of the Living God. Jesus didn't falter. He released His confession and His faith mixed with the Word of God: "It is written"!

Three times He replied to the devil, "It is written."

> **It is written,** *"Man shall not live by bread alone, but by every word of God."*
>
> —Luke 4:4

*And Jesus answered and said to him, "Get behind Me, Satan! For **it is written**, 'You shall worship the Lord your God, and Him only you shall serve.'"*

—Luke 4:8

*Jesus said to him, "**It is written again**, you shall not tempt the Lord your God."*

—Matthew 4:7

What the devil was tempting Jesus with was hell's economy and its entire system. He was offering Jesus control of the commerce that he himself possessed in an old world. He offered Jesus a reputation with the entire world and to sit as king over the earth—of course, with the devil seated in the place of God. The thing the devil may not have realized is that Jesus wasn't in the devil's arena; the devil was now in His. Jesus had arrived to legally claim back what the devil had taken by deception from Adam and Eve. Jesus was here to set up the kingdom of God and empower a whole new generation with His words and authority to drive the devil and his influence out. This was a purely savage move by God the Father and Jesus the Son. He humbled Himself and became a man to have revenge on the prince of darkness and give every living person the opportunity to be free once and for all time!

Jesus was the first born among many brethren; He was the prototype for how we are to treat the devil and the kingdom of darkness and every demonic adversary. Nothing has changed—the devil is still the author of stealing, killing, and destroying. Jesus said while addressing the Pharisees that the devil was a murderer from the beginning and that his native tongue is lying.

You are of your father the devil, and the desires of your father you want to do. He was a murderer from the beginning, and

does not stand in the truth, because there is no truth in him.
When he speaks a lie, he speaks from his own resources, for he
is a liar and the father of it.

—John 8:44

A REVELATION OF JESUS

There is a way to break free from hell's economy with lasting results. It begins with understanding the gates of hell and its economy. Similar to the kingdom of God, the gates of hell (which we could call the kingdom of hell) is a system that operates by rules. Going back to Matthew 16:18, Jesus said to Peter, "upon this rock I will build My church; and the gates of hell shall not prevail against it" (KJV). What a strange thing to say, "the gates of hell will not prevail against the church." First, it's worth mentioning that Jesus was not talking about Peter being the rock He would build His church on. Rather you must investigate the context leading up to Jesus' remarks. He was asking the disciples who they thought He was. Peter was the only one to speak up, saying, "You are the Christ, the Son of God." It was to this statement made by Peter that Jesus was referring. Although Peter's name does indeed mean "the Rock," Jesus was pointing out that it was Peter's revelation of Jesus as the Christ and Him being the Son of God that His church would be built on. A simpler way of saying it would be, "The church is built on the revelation of Jesus!"

Your Presence Should Demand
an Explanation

*For whatsoever is born of God overcometh the world: and this
is the victory that overcometh the world, even our faith.*

—1 John 5:4, KJV

First John 5:4 is a parallel scripture reference that defines the gates
of hell from another vantage point. The word translated as *world* has a
deeper meaning when it is seen in the Greek. It is the word *kosmos*. The
word *kosmos* might lead some to believe this is a description of outer
space or some off-world region. That would be an easy conclusion at
first glance and even upon pronouncing the Greek word. What it really
means is the public, the culture, or society.

Much like the words of Jesus regarding the gates of hell not prevail-
ing against the church, this scripture says those who are born of God
overcome the world! How? By our faith. What powerful insight into
how the gates of hell will not prevail against the church. Not only will
the gates of hell not prevail, or the society of darkness not prevail, but
here we see how we go on the offensive. It is our faith that overcomes a
society of darkness.

Look how *The Message* says it: "Every God-born person conquers the
world's ways. The conquering power that brings the world to its knees is
our faith" (1 John 5:4 MSG).

Did you catch that? If you are born of God, by default, you are
supposed to conquer the world's ways! The power you use to conquer
with is faith! *The Message* takes it a step further and says your faith is the
power that brings the world to its knees! That means the world's ways,
its systems, and all the nefarious dark agendas it can muster are brought

to their knees by your faith. The believer is called to drop the world to its knees simply by showing up full of God!

I like to say it this way: "Your presence should demand an explanation!" In other words, someone with actual horsepower just showed up. When you are surrendered to God and filled with faith, you are an unstoppable force against the kingdom of darkness.

> *And I will give you the keys of the kingdom of heaven, and whatever you bind on earth will be bound in heaven, and whatever you loose on earth will be loosed in heaven.*
>
> **—Matthew 16:19**

The Word of God refers to the "kingdom of Heaven" on several occasions; it is a location. Romans 14:17 unveils another aspect of God's rule found in the terminology "the kingdom of God."

> *For the kingdom of God is not eating and drinking, but righteousness and peace and joy in the Holy Spirit.*
>
> **—Romans 14:17**

> *And when he was demanded of the Pharisees, when the kingdom of God should come, he answered them and said, The kingdom of God cometh not with observation: neither shall they say, Lo here! or, lo there! for, behold, **the kingdom of God is within you.***
>
> **—Luke 17:20-21, KJV**

The profound reality of the kingdom of God is that rather than a location, it is a manifestation of righteousness, peace, and joy. Another earth-shaking reality of this manifestation is that it takes place within you, the believer!

Who Are You Giving Territory to?

There is nothing equal to or even worthy of comparison when it comes to God and the devil. They are not even polar opposites. One is the creator of the universe, the other is a failed being with a story that is highly pitiful. Not only was Lucifer a created being with splendor, but he couldn't even maintain what God made and gave him temporary control over. He was filled with self-adoration, failing at his station, and falling like lightning. The only relevance he has is that he managed to take God's prized children hostage through persuasion and trickery. This gave a very insignificant player authority on earth and over mankind. This, of course, is why Jesus came, as we explored earlier.

The main power the devil possesses is persuasion, and in this arena he is a master. Why persuasion? Because he has no authority over humanity after Jesus died and was resurrected, except for those who are under his persuasion. This means the devil is territorial, and his entire game is to take territory in your mind and ultimately your life.

Discovering that both God and the devil are territorial is to understand the entire battle. God wants the territory of your mind and thoughts, but so does the devil. He learned it from God. Whoever has control of the mind and influence over the decision of free moral agents will rule them. Ultimately, with enough people under the influence of the devil, he can persecute God's people and alter the culture to fulfill his desires. Therefore, the gospel being preached is really a war for not only the souls of humanity, but it is a war for the culture as well!

Both God and the devil are territorial. Both are speaking and both are begging the question—who will you listen to?

No man can serve two masters. God is calling you to your highest and best. Jesus fought for you and won; it is now up to you to advance in understanding and the practice of His kingdom. His voice is calling you to follow His plan and take your place within His kingdom system.

Chapter Four

THE KINGDOM OF GOD IS NOT A DEMOCRACY

For the kingdom of God is not eating and drinking, but
righteousness and peace and joy in the Holy Spirit.

—Romans 14:17

Often when teaching or speaking, I will say, "The kingdom is not a democracy." This means that the kingdom is not a system of voting where the majority rules. Rather, the kingdom of God is a system with a king at the head. I also like to jokingly say the kingdom is a theocracy and God's name is Theo!

This is an important point when considering the two kingdoms. *Ultimately, each kingdom cannot be altered, they can only be entered.* By entering the kingdom of God, you are empowered with rights to manifest everything Jesus paid for. Likewise, the kingdom of hell makes it easy to be empowered by the wisdom of the world and the devices of darkness. The rules to each kingdom oppose one another.

When referencing kingdoms, it is helpful to keep in mind that there is a difference between the kingdom of heaven and the kingdom of God. The Scripture refers to the kingdom of heaven on several occasions; it is a place, a location, the realm of heaven with all its attributes—saints, angels, and the very throne of God! By comparison, the kingdom of God is different, yet of the same substance, with a far greater application. It is spoken of in Romans 14:17:

> *For the kingdom of God is not eating and drinking, but righteousness and peace and joy in the Holy Spirit.*
>
> **—Romans 14:17**

The kingdom of God is a system within believers, a system of righteousness, peace, and joy! In the same way, the gates of hell is a system working in a dark society, and it consists of stealing, killing, and destroying.

Kingdoms are made up of citizens who follow a set of rules and means of operation. In the comparison between the kingdom of God and the gates of hell, it becomes clear that each one has systems empowered by and for the citizens of the kingdom they occupy.

KINGDOMS

Kingdom of God

- Constitution—Word of God
- Military—angelic protection military
- Mental health—peace that passes understanding
- Healthcare—by His stripes you are healed
- Family—brothers and sisters
- Economy—blessing and prosperity
- Social system—local church

Gates of Hell

- Constitution—deception
- Military—demonic assailants
- Mental health—confusion and chaos
- Healthcare—sickness and death
- Family—usury and false love
- Economy—mammon (love of money)
- Social system—wisdom of the world

The comparisons above are a mere sample of the differences between these two kingdoms. Each one carries its own system—one the original, the other a perversion of what God intended. The two are separated by mankind's free moral agency, or a simpler way of saying it would be *mankind's choice*. Choice is the determining factor by which we have access to either of these two kingdom systems. By choosing the kingdom of God, you have declared war on the kingdom of darkness. This is what Jesus did when He stepped onto earth as a Man. Your choice for the kingdom of God does the same. It gives you the power to declare war on the devil in similar fashion to Jesus. "The Son of God appeared for this purpose, to destroy the works of the devil," (1 John 3:8 AMP); and "as He is, so are we in this world" (1 John 4:17). This empowerment grows and becomes more potent by increased revelation.

As stated at the outset of this chapter, the kingdom of God is not a democracy, neither is the kingdom of hell a democracy. It should be said again, these kingdoms cannot be altered, only entered. Once entered, an individual has the opportunity to experience all that kingdom has to offer. The deception of the kingdom of hell is that it is logical. It lines up with the five senses. It is carnal and possesses what would seem like a gateway that leads to everything a person might suspect they desire. Yet we know through the Word of God there is a label for this type of carnal expectation. It is known as the wide gate, and many are they who go in by it.

> *Enter by the narrow gate; for wide is the gate and broad is the way that leads to destruction, and there are many who go in by it. Because narrow is the gate and difficult is the way which leads to life, and there are few who find it.*
>
> —Matthew 7:13-14

It is a sad reality that most people will choose to follow the wide gate and broad way. These references are also known as the gates of hell.

STOP VOTING, START SURRENDERING

The purpose of the statement "the kingdom is not a democracy" has meaning. Let me explain. Often individuals feel they can live how they see fit in whatever kingdom they are in. To a certain extent this is true, although this only works for someone living in the gates of hell. Why? Because hell's system doesn't really care what you do, as long as you don't challenge it.

A person could live out a good moral life, even show kindness and responsibility toward their family and fellow man. This is fine with hell's system if there is no discovery of Jesus. It is when Jesus is discovered for real, that hell's system will throw a fit! The closer someone is to stepping into the kingdom of God through Jesus, the more the gates of hell will begin to cause issues. Suddenly strife, difficulty, stress, and a host of unforeseen issues will arise. This is warfare waged by the powers of darkness. These acting agents from hell's system will stir up anything and everything they can to induce fear, doubt, anxiety, and the like, to be embraced. These induced elements are the fuel needed by darkness to keep taking ground in a person's life who will give place to them. Much like the Parable of the Sower, these crisis-based things come to steal the Word of God out of the hearts of those hearing and on the verge of believing.

> *Therefore hear the parable of the sower: When anyone hears the word of the kingdom, and does not understand it, then the wicked one comes and snatches away what was sown in his heart. This is he who received seed by the wayside. But he who received the seed on stony places, this is he who hears the word and immediately receives it with joy; yet he has no root in himself, but endures only for a while. For when* **tribulation or persecution arises because of the word, immediately he stumbles.** *Now he who received seed among the thorns is he who hears the word, and the cares of this world and the deceitfulness of riches choke the word, and he becomes unfruitful. But he who received seed on the good ground is he who hears the word and understands it, who indeed bears fruit and produces: some a hundredfold, some sixty, some thirty.*
>
> **—Matthew 13:18-23**

The good news for someone who understands this is they can see this trap and embrace the Word of God no matter the difficulty! This is how winning is done!

The kingdom of God will not fight you with difficulty; just the opposite is true. What is vital to understand regarding God's kingdom is that it is indeed a kingdom, and as such those who abide in it must do so according to what the kingdom prescribes. To not do so will result in not experiencing the highest and best results God has to offer.

This especially becomes clear when understanding that God's kingdom is not a democracy—it is a system built on His Word. When a believer begins to operate by the Word of God as their standard for living, the full potential of all God has is now realized and available.

This is not a democratic system; this comes by surrendering your will and entire process to the written Word mixed with your faith. A person can vote, but if their vote or choices are not founded and executed on God's Word, the results can be frustrating. Believers on the road to salvation, who've not yet surrendered to the Word of God, are still voting and making the mistake that they are in a democracy that can be altered by casting their choice. This is the mindset of infant believers who will never receive the amazing things God has in store until they quit voting and begin surrendering!

SEEING THE HEAVENLY CULTURE

As a believer, God has given you far more authority in this natural realm than you might realize. The kingdom of darkness works constantly to limit you. But when you discover the truth about God's economy, you can easily break these limitations.

In John 10:10, Scripture tells us Jesus came to give life more abundantly, but the devil comes to steal, kill, and destroy. To break hell's economy, you must see yourself as part of a kingdom with its own economy, culture, and system. Malachi 3:10 gives us a glimpse into this heavenly culture. It says:

> *"Bring all the tithes into the storehouse, that there may be food in My house, and try Me now in this," says the Lord of hosts, "If I will not open for you the windows of heaven and pour out such blessing that there will not be room enough to receive it."*
>
> —**Malachi 3:10**

BIBLICAL RETURN

My wife, Heather, and I have changed our terminology from, "I want a harvest" to "I want a return of biblical proportions." This terminology adjustment came from placing more value on what the Word of God has to say concerning matters of economics versus what society says or even our own tendencies might sway us to believe. When you realize God's Word promises blessings, you find favor and victory. You'll see how God's ways are higher than our ways. The windows of heaven will open and pour out such a blessing you will not have room to contain it.

What I'm saying isn't only a good, liberating thought process—it is a word from God that destroys yokes and shackles. You will experience unmatched liberty as the windows of heaven open and blessings flow freely. Proverbs 10:22 says, "The blessing of the Lord makes one rich, and He adds no sorrow with it." When the windows of heaven pour out, the potential of the blessings is so great the Bible tells us that there is not room enough to receive it! Not having room enough to receive what God is pouring out on you is a return of biblical proportions!

BREAKING THE DEVOURER

> *"And I will rebuke the devourer for your sakes, so that he will not destroy the fruit of your ground, nor shall the vine fail to bear fruit for you in the field," says the Lord of hosts.*
>
> **—Malachi 3:11**

When this verse says "I," it is talking about God. It's predicated on the understanding we take the system of God and His way of doing things and obey it. According to verse 11, when we seek the system of God through this process, God rebukes the devourer. He roams the earth like a roaring lion seeking whom he may devour. He entices you to bow to him and enter his economy. When we give way to fear, we pull back from God's system. We doubt. We no longer give, or pray for the sick, or believe in God's blessings, or even believe the words of Jesus. We step back from God and step into the kingdom of darkness.

To step out of hell's economy, we must first seek the kingdom of God and His righteousness by sowing and reaping. When you step into God's supernatural economic system, you are destroying the kingdom of darkness in your life. This is where God rebukes the devourer for your sake.

What does that look like? It looks like the things that come against your health and your children are being broken off. This is the Word of God coming true. In Malachi 3:11, the Scripture says, "I [God] will rebuke the devourer for your sakes, so that he will not destroy the fruit of your ground." He will not be able to touch the labor of your hands or the things God has called you to do!

A Delightful Land

When I envision God rebuking the devourer, I see God punching the kingdom of darkness in the mouth. God is a God of war. He's a mighty God with mighty angels fighting on our behalf.

Malachi 3:12 goes on to say, "'And all nations will call you blessed, for you will be a delightful land,' says the Lord of hosts." *Delightful* implies your land and life will continue to increase, break through, and overflow to the pleasure of God. Delight is a more permanent pleasure than joy. Delight is God using your life to shine and break the influence of darkness over nations. There will be a battle, but stand strong. That's when you will see a breakthrough.

God wants to make you a delightful land so He can place you on display for His splendor (see Isa. 61:3 NIV). Isaiah 60 also echoes that thought when it says, "Arise, shine; for your light has come! And the glory of the Lord is risen upon you. ...The Gentiles shall come to your light" (Isa. 60:1,3). On your day of adversity, you must stand firm and not grow weary or shrink back. God is calling you forward with great horsepower. Even though you may not feel it, you are breaking through even now! You are increasing and expanding. As you seek first the kingdom of God today, I charge the angels concerning you to bring forth heaven's culture in your life, that you may experience the fullness God has for you and the powers of darkness coming against you will be destroyed. May you be a delightful land!

JESUS IS LORD

The narrow gate, with a difficult way that leads to life, is the path to the kingdom of God. Let's be clear—Jesus is the only way to God the Father and to experience eternal life. He is the narrow gate, the difficult way which leads to life. Jesus Himself said there are few who find it. As sobering as this is, if you are reading this right now and haven't made Jesus the Lord of your life, stop what you are doing and do it right now! Repent of your sins, ask Jesus to forgive you, believe in your heart that God raised Him from the dead, and confess Him as your Lord.

If you receive Jesus or simply want more information on how to give your life to Jesus, please contact our ministry. We will give you free materials explaining salvation and what you receive when you ask Jesus to rescue you. If you have made Jesus Lord of your life, then rejoice—you are walking the narrow path that leads to life!

There is a dramatic difference when we pray for God's will to be done on earth as it is in heaven; we're recognizing heaven as a place with its own economy, structure, culture, armies, and its own healing system. When we talk about seeking first the kingdom of God, like in Matthew 6:33, we see a system that gives you access to the path that ultimately leads to the kingdom of heaven. When we seek the kingdom of God and His righteousness, everything in heaven is added to you as a natural manifestation of heaven's supernatural culture.

Chapter Five

A CORPORATE SUPERPOWER

Everything we have talked about up to this point has been preparatory. You must have the right mindset and belief system in place if you are going to begin breaking hell's economy off your life. It takes revelation and intensity!

If the devil can't steal your vision, the next thing he tries to steal is your resources. Why? To delay your breakthrough or derail it all together, he will throw everything at you that interrupts your encouragement and will fight to shake your confidence. You must fight back by writing down your vision, believing it, and standing on it.

> *And the Lord answered me, and said, Write the vision, and make it plain upon tables, that he may run that readeth it. For the vision is yet for an appointed time, but at the end it shall speak, and not lie: though it tarry, wait for it; because it will surely come, it will not tarry.*
>
> **—Habakkuk 2:2-3, KJV**

Your time to increase is now. Your calling, your mandate, requires it. It's calling you to break through, to increase, and to overcome all to fulfill God's purpose for your life. Deuteronomy 8:18 says, "And you shall remember the Lord your God, for it is He who gives you power to get wealth, that He may establish His covenant which He swore to your fathers, as it is this day."

Prosperity from God has a purpose, which is to establish His covenant around the earth. In other words, He wants the message of the gospel to spread across the globe. Your vision, and the ultimate purpose of your vision, is a piece to the larger puzzle, which is the gospel reaching every person in the world.

The Missing Truth of Corporate Prosperity

Understanding the value of your piece in the puzzle, your part to play in the big picture, is vital! Without knowing we are called to stand together, unified and empowering one another, the highest potential available will not be reached. Corporate prosperity is not a given; it is something we must rise to. As I often say, "The devil couldn't beat the church, so he did the next best thing—he joined it." This denominating of the nation has caused tremendous loss and wasted potential for all believers.

If the body of Christ ever unlocks what is available to them, it would be the number one financial superpower in the world! The blessing is without measure. Limits come from religion, man's limited thinking, and the influence brought on by the kingdom of darkness resulting in a broken ideology throughout the ranks of the people of God. He knew he couldn't beat the church in this area, so the devil joined the church, doing his best to influence the church's economics.

How is it that men like Abraham, Isaac, and Jacob were the wealthiest individuals of their time, and yet the church that is living in a *greater covenant* has been so far behind in these arenas? Hell's system has effectively influenced the idea of preachers with great financial means as an evil thing.

Hell's economy, the mammon way of thinking, has induced two different extremes—either keep the church broke or make them obsessed with money. We are the body of Christ; we are made up of many individuals but collectively are one in Jesus. When Scripture explains to us we have many members as one body (see 1 Cor. 12:12), this imagery is a reference to a corporate understanding. The body works together for a common purpose.

Regarding monetary wealth, prosperity, increase, and similar terms, the focus has been on the individual. Although correct, this picture is not complete; it is very limited. Individually you are to have all things to richly enjoy; you are absolutely supposed to do well and experience good things regarding possessions and resources. God's kind of monetary wealth was never meant for one person. One person can only accomplish so much. Teamwork is required in every area of God's kingdom such as missions, the daily operation of a church, crusades, written materials, television outreach, and the like.

Words such as "wealth transfer" and "the wealth of the wicked being stored up for the righteous" aren't about one person. This is referencing generational purpose and resource far more than an individual bank account.

Knowing that Jesus provided everything physically, financially, and so much more, it becomes simple. All He has is ours. He has given us all things that pertain to life and godliness. The big revelation is to see and know what John the revelator stated: "As He is [present tense, right now] so are we in this world." Jesus is the Son of the living God, the One who created everything. He owns cattle on a thousand hills. The sea, the sky, the forests, all land, all space, time, and the stars alone are beyond our comprehension in magnitude. He owns them all. As He is—His position, His influence, His ownership—so are we, corporately, in this world. We are the body of Christ. We are called to preach the gospel, but also notice we are to make disciples of nations.

*And Jesus came and spoke to them, saying, "All authority has been given to Me in heaven and on earth. Go therefore and **make disciples of all the nations**, baptizing them in the name of the Father and of the Son and of the Holy Spirit."*

—Matthew 28:18-19

What a statement! How do you disciple a nation? Or nations! By us all doing the same work, with the same mind, spread out all over the world! This also means we influence every area of the culture. We cannot disciple nations without having a corporate presence in every nation. Should Jesus tarry, this is the path to corporate prosperity—this is the avenue of becoming a global superpower of influence and culture. God will finance His corporate people who widely influence every aspect of the culture for the sake of the gospel.

The revelation we all need is that the wealth transfer from the wicked to the righteous is to be done as the body of Christ. One person is not enough, nor is it God's design that just one individual single-handedly becomes the number one financial superpower in the world. It's a culture, similar to the Josephs in Egypt, the Solomons carrying on a legacy, the artisans who built the temple, and it's you and me. We are to do our part by stepping into God's economy; this will induce multiplication in a way we have never imagined. Our answer to solving global debt is based on where the righteous superpower has influence. Rightsizing cultural issues would be in the hands of the corporate body if we acted on this understanding.

It has been said that less than 5 percent of church attendees are the actual givers and tithers in most churches. This is horrible as it shows us the predicament. Still, so much gets accomplished all over the world by a small percent of the body with a revelation of God's economy. Imagine if the entire corporate body acted in the same way the 5 percent do. Churches and ministries would never have debt. Building projects would be instantly executed. Vision would be the conversation of local churches and ministries. Taking territory would be the real conversation. The answer to rescuing the unborn and human trafficking would be brought to an end much faster. His truth would march on rapidly! Jesus might even return much sooner than planned. Why? Because mission accomplished! That's why.

It's hard for people to enter God's economy without doing what is required according to His Word. This is the cause of lack and sadly the financial empowerment of darkness. It's time to make a change. It all begins with placing a priority on tithing, giving, and doing all the biblical steps required to experience God's economy. Every local church and ministry that is wildly increasing according to the grace given them is foundationally called to send out laborers. Business missionaries, entertainers, politicians, educators, scientists, and military are all connected to the body of Christ. They are subject to expanding the gospel footprint to reach every nation as the initial step in discipling nations.

Making God Rich

God's economy for you has an ultimate purpose—to be Christ-centered and expand the gospel's reach to every corner of the earth. Corporate increase exists to make God rich. Someone might ask, "God? Rich? How could we possibly make Him rich? He has it all." That is not true.

He does not have it all. He still doesn't have some of the people you love, some of the lost and wandering souls around the world. Millions and millions of people will one day enter the real hell without ever truly knowing Jesus as their Lord and Savior. This is what God does not have—enough souls.

A Father who wants all His kids home—that is our God. Sadly, we know through His Word that many will enter eternity without knowing their true Father by Jesus His Son. Our part is to win as many as we can before the end. The way we make God rich is to bring His lost kids home to Him. To win the lost, we must bring as many as we can to the saving knowledge of Jesus Christ.

If the body of Christ realized that this is what wealth and prosperity was really about, God would get behind their finances like this world has never seen. It still begins by sowing and reaping God's way, through marshaling the prosperity He gives us to not only enjoy life but to share the gospel around the world!

His purpose may best be represented by the waters that surround the earth. In Revelation 14:2, it says, "And I heard a voice from heaven, like the voice of many waters." Habakkuk 2:14 also uses this image to illustrate the knowledge of God's glory: "For the earth will be filled with the knowledge of the glory of the Lord, as the waters cover the sea."

The sea represents the people and the nations. What the Word of God is telling us is that the earth is desperate to hear the knowledge of the Lord! God's desire is for the knowledge of His glory to touch every place and person the same way the oceans and seas cover the earth. What a picture that is—God wants to saturate the earth with the revelatory knowledge of Him and the gospel. The end result translates to a mass number of individuals coming to know Jesus as Savior.

This is where individual and corporate increase comes into play. God's economy is a system given to us to fulfill God's ultimate purpose and proclaim the knowledge of the glory of the Lord.

Arise, shine; for your light has come! And the glory of the Lord is risen upon you.

—Isaiah 60:1

Our calling is to present the glory of the Lord through the birth, life, death, and resurrection of His precious Son, Jesus Christ. Therefore, it's imperative that we stop our limited thinking, our limited believing, our limited giving, and our limited understanding concerning God's desire for our breakthrough.

Individually your dream is God-given and it is for an appointed time. It is your duty to participate in this large tapestry and global superpower, as the body of Christ, corporately taking territory through influence and purpose.

Let me say a prayer over you right now. In Jesus' name, I declare that your day of increase is manifesting. I call it forward—your positioning and your harvest on seed that is sown. Right now, I speak over you, dear reader, that your generational purpose would rise in your life and a position would unfold for you to discover your place. God bless you! May the Spirit of the Lord be upon you! Be bold, do not shrink back— your day of increase is coming. Whatever you have struggled through, whatever challenges you've faced, it is time to stand and declare the glory of God throughout all the earth. You are needed and highly valued, amen.

CREATION IS BEGGING FOR YOU TO SHOW UP

According to Romans 8:22, the chaos we're seeing in the world is due to God's children not standing up and fulfilling His purpose. The Scripture tells us, "We know that the whole creation has been groaning as in the pains of childbirth right up to the present time" (NIV). Around the world, volcanoes are erupting, tectonic plates are shifting, and God's people are settling for soulless entertainment instead of a true anointing from God.

The earth is literally quaking and groaning to see the manifest sons and daughters of God revealed. Remember when Jesus rode into Jerusalem. We're told in John 12:13 that the people shouted, "Hosanna! 'Blessed is He who comes in the name of the Lord!'" In Luke 19:39-40, the religious leaders tried to stop them: "But He answered and said to them, 'I tell you that if these should keep silent, the stones would immediately cry out.'"

Believers are called to do what God has called them to do. Jesus fulfilled His calling, and the disciples fulfilled the call of God on their lives so passionately that most of them pursued their call to the point of death.

Hitting the target requires maturity, which I believe means moving from conversion to sonship.

But as many as received Him, to them He gave the right to become children of God, to those who believe in His name.

—**John 1:12**

Sons and daughters are those who have gone from the point of getting their "fire insurance" to stepping into a revelation of what Jesus provided. The beginning of this journey is the path of maturity. It is a lack of this type of believer that causes the earth to cry out. Groaning is induced by a lack of mature believers. Creation was made to glorify God and is violated when evil-minded free moral agents are running the show. It also reveals fewer mature believers are taking their authority. The culture of unsaved, perverse, and ungodly agendas is propagating and further empowering the spirit of antichrist.

This causes great strain on creation; its only response is to cry out in the form of earthquakes, tsunamis, extreme weather, signs in the heavens, and a variety of natural phenomena. This is all due to a void and lack of manifestation in more sons of God. Every time we see earthquakes and natural disasters, remember, that is God's handiwork saying, "Help! Where are you?" Creation crying out is like a dog who was lost by its owner and forced to become defensive, ultimately biting unknown bystanders for provoking it while the dog is desperately searching for its owner.

Have you ever seen a loyal dog separated from its owner and later reunited? It's emotional. This is the state of creation searching for the ones God told to occupy and subdue His handiwork until He returns. Creation desires the righteous to oversee the planet, like Adam all the way back to the beginning. The thousand-year reign of Jesus mentioned in the Book of Revelation will be what corrects this injustice.

Creation needs believers stepping into their calling and standing up for the Word of God. When manifested sons and daughters fulfill their purpose, the glory of the knowledge of the Lord will cover the whole earth—like the waters. That is why it's crucial and why the earth is crying out.

We must step forward, like David facing Goliath, and take the Word of God to all corners of the earth.

That destiny starts with me, and it starts with you.

Chapter Six

INSTITUTION OR EKKLESIA

And I also say to you that you are Peter, and on
this rock I will build My church, and the gates
of Hades shall not prevail against it.

—Matthew 16:18

In this time or dispensation of grace, also known as the Church Age, we, the corporate body of Christ, have the power to stop the gates of hell. This is a distinction on the church during the Age of Grace, meaning the time of the New Testament. Shortly following the resurrection of Jesus, a tremendous encounter took place. Acts 2 describes this divine occasion. It is when the Holy Spirit was poured out in power upon all gathered in the upper room. Not only did the baptism in the Holy Spirit occur, causing the believers to speak in different tongues, but it was the arrival of a new power with new authority. The church now being born during this event kicked off the last days and arrived to enforce something that had never been seen before. A united group of people were given the authority of God to enforce what Jesus accomplished.

New terminology was used, such as "believers," "brothers and sisters," "baptism in the Holy Spirit," even the terminology "the church" was brand new. Never had anyone been empowered by the Holy Spirit in this manner. God came and dwelt among men through Jesus and took it a step further by making a way for man to become that habitation of God. Anyone who called on the name of Jesus could be saved! Powerfully united against the present evil age, these brand-new species of believers, filled up with God, became a global power to be reckoned with.

These who have turned the world upside down.

—Acts 17:6

THE CHURCH CANNOT BE OVERCOME!

The Book of Revelation in chapter 13 speaks of an end-time scenario when the antichrist will be in power on the earth. He will also be granted the ability to make war with the saints—and to overcome them.

And it was given unto him to make war with the saints, and to overcome them: and power was given him over all kindreds, and tongues, and nations.

—Revelation 13:7, KJV

In that dispensation, it will be different from the current time we are living in. We are in the church age and Jesus declared in Matthew 16:18 that "the gates of hell shall not prevail" against His church. Those saints who are on the earth at that time will be overcome by the antichrist. Many speculate this is because the church of Jesus Christ will be caught up to meet the Lord in the air before this dreadful time. Those that remain will still be able to discover the truth of Jesus; some will give their lives to Him, becoming end-time saints. This, however, is not the experience of the believers today. We cannot be overcome by the gates of hell unless we give it permission or we lie down, not enforcing our authority.

And I also say to you that you are Peter, and on this rock I will build My church, and the gates of Hades shall not prevail against it.

—Matthew 16:18

"Church" was a new moniker. The Old Testament never mentioned it; you might say it was concealed. Many thought the Messiah would come and deliver Israel from all the outside governmental oppression. Groups such as the zealots pressured Jesus to "storm the castle," so to speak. Yet He explained the purpose of His coming was not for that; it was to seek and save that which was lost. In His second advent, He will come and take over the world. First, He arrived as the Lamb of God who takes away the sin of the world. His second coming will reveal Him as the Lion, as King Jesus.

"Grace" is the label given to the age we live in—a unique moment in all of history when the gospel is to be preached to the ends of the earth, then the end will come (see Matt. 24).

Jesus referred to the body of believers as His church, and the gates of hell would not prevail against it. The word *church* here is the Greek word *ekklesia*.

THE EKKLESIA

Ekklesia was a governmental word used in ancient history meaning "the called-out people or assembled body of free citizens in the public affairs of a free state."

The *ekklesia* was summoned by a "herald" or "messenger" with public authority to represent the kingdom they served. A clearer picture would be the local church coming together at the summons of a preacher.

A broader definition of the *ekklesia* reaches beyond the local church and includes the global body of believers. In the Greek it is defined this way: "those who anywhere, in a city or village, constitute a company, and are united into one body, making up the whole body of Christians scattered throughout the earth." What's presented here is a working picture of the church, both locally and globally.

Understanding the *ekklesia*/church that Jesus told Peter about makes it clear that it is a powerful entity built by Jesus Himself! Hell with all its systems and evil cannot withstand the actual church!

How is it then that we do not see more victory and taking of territory? Allow me to present you with a thought. What many label the church today might in fact not actually be the church, at least not the church Jesus described. What many well-intending believers have labeled as their church might in reality be an institutionalized version of an effectual church impacting the culture.

THE INSTITUTIONALIZED CHURCH

For a large portion of believers, the institutionalized church is being confused with the actual church. When speaking of the institutionalization of the church, I'm grateful to the work of George Barna for his insights regarding ministries and churches. His research shows an arc comprised of four phases revealing the typical lifespan of a church or ministry. They are as follows:

1. The infancy or "birthing" phase.

2. The development or "growth" phase.

3. The mature phase. The group begins to focus more and more on its history rather than its future.

4. The declining phase. This is every ministry's "final frontier."

Institutionalization becomes solidified in the mature phase. Institutionalization is the sum of what it took to build the platform or position they possess, along with the unique message they preached, and the overall cultural values they have developed with the doctrinal towers they stand on.

All these things have become a place of familiarity and are good, yet they can become the very enemy of a ministry's original purpose once it arrives at its declining phase.

Decline begins at the point of fulfilled vision or the end of a movement. Decline often takes place when the next generation takes over, and by placing extreme value on the principles of what achieved the entity's position. This is what fortifies institutionalism. By the time a former revelation—now with extreme value turned into rules—finds its way to the third generation, it is most often completely institutionalized. No more life, nothing new, the past is celebrated more than the future.

WHEN THE HORSE IS DEAD, DISMOUNT!

Several decades ago, my mentor coined a saying, "When the horse is dead, dismount!" This perfectly describes an entity that was once alive and thriving coming to its conclusion. There are times and seasons for things. Ministries must focus on the gospel and making disciples rather than their own legacy and future. When that horse is dead and no longer capable of carrying on, it's time to dismount. There is nothing wrong with that.

A dark side of institutionalized movements can be revealed when they arrive at their decline. Churches and ministries that discover they are in a state of decline will begin to understand that their time of influence is over. They often find their days of being "cutting edge" are out of date. As they come to this realization that they're no longer relevant, a church or ministry can become violently committed to their own self-preservation. The result is a deformed ministry. If God birthed it, then the blessing of the Lord will keep something going for its designated target. If man birthed it, then man will keep it going through every carnal avenue available.

WHATEVER THE INSTITUTION CANNOT CONTROL, IT MUST KILL

History is filled with the institution desiring to keep its former relevance. As a result, whatever the institution cannot control, it must kill. The irrelevance of an institution can often be gauged by the level of persecution it shows reformers. Most often this is by the leaders fearful of losing a perceived relevance. Institutions are often filled with genuine believers who truly love the Lord and are led by generational leaders who do not carry a "now word" for their generation.

> *I do not write these things to shame you, but as my beloved children I warn you. For though you might have ten thousand instructors in Christ, yet you do not have many fathers; for in Christ Jesus I have begotten you through the gospel. Therefore I urge you, imitate me.*
>
> —1 Corinthians 4:14-16

Verse 15 of the above Scripture mentions ten thousand instructors. The literal rendering of it means "boy instructors." Paul is saying though you have ten thousand "boy instructors" you have not many fathers. He goes on to define what he means. A father is someone you can imitate. Paul urged them to imitate him! He was saying, "Hey! Act like me!"

Fathers are originators; boy instructors are those who parrot what they have heard. Now, we should all thank God for boy instructors—without them we would not have widespread teaching and discipleship. It is, however, boy instructors who typically are holding the reins of an institution during its decline. This leads to a mutation of the original intent. Examples of healthy legacy happen more often than not, and a revelation becomes institutionalized at the hands of boy instructors.

Opposite of God's highest and best is an institutionalized church whose relevance is found in persecuting those with a "now word" for their generation. Understanding the words of John the Baptist is the way of real kingdom-minded leaders: "I must decrease, He must increase." At the heart of real fathers and mothers in the faith is this statement. Originators desire to see what they built outshine them through those who carry on with the message; they are gospel driven. Discipleship and reaching a lost world through every available means is the legacy they care about first.

Leaders willing to give up, to go up, to pass the baton, and celebrate those they pass it to, are the lifeblood of generational growth. Corporately and globally, the body of Christ should produce legitimate reformers in each generation.

Healthy reformers taxi the good from the last movement while merging it with the next. These are experts in retrofitting a movement's message and values. I call this breathing life into the institution. It must be stated that reformers are not called to destroy the institution; rather, they are to breathe life into the institution!

The following Scriptures reference several times when the word *ekklesia* is used in the New Testament.

And I also say to you that you are Peter, and on this rock I will build My church, and the gates of Hades shall not prevail against it.

—Matthew 16:18

Therefore take heed to yourselves and to all the flock, among which the Holy Spirit has made you overseers, to shepherd the church of God which He purchased with His own blood.

—Acts 20:28

So great fear came upon all the church and upon all who heard these things.

—Acts 5:11

And He put all things under His feet, and gave Him to be head over all things to the church, which is His body, the fullness of Him who fills all in all.

—Ephesians 1:22-23

Till we all come to the unity of the faith and of the knowledge of the Son of God, to a perfect man, to the measure of the stature of the fullness of Christ.

—Ephesians 4:13

And if he refuses to hear them, tell it to the church. But if he refuses even to hear the church, let him be to you like a heathen and a tax collector.

—Matthew 18:17

Praising God and having favor with all the people. And the Lord added to the church daily those who were being saved.

—Acts 2:47

This is he who was in the congregation in the wilderness with the Angel who spoke to him on Mount Sinai, and with our fathers, the one who received the living oracles to give to us.

—Acts 7:38

Now Saul was consenting to his death. At that time a great persecution arose against the church which was at Jerusalem; and they were all scattered throughout the regions of Judea and Samaria, except the apostles.

—Acts 8:1

As for Saul, he made havoc of the church, entering every house, and dragging off men and women, committing them to prison.

—Acts 8:3

Then the churches throughout all Judea, Galilee, and Samaria had peace and were edified. And walking in the fear of the Lord and in the comfort of the Holy Spirit, they were multiplied.

—Acts 9:31

Then news of these things came to the ears of the church in Jerusalem, and they sent out Barnabas to go as far as Antioch. When he came and had seen the grace of God, he was glad, and encouraged them all that with purpose of heart, they should continue with the Lord. For he was a good man, full of the Holy Spirit and of faith. And a great many people were added to the Lord. Then Barnabas departed for Tarsus to seek Saul. And when he had found him, he brought him to Antioch. So it was that for a whole year they assembled with the church and taught a great many people. And the disciples were first called Christians in Antioch.

—Acts 11:22-26

Now about that time Herod the king stretched out his hand to harass some from the church.

—Acts 12:1

Peter was therefore kept in prison, but constant prayer was offered to God for him by the church.

—Acts 12:5

Now in the church that was at Antioch there were certain prophets and teachers: Barnabas, Simeon who was called Niger, Lucius of Cyrene, Manaen who had been brought up with Herod the tetrarch, and Saul.

—Acts 13:1

So when they had appointed elders in every church, and prayed with fasting, they commended them to the Lord in whom they had believed.

—Acts 14:23

Now when they had come and gathered the church together, they reported all that God had done with them, and that He had opened the door of faith to the Gentiles.

—Acts 14:27

So, being sent on their way by the church, they passed through Phoenicia and Samaria, describing the conversion of the Gentiles; and they caused great joy to all the brethren. And when they had come to Jerusalem, they were received by the church and the apostles and the elders; and they reported all things that God had done with them.

—Acts 15:3-4

Then it pleased the apostles and elders, with the whole church, to send chosen men of their own company to Antioch with Paul and Barnabas, namely, Judas who was also named Barsabas, and Silas, leading men among the brethren.

—Acts 15:22

And he went through Syria and Cilicia, strengthening the churches.

—Acts 15:41

So the churches were strengthened in the faith, and increased in number daily.

—Acts 16:5

And when he had landed at Caesarea, and gone up and greeted the church, he went down to Antioch.

—Acts 18:22

Some therefore cried one thing and some another, for the assembly was confused, and most of them did not know why they had come together.

—Acts 19:32

But if you have any other inquiry to make, it shall be determined in the lawful assembly.

—Acts 19:39

And when he had said these things, he dismissed the assembly.

—Acts 19:41

From Miletus he sent to Ephesus and called for the elders of the church.

—Acts 20:17

Now you are the body of Christ, and members individually.

—1 Corinthians 12:27

For you have heard of my former conduct in Judaism, how I persecuted the church of God beyond measure and tried to destroy it.

—Galatians 1:13

There is one body and one Spirit, just as you were called in one hope of your calling.

—Ephesians 4:4

Not forsaking the assembling of ourselves together, as is the manner of some, but exhorting one another, and so much the more as you see the Day approaching.

—Hebrews 10:25

But you are a chosen generation, a royal priesthood, a holy nation, His own special people, that you may proclaim the praises of Him who called you out of darkness into His marvelous light.

—1 Peter 2:9

THE HISTORICAL LIFE OF JESUS

Chapter Seven

JESUS AND ANCIENT MYTHS

My people are destroyed for lack of knowledge:

—Hosea 4:6

W hat you don't know can hurt you. Ignorance to what you have been given can cause unnecessary grief. Any area where ignorance is present causes loss of opportunity. Not knowing your rights about a specific issue will limit your authority regarding that same issue.

In a court of law, what is fair is not the discussion. What is discussed and argued over is what the law says or permits. Was the law broken? Who is at fault? Who should be compensated, rewarded, or punished? Going into a court of law to plead a case and hoping for a desired outcome has great effectiveness when the individual stating the case knows the law.

As believers, we have the greatest Jewish attorney who has ever lived pleading our case. He never loses if His clients listen to Him. Arguing a case on an individual level requires knowing your rights. Likewise, if we are to have success and exercise the authority required to break hell's economy off our lives, proper understanding is in order.

For ye know the grace of our Lord Jesus Christ, that, though he was rich, yet for your sakes he became poor, that ye through his poverty might be rich.

—2 Corinthians 8:9, KJV

Jesus was sent to earth because God loved you. Think about that! God loved you and your family so much that He sent Jesus to pay for your eternity should you choose Him as your Lord. In sending Jesus, He also provided an avenue for your provision.

Perverting the foundation and purpose for this provision is a tactic brought on by the kingdom of hell to ultimately hinder the gospel. The devil, as we have said, couldn't beat the church, so he joined it. The kingdom of darkness utilizes wrong ideologies that have effectively limited the *ekklesia's* great commission.

One such way is the notion that somehow the church, preachers, and believers should not have means to accomplish their calling, thereby making poverty a part of holiness. Thankfully in recent years, there has been growth and better education regarding Christians and money. Sadly, a vast majority of the body of Christ, as well as those in the world, have a misunderstanding when it comes to the topic.

Make no mistake, the devil and the spirit of the age would love to see the church bankrupt and have been trying for generations to accomplish that.

Institutionalized religion, going as far back as the dark ages, made sure the people were ignorant and broke, while they themselves hoarded resources in the name of the Lord. These blind guides poured on guilt and shame, then collected resources by benefitting from people's ignorance. Much like a socialist government taxing the citizens to no end, while the leaders live posh, high-end lifestyles.

It is very important to note that imbalances abound on both sides of the issue, including off-the-rails money preaching. Explained differently, they have an end goal of getting bigger offerings. No different than the religious leaders during the dark ages, many modern preachers keep followers ignorant through preaching out of context, half-truths, and sensationalizing money for the purpose of fleecing the listeners. Of course, with the negatives there are alternately many excellent preachers who have a very healthy grasp on the Word of God, teaching their followers properly. These always point to Jesus and teach a truth-filled message empowering the listeners to receive everything Jesus provided.

What Is Real Wealth?

We are about to enter the subject matter concerning myths about Jesus. Just before we do, let's put some terms in perspective. We'll start off by defining the word *wealthy*.

The concept of being wealthy probably means a lot of different things to different folks. In certain parts of the world, one definition describes wealth as "access to an abundance of money or owning a lot of things."

Someone once said, "The wealth of a nation is determined by how much excess they display, without affecting the population's normal living routine." Others have said, and I disagree, that wealth is based on how much someone is able to borrow from a bank. This way of thinking is common in today's American culture.

Here is one of my personal favorite definitions regarding wealth. Wealth is defined as a man or woman who has a family and children who love them. I think that's an amazing concept. Whether it's a man or a woman, I think this is a very healthy way to view wealth. This is because when you truly think about it, a family is a little kingdom. If love exists in that kingdom, it creates a healthy environment for growth and increase, which is what makes up the bedrock of true wealth.

One of the highest definitions of *wealth* is "one who is *able*." In other words, someone is wealthy if they are able to accomplish what is necessary at any given moment or occasion, no matter the cost. What a revelation! This definition becomes powerful when lined up with the great commission. Imagine it this way—being able to reach significant numbers of people on the planet with the gospel is a powerful way to consider wealth!

The term *wealthy*, for most, represents convenience and comfort. How often have you thought to yourself, *If only I could get this or do that?* We all associate wealth with the ability to provide or purchase something quickly, which is what many who define wealth emphasize.

As we progress, we need to lay a foundation. This foundation is important because many people have misunderstood this concept for so long. Now, if you don't believe something, you can't receive it, which is why the ultimate truth being attacked by the spirit of the age is the identity of Jesus. There is widespread teaching in Christianity that says Jesus was poor, homeless, and broke. The spirit of the age paints Him in all these negative beliefs knowing that by attacking Jesus, the messenger, the author and finisher of our faith, it can weaken our resolve about ourselves. By spreading the falsehood that He was poor, it makes Christians comfortable with the concept of poverty.

JESUS IS OUR PROTOTYPE

A genuine paradigm shift takes place when it is understood that Jesus came as our prototype! He is the firstborn among many brethren. Since this is true, we should become well versed in every part of His life, including His part in God's economy.

Jesus is head of the church. The *ekklesia* is His. He founded it and we comprise it. As the world is plunging into times of great difficulty, we, the *ekklesia*, are smooth in the middle of it. These are indeed the last of the "last days." If we are to accomplish the high call of God with our short time here, it is imperative that we discover God's supernatural economy to finish our race strong. To do this, we must have a deeper understanding of Jesus.

In the pages ahead, we are going to take a detailed look at Jesus, His involvement in God's economy, including what He provided for you. We will also confront a variety of religious staples that are not based in reality. Some of this might come as a surprise, but it will be a rewarding journey.

DEBUNKING ANCIENT MYTHS

A lot of us have been duped by religion over the years. We have not understood the truth about Jesus. We were taught to think Jesus was poor. Through the Word of God, we're going to uncover the truth about Jesus and the resources He had available to Him while on earth. We're going to let the Word of God speak for itself.

The "Jesus Was Homeless" Narrative

Another popular belief, which quite frankly I cannot fathom how it became so deep-rooted, is the "Jesus was homeless" narrative. A lot of people say Jesus was homeless. He had no place to live. He had no place to dwell. They look at Jesus like He was a vagabond or someone wandering to and from places trying to find His way through life. I don't know if He had a GPS to direct Him while He wandered and slept in the middle of nowhere. Well, that is not a fact we get from the Bible. A lot of the time, we've misunderstood Christ and His teachings by making them fit into our own ideologies rather than what they really are.

So many people hold strongly to the verse that says, "Foxes have holes, birds of the air have nests, but the Son of Man has no place to lay His head," and they say, "See brethren, do you not see? Jesus was so broke, He couldn't afford to live anywhere, nor could He handle anything." This shouldn't be our narrative of Jesus. How can the Savior of the world be so helpless and unable to fend for Himself?

Let's examine this perspective. Considering the Scriptures, Matthew 8:19-20 says:

> *Then a certain scribe came and said to Him, "Teacher, I will follow You wherever You go." And Jesus said to him, "Foxes have holes and birds of the air have nests, but the Son of Man has nowhere to lay His head."*

If we read even further, verse 21-22 says:

> *Then another of His disciples said to Him, "Lord, let me first go and bury my father." But Jesus said to him, "Follow Me, and let the dead bury their own dead."*

Let's ponder on this passage before we move forward. I think Jesus was in a little bit of a mood when He said some of these things. This scenario is very similar to the encounter He had with the apostles on the boat when they thought they were drowning. He rebuked them and snapped at them a little bit. At that moment, He was probably disappointed with their progress. It was obvious that Jesus was irritated when He said, "Oh, unbelieving generation, how long shall I put up with you?"

Just like the boat experience, Jesus was obviously irritated when He made the statement "foxes have holes and birds of the air have nests, but the Son of Man has nowhere to lay His head." If you take this at face value, then you'll fall into the category of people who believe Jesus was homeless. However, if you look at this story in Luke 9, just previously in this Scripture Jesus had sent messengers to Samaria. In this area where He was going to rest, they completely rejected Him. At that moment, as they brought Him the news of this rejection, you had this man saying to Him, "I'll follow You wherever You go." Jesus could as well have said, "Foxes have holes, birds of the air have nests, but *sometimes* when you follow Me, we're not always welcome in a town." Simply put, you aren't always guaranteed a place to sleep.

Because of this, people say Jesus was homeless. He had no permanent home to dwell in. They assumed Jesus just came and went, floating around with no place to stay. I want to bring another perspective to this. In John 1:38-39:

> *Then Jesus turned, and seeing them* [two of His disciples] *following, said to them, "What do you seek?" They said to Him, "Rabbi" (which is to say, when translated, Teacher), "where are You staying?" He said to them, "Come and see."*

Simply put and without hesitation. If we read on, the Bible tells us that they went with Him and saw where He was staying, and they remained with Him that day.

The Capernaum Scenario

The Greek word used in this passage is the same word you would use to identify where a person lived. It would be used in conversation saying, "That's their house." Use of the word *staying* in the Greek is to say, "This is where He lives." In other words, it was defining His residence.

It's crucial that you understand this point because it will serve as the basis of this discussion. Jesus was saying, "Come to My house." Now, some commentators believe Jesus' house was in Capernaum, which I'm persuaded to agree with. So when He said, "Come and see," they went with Him and saw where He was living and remained with Him the entire day. This incident happened around the tenth hour. Let's pause and think about this. Would they have remained with Him for very long if it wasn't His house? Certainly not!

I'll give you another example to reinforce the fact that Jesus had his own house. In Mark 2:1 it says, "And again He entered Capernaum after some days, and it was heard that He was in the house." Note the use of the definite article there. It says "the house." It's like saying He was in His house. If you were to say to your family, "Let's go back to the house," what would that mean to them? They wouldn't need you to explain further, as they'll understand what you mean immediately. Let's continue on with this reading. Verse 2 says, "Immediately many gathered together, so that there was no longer room to receive them, not even near the door. And He preached the word to them." Verses 3-4 say, "Then they came to Him, bringing a paralytic who was carried by four men. And when they could not come near Him because of the crowd, they uncovered the roof where He was." Every single time I read this I find it mind boggling. They didn't just give up and go away; what did they do? They uncovered the roof where He was. They were relentless, hallelujah!

I digress. We know the rest of that story. Jesus made him well. But notice very clearly, first, we see in Mark 2:1 the phrase, "He was in the house." It's like, hey! I'm back at my house. Going further, we see how they lowered somebody through the roof. Now, imagine if you would that you're out of your house, and you've decided to spend some time at a friend's house. The next thing you know, some people show up with shovels in their hands; they have pitchforks, hammers, and crowbars.

Suddenly, they rip the roof off your friend's house. Don't you think somebody might voice a concern over that? Don't you think somebody would have said, "Hold it, hey!" I expect a lot of people would say, "Wait, this is Peter's house, or James' house, or even Andrew's." But no one did any of that because it wasn't necessary. Do you know why? It was because the owner of the house was looking right at those five men and probably chuckling to Himself about their grand entrance.

Everyone must have thought to themselves, *It's His house and He's letting it happen.* This took place and nobody freaked out. Nobody shouted and Jesus probably made a mental note to get it fixed later. Capernaum was Jesus' hometown, and I strongly believe this theory that He had a house there. So we must understand that a lot of the time when Jesus made statements like "the Son of Man has no place to lay His head," He was just being figurative and not literal.

The Rich Young Ruler

Let's look into another very popular narrative. This story can be found in Mark 10:17-22. Here, Jesus is talking to the rich young ruler, a story that has stirred up controversy for generations when it comes to the topic of being rich.

Mark 10:23 says, "Then Jesus looked around and said to His disciples, 'How hard is it for those who have riches to enter the kingdom of God!'" Now, He had just been dealing with this rich young ruler. Remember the story? The rich young ruler came to him in the previous verses, saying, "Lord, I've done it all. I'm amazing!" Then Jesus said, "Keep all the commandments, love your neighbor." The rich young ruler said, "I've kept all those since I was a young man. Anything else?"

At this point, the Bible says Jesus looked at him, and in Mark 10:21 it says, "Then Jesus, looking at him, loved him, and said to him, 'One thing you lack: Go your way, sell whatever you have and give to the poor...and follow Me.'" This is the part where we read that the man's heart sank because he had many possessions. Now that's a strong understanding that we've got to get into. A lot of people think he was rich; that's why Jesus rebuked him.

There are a couple of points in that verse I want you to notice. He was rich, but he was also young, hence the name "the rich young ruler." There's something to be said about age. When you look at people's age in Scripture, there's a lot to do with that note, as age has to do with the definition of one's experience and how he'd work things through.

For most young people, we know that oftentimes they are filled with idealism. What Jesus was doing in that passage was confronting that fact. He was saying, "Hold on, son, you haven't really figured it all out yet, have you?" He needed the rich young ruler to understand that one thing was closer to his heart than Jesus. The rich young ruler loved his wealth more than God, and Jesus knew it, which is why Jesus touched on that very topic and began to tell him to give all he had to the poor.

Fast forward to verse 23 of that chapter. After that encounter, "Then Jesus looked around and said to His disciples, 'How hard it is for those who have riches to enter the kingdom of God!'" Another way of saying this would be, "How hard is it for those who are *had by riches* to enter the kingdom of God!" Jesus wasn't addressing those that possess riches, but those with riches that possess them, just like this circumstance.

The rich young ruler had riches that possessed him. Verses 24-25 are very revealing:

> *And the disciples were astonished at His words. But Jesus answered again and said to them, "Children, how hard it is for those who trust in riches to enter the kingdom of God!" It is easier for a camel to go through the eye of a needle than for a rich man to enter the kingdom of God.*

The Eye of the Needle

Let's talk about this camel and the eye of the needle for a minute. A lot of people have said this "eye of the needle" is a small, special gate in Jerusalem, Israel. When it's locked, a camel must get down on its knees and trudge across the ground, attempting to get into the city. As this camel is doing an army crawl, fully loaded, it is a picture that the camel must humble itself and break off all the packages from its back and crawl down with nothing on it to enter the gate.

This sounds pious and noble, with only one thing going against it—there is no gate called the eye of the needle in Jerusalem. Theologians and commentators all agree that it's very disputed at best. Most reputable commentators and theologians agree it probably doesn't exist and never did.

What did Jesus mean when talking about "the eye of the needle"? Many people still believe today that Jesus was referring to a camel and that tiny (non-existent) gate. They claim it means that the camel can get through but not without a lot of effort. Let's get this straight, because that's not what Jesus is saying. Instead, Jesus is saying it's not difficult for the camel to get through the eye of the needle—it's impossible!

In other words, it's not difficult for a rich person or someone who trusts in their own strength to get into the kingdom. No, it's impossible. However, He goes on to say that all things are possible with God. The rich person simply needs to call out to Jesus and they will be saved.

If we look at verse 26, after Jesus mentions the idea of a camel going through the eye of the needle, He uses it to signify a rich man's inability to get into the kingdom. The response by the disciples is really revealing. Verse 26 says, "And they were greatly astonished, saying among themselves, 'Who then can be saved?'" Let's think deeply about what this verse is pointing at. Why would the disciples look at each other and say, "Who can be saved?" Why did they all seem afraid? It's because they all had money. They were all business owners who were wealthy men in their own rights.

Can you even begin to imagine how confused they felt? They must have thought, *How is this possible? If we can't be saved, then who can? If what You're saying is true, Jesus, what hope do we have?* In verse 27, Jesus goes on to say, "With men it is impossible, but not with God; for with God all things are possible." In other words, man with his own strength cannot save himself no matter how hard he tries. In verse 28, it says, "Then Peter began to say to Him, 'See, we have left all to follow You.'" This is where it gets very interesting. In verses 29-30, it reads:

> *So Jesus answered and said, "Assuredly, I say to you, there is no one who has left house or brothers or sisters or father or mother or wife or children or lands, for My sake and the gospel's, who shall not receive a hundredfold now in this time—houses and brothers and sisters and mothers and children and lands, with persecutions—and in the age to come, eternal life."*

If we move on to verse 31, it further says, "But many who are first will be last, and the last first." At this point, I need you to fully internalize the idea that Jesus was stating. Jesus was saying that if you've given up these things, you're going to receive one hundred times as much now in this present time. All He really wants from anyone is to put the kingdom of God over self-preservation. Anyone who chooses to let go of any and all earthly comforts for the sake of Jesus and the gospel will receive a multiplied reward in this present time!

If You Do the Difficult, God Will Do the Impossible

We still find a lot of people preach that there's no such thing as a hundredfold return. The only reservation I have with that is that the Bible happens to say there is. In Mark 10:30, it says, "who shall not receive a hundredfold now in this time—houses and brothers and sisters and mothers and children and lands, with persecutions." It doesn't get any clearer than this! Jesus in essence is saying, "If you give up, you will go up! If you do the difficult, watch God do the impossible!" The impossible in this Scripture means an exponential curve of return that, most certainly, will release exponential growth.

I believe the reason the church has not tapped into this is because it has not created a faith-based mental picture of the kind of return or economic horsepower the body of Christ could have. Dear reader, you need to understand that your sufficiency is from the Lord and no one else. When you fully grasp this concept and let go, only then can you truly allow God to work His blessings in your life.

Chapter Eight

THE SUPERIORITY
OF JESUS

In the previous chapter, we established that Jesus had a house. Another thing we should acknowledge is that Jesus had a tomb. A tomb that was effortlessly provided for Him. Now, this is major! In Matthew 27:60, there's a whole scenario where He was laid in a new tomb, which had been hewn out of a rock. From this passage, we begin to see that Jesus's burial scenario was the type reserved for the very rich. However, we know from the Scriptures that He didn't pay a dime for that tomb. He had the ability to obtain that which was immediately required.

It's amazing at this point, because we can now see that Jesus not only had a house, but He also had a tomb provided for Him. This was a tomb reserved for Joseph of Arimathea who donated his own tomb for Jesus. The picture changes when you begin to understand that Jesus could come and go at will, and He had provision for everything He needed. Jesus was buried in a rich man's tomb, He had a house, and He had various places to stay.

THE TRIUMPHANT ENTRY

Another major event in Jesus' life is His triumphant entry into Jerusalem (see Matt. 21:1-11). That event was so spectacular, if I had to guess,

I'm sure there were several people who saw Jesus for the first time as the man He had always proclaimed He was. What was so spectacular about riding on a donkey, you may ask? Well, I'll tell you. Did you know that the donkey had never been ridden before? I'm not saying maybe it was ridden once or twice. No, the Bible confirms that it had never been ridden by any man or woman before the Son of God. This is a miracle, isn't it? For a donkey to grow to that age where it can be ridden and remain untouched. Who else could have made that happen, if not Jesus? If you remember this story, you'll recall how those waiting for His arrival upon seeing Him began to cry out "Hosanna!"

A lot of people say Jesus wouldn't have bought something new. Jesus would have been frugal. He would have bartered and gotten the best bargain at a cheap rate. They might go on to say, "He would have done this, or He would have done that," based on their own ideas. Perhaps that would have been so if He was involved in a business deal, but that's not the case here.

What we read is that Jesus rode a donkey that no man had ever ridden. In these times, it would have been like driving a brand-new car that nobody had ever driven. Have you ever asked yourself why Jesus didn't just get a beat-up old donkey and an old coat, which would not have cost more than a few shekels? He could have gotten a used donkey and rode into the city. He could have even gotten a donkey that was limping into town, right? Who cares how He enters? What matters is that He does, and it was important enough to be pointed out in Scripture.

I'll tell you why it mattered so much. It's because Jesus didn't have a "broke" mindset or a "broke" belief system. Whatever He was going to use, it had to be the very best.

Mansions in Heaven

Let's move on to another concept that people find hard to believe. Jesus talked of riches with His disciples. In John 14:2, Jesus was talking to his disciples, and He said, "In My Father's house are many mansions." This is a huge point of controversy for many. I've heard people argue on this issue from several points of view. Let's note that this was Jesus talking, and if Jesus is talking, I pay very close attention and so should you. After Jesus mentioned, "In My Father's house are many mansions," He went on to say, "if it were not so, I would have told you. I go to prepare a place for you."

I want you to pay very close attention to the word *mansions* mentioned here. I thought it meant something else because I've heard people argue against it. I've heard people say, "Oh, it just means a place to live." It just means space. They're going to get a little portion on the ground just enough to stand with a flag and wave at Jesus, right? Or maybe it's like being at a concert where you'd only get to stand in a particular spot. Nope. He says, "If it were not so I would have told you." There's a predicated understanding. He said something so profound. He said, paraphrasing, "And if it's not so, I wouldn't have even brought it up."

I looked up the Greek word for *mansion* and I discovered that *mansions* here means "dwelling." You could say a place of dwelling. In every reference I looked at, the Greek reference for the word *mansion* means a "huge, ornate house." So when He says you will have many mansions, it means there will be mansions for you in God's house, God's kingdom. Another way to phrase it means in "God's place" you'll have a mansion. Jesus was not being figurative here; He meant the word *mansion* literally. It means I'll have a place to dwell in, a home, a beautiful mansion in heaven.

My Wife Died and Saw Her Home in Heaven

Many years ago, my wife broke her neck in a gymnastics accident. It was the same break that paralyzed Christopher Reeve (the actor who played Superman in the '80s). While Heather was lying on a CAT scan table, she died. She vividly recalls drifting up out of her body, even looking down on her body still lying there. From this moment, she traveled to heaven. She saw and experienced things that are difficult to describe. While relaying her experience and journey to heaven, she explained that in heaven you're capable of traveling at the speed of thought. When thinking about a location, you can suddenly be there. You are able to pass through walls as well as display many other fascinating abilities. One of the things I found fascinating was when she began to describe a moment when she was standing in a beautiful, enormous home, and she was looking out over a field. As she looked out a window scanning this field, she saw the Lord standing in the field and said, "I want to go and stand there." Even before she was done thinking about it, she went through the wall and was standing on the field. She then understood that you travel at the speed of thought in God's realm. You're here one moment and there in another. After her journey, she explains there are structures in heaven because she's seen them.

When something lines up with the Word, I happen to believe it. People ask, "Why would He build a house in heaven? That's goofy." Well, I believe it's because Jesus loves to absolutely give you His best. If He says *mansions*, and the Greek word translates into *mansions*, I think I'm going to believe the word *mansions*. Praise God! That's a strong understanding right there. He said, "I go to prepare a place for you." In other words, He's been constructing this. He's been waiting on this. He's been desiring this for you. It's so powerful, isn't it? It's so good. You need to say to yourself, "He has a mansion for me." Isn't that amazing?

Heather said the house she was in was very large and beautiful. She knew while she was there that this mansion was hers. The large home she was standing in and admiring was the place Jesus prepared for her. She loved everything about it. Sometimes for encouragement, I will ask her to tell me about heaven again.

Jesus Emptied Himself for You

Let's continue traveling down the road and narrative that "Jesus became poor." This narrative usually starts out in Philippians 2:5.

> *Let this mind be in you which was also in Christ Jesus, who, being in the form of God, did not consider it robbery to be equal with God, but made Himself of no reputation, taking the form of a bondservant, and coming in the likeness of men. And being found in appearance as a man, He humbled Himself and became obedient to the point of death, even the death of the cross.*
>
> **—Philippians 2:5-8**

Abasement

I want you to pay very close attention to the Greek word that is used for "made Himself of no reputation." It's the Greek word *keno*. From *keno* you get the word *kenosis*. *Keno* means "to make empty." Figuratively, it means "to abase or to neutralize." *Technically*, when He made Himself of no reputation, He made Himself empty. He emptied His ability to look like a deity. He emptied His ability to look like the Father, God. To come down to us, He abased Himself and neutralized anything that would cause Him to look like He was from heaven. When you look at it from this angle, you catch a glimpse of Jesus' glory in heaven and the implication of what He gave up for all of us. He had to strip Himself, completely, of all glory. What we can infer from this is, despite His deity in heaven with God, He was also fully glorified. He had the full ability to be radiant, shining with power, and prosperous beyond imagination. He had all the glory of heaven shining through Him and on Him.

GLORIFIED ON EARTH

In John 17:4-5, Jesus said, "I have glorified You on the earth. I have finished the work which You have given Me to do. And now, O Father, glorify Me together with Yourself, with the glory which I had with You before the world was." Please pause and read that again. What a prayer! In essence, His prayer was, "I'm about to finish My race here on earth, God. I'm about to finish My race, Father." He was asking God to restore that which He had put away before coming to earth. I believe Jesus was missing that glory. I think He was a little homesick for God, the Father, and at that level He was saying, "Let's go back to the beginning. Let's go back to what it was like before I took this off for the people of God." Here we see Jesus who made Himself of no reputation, spiritually. In other words, He looked just like us. He took on the form of one of us—a bondservant, a human. He stepped down from His authority to be one of us so He could rescue us.

Now remember, I'm laying the foundation so we can talk about the wealth of Jesus. There was nothing more humbling than when Jesus became a man, because:

1. He had to renounce the wealth given to Him in spiritual glorification.

In other words, He had this glorification, but He took it off. There are two things we should note here. One, He had a supernatural sense of supernatural wealth, because He came from a place where the streets are made of gold. We also see Him put off the wealth given to Him in His infancy. I know you're wondering what I mean by wealth in His infancy. Remember, when the people popularly known as the "three wise men" visited Him, Jesus was given wealth even as a child. While in the manger, a lot of wealth came to Him through the "wise men" or the "magi." We can deduce that these gifts remained with Him by His right. He did not utilize that wealth in His ministry.

2. He faced a humiliating death on the cross.

These are the two very humbling scenarios for Christ. He did not use all the wealth that was given to Him, and there's a purpose for that. Ultimately, we see Jesus face two levels of humiliation with His wealth at His fingertips the entire time.

> *For you know the grace of our Lord Jesus Christ, that though He was rich, yet for your sakes He became poor, that you through His poverty might become rich.*
>
> **—2 Corinthians 8:9**

Now, we recognize that He was rich in heaven, and He was also rich on earth, especially at His birth. We're not talking about a spiritual kind of wealth here, but physical riches. A lot of people think otherwise, but that's just because they've not given themselves to study. The Word of God is ever insightful to those who search through it for the right answers.

Jesus Modeled How to Prosper from Nothing

I am sure the question on your mind now is, if Jesus was given a powerful amount of wealth by the magi, why didn't He avail Himself of the wealth? Why did He not flex His muscles and show off all the wealth He received from the magi as a child? A worthy question that deserves a good answer. Jesus began His earthly ministry when He was 30 years old. Before His earthly ministry began, somewhere between when He was younger and the beginning of His ministry, I believe Jesus made the choice to become poor. This doesn't translate to a life of lack. All wealth in the world was at His fingertips, and He had a right to everything He created, including the gifts delivered by the magi. Yet He chose not to touch it. Why, you ask? I believe Jesus wanted to give those around Him an opportunity to cultivate blessings. He wanted to allow those in His ministry to sow into Him like the wise men from the east did. I believe Jesus wanted to give us a model. He became poor so He could demonstrate how to prosper from nothing, even in this natural life.

His ministry was largely financed by partners. This is because Jesus understood the law of sowing and reaping. When people supported "Jesus of Nazareth Ministries International," they began to be blessed in ways they could never understand. They began to understand increase, and I also believe that there was a multiplied anointing on Jesus' life. If He had self-financed the whole thing, He probably would have disrupted the benefits gained by those who sowed into His ministry.

Paul the apostle said in Philippians 4:16-17, "For even in Thessalonica ye sent once and again unto my necessity. Not because I desire a gift: but I desire fruit that may abound to your account" (KJV). This is what Jesus did. He became poor so that we might become rich. We see from Scriptures that even His immediate followers could sow into Him and receive blessings in return. As we progress, we'll delve deeper into this.

Let's go back to 2 Corinthians 8:9, which says, "For you know the grace of our Lord Jesus Christ, that though He was rich, yet for your sakes He became poor, that you through His poverty might become rich." He emptied Himself of the glory of heaven, the external, radiant glory of heaven. If He had come down floating from the sky and landed on the earth and said, "I am here, thou shalt receive me, My children," I think a lot of people would've run to Him. But He emptied Himself of that so they could have a proper relationship with Him by believing His Word over what they could see.

Blessed are those who have not seen and yet have believed.

—John 20:29

Forsaking Physical Wealth

Jesus became poor and paid the price just so we wouldn't have to. Jesus chose not to use His rightful physical wealth. He died on the cross so that we wouldn't have to and became poor so that we would not have to live poor. He set the earthly wealth He had in His ministry to the side; maybe He had it the whole time, but He set it to the side and God prospered Him. From birth, Jesus had influential supporters like the wise men. Jesus had a treasurer who was a thief. He also had a ministry that contained enough wealth that it required the services of a "treasurer." This treasurer, named Judas, also stole from Jesus, but the others did not notice. If others do not notice, there must be enough in the "account" that anything missing went unnoticed. Think about it—if there wasn't enough money in the account to buy what they needed, when they needed, they would have caught on, but there was never any suspicion raised.

Sometimes when I preach, people get stirred by the Holy Spirit and great things begin to happen. I can remember preaching once in a meeting about "God wants you to increase." After speaking, I wanted to take an offering and bless the place we were ministering in and bless the people who helped us. When we got to the back, we realized that the offering was really small. There was almost nothing there. They said, "Yeah, nobody gave tonight." However, I found it odd that we had such a blessed service, yet that night nobody gave.

It turned out that one of the individuals who collected the offering decided to steal some of it. They said, "You don't understand, I have bills. I have stuff to take care of." They decided to come clean with us. At this point, we discovered they had already spent the money, but we made them pay it back. Thankfully, they did refund it and repented of what they did.

Because of believing in the blessing of God, we decided to help this person with their bills. They couldn't believe it and were profoundly impacted by Heather's and my action toward them. Today they are still serving the Lord. God takes care of His own, especially when you have integrity.

Chapter Nine

SUPERNATURAL ABUNDANCE

L et's get back into the subject of Jesus' wealth. It is imperative for us to define some things about His riches. We'll look at what Jesus possessed both on earth and in heaven. Supernaturally, Jesus was not broke. He was never broke, and there are a lot of circumstances in the Scripture that prove this and quite clearly too. John 19:23-24 talks about the crucifixion site. Here we can gain an understanding in the quality of clothes that Jesus wore. It says, "Then the soldiers, when they had crucified Jesus, took His garments and made four parts, to each soldier a part, and also the tunic. Now the tunic was without seam" (John 19:23). Did you see that? The tunic was without seams! This means that it was one woven garment, woven from the top, all in one piece. This implies that Jesus' garments were valuable.

JESUS' GARMENT

The tunic or garment that Jesus had was a very fine article of clothing. Assuredly, we know that Jesus wasn't wearing rags. This could be likened to wearing a fine suit or a very expensive gown. It would be like wearing something ornate and expensive, to the extent that the soldiers said, "We want it." John 19:24 states, *"They said therefore among themselves, 'Let us not tear it, but cast lots for it, whose it shall be.'"*

This tells us Jesus wore clothes like someone who shopped at the high end of town. In fact, He shopped in the most expensive part of town. In other words, He had clothing made from material that was of such quality that people fought over it at His death. They actually drew straws or rolled dice for it. Imagine the quality it must have been for soldiers to leave their duty for a moment and cast lots for it.

As you've begun to see by now, Jesus was anything but broke. He had a treasurer and a house. He had a place to stay whenever He needed to rest. He also had ministry supporters, and as a child He had the magi who brought Him great things of immense value. I say again, Jesus was not broke! Ladies and gentlemen, Jesus was very well off, and I believe He didn't use the abundance of the wealth He had but rather chose not to access it. He became poor to show us how to grow our own finances. I really believe this, even as I believe this is what Jesus is saying to us today, "I did this so you don't have to, so that you can live, supernaturally, in abundance."

HEAVENLY ESTATES

Let's go beyond just the fact that Jesus had earthly things. People don't recognize that Jesus also has heavenly estates. Think about heaven and all its possessions. Remember, Jesus is the creator of the universe. God, with Him, formed all these things including the natural things on earth. Even when the magi brought Him all that wealth, they could be considered as dirt compared to the wealth Jesus was in possession of.

> *Lift up your heads, O you gates! And be lifted up, you everlasting doors! And the King of glory shall come in.*
>
> **—Psalm 24:7**

Look at those plural words *doors* and *gates*. Then it goes on to say, *"and the King of glory shall come in."* There's a lot we can get from here. It's the narrative where Jesus was leaving captivity. He was leading it right out of Abraham's bosom, or paradise, and going up to heaven.

In that passage, we get a quick glimpse of something—the word *gates*. You get a glimpse of everlasting doors, and you see the mention of ancient gates because it says, "be lifted up, you everlasting doors." In Revelation 21:21, it says, "The twelve gates were twelve pearls." Here we begin to see a connection between heaven and the New Jerusalem. This reference to "the gates" and then the reference to "the gates that are to come" begins to define them.

Here, you see heaven and the 12 gates. When you look at the opulence and magnificence of what God has and weigh it with what people would consider as wasteful, you tend to ask, "Is this necessary?" The answer is, to God, yes, it's necessary because He likes it.

Let's look at Revelation 21:21 again, "The twelve gates were twelve pearls." May I present to you, "the gates that were lifted," these everlasting ancient gates, are giant pearls. It says each one of the gates is made from just one pearl! The main street of the city is pure gold, like transparent glass.

Reflect on that for a moment. The streets are constructed of gold. Do you know what gold is called in heaven? Pavement. Now, gold has value in heaven, and I believe gold has value everywhere.

On each individual gate was one giant pearl. Can you imagine enormous gates coming into a giant city? And as they lifted, the King of Glory came in; I believe angels must have broken into different ranks and regiments, went around it, and then entered through all the 12 gates. I believe it was like spokes in a wheel coming into the city of God and entering heaven. The priceless value, in monetary terms, of these ancient pearls on these gates is beyond our imagination. You know what? The gold-laced streets of heaven and the ancient pearls from before time began are owned by Jesus.

THE EARTH IS THE LORD'S

Psalm 24:1 drives this point home even further. We've talked about heaven and the ancient gates; let's go back to earth. Psalm 24:1 says, "The earth is the Lord's, and all its fullness, the world and those who dwell therein." You could view it this way: Jesus and His Father own the largest cattle ranch on the planet. This includes the mines and everything on Wall Street. It includes every mineral, every shipping industry, every precious metal, and every valuable thing on this planet, which belongs to God.

> *For every beast of the forest is Mine, and the cattle on a thousand hills. I know all the birds of the mountains, and the wild beasts of the field are Mine.*
>
> —Psalm 50:10-11

God owns it all, and by inference this means Jesus owns it all. Jesus is wealthier than any millionaire or billionaire you can ever imagine, both individually and combined. Jesus owns heaven and He also owns the earth. As men, we're called to take dominion and occupy the earth. We are to enforce His kingdom on earth as it is in heaven.

Think about this for a second: do you really think heaven is struggling to pay its bills? Do you really think that heaven is having a hard time making things happen? I must emphasize the saying, "As it is in heaven, so let it be on earth." This is one of the prayers: "Your kingdom come, Your will be done (this is Jesus' word); as it is in heaven, so let it be done on earth." With this statement, I believe there's a great breakthrough in the body of Christ that hasn't been tapped into yet. Jesus set aside His natural wealth to prove to us that we can receive supernaturally in our lives right now, just like He did.

You can do it using what's in front of you. As a child, maybe you didn't get a disbursement of millions or billions of dollars. Instead, what you did get is the ability to hear the Word of the Lord and see that, as it is in heaven, it can also be on earth. Jesus is the Lord of heaven and earth. Jesus owns all the cattle on earth, all the pearly gates in heaven, and all the streets of gold. When we remove greed and the love of money and go into a place of trust with Him, that is when we will begin tapping into what He possesses.

DEAR READER

Dear reader, Jesus loves you. He humbled Himself and chose to become poor so He could be an example for us all. You don't have to be broke or poor, nor do you have to lack in any area. The "hundredfold promise" is real, and Jesus wants you to live, move, and have your being in this truth.

Your mind renewed to the truth of God's Word will set you free from extremes on either side of this subject. We are laying a foundation for you to stand on. God definitely wants you to increase and to do well and not be limited in any fashion. He also wants you free from the love of money. Liberty occurs through growth of understanding, which leads to faith-filled action.

God wants good things for you. He also wants a life committed to Him. Jesus attained victory for you. It is to our benefit to offer our lives to Him in both good and reasonable service as a living sacrifice in thanks and gratitude. This is the ultimate offering in God's economy.

Chapter Ten

THE AUTHORITY
OF JESUS

We're going to delve into a lot of truths that will be directly beneficial to you. The life of Jesus is not only calling you to the gospel, but He is also calling you to live out the destiny God has ordained for you. When you have a vision, a dream, a desire to do something for God, it takes resources. No matter where you are financially, God wants to get His "super" on your "natural." The revelation that Jesus is above our natural economy opens doors to His supernatural provision.

JESUS IS ABOVE THE NATURAL ECONOMY

And Jesus came and spoke to them, saying, "All authority has been given to Me in heaven and on earth."

—Matthew 28:18

Did you read that? All authority has been given to Jesus, both in heaven and on earth. A lot of people have authority in different places. You have natural authority over different things, but Jesus had *all* authority, both in heaven and on earth. This right here is a powerful part of our hope in Jesus. If we read on, verses 19 and 20 say, "Go therefore and make disciples of all the nations, baptizing them in the name of the Father and of the Son and of the Holy Spirit, teaching them to observe all things that I have commanded you; and lo, I am with you always, even to the end of the age." I'm sure you've read that passage again and again, but let's pause for a second and look at it with new understanding.

FIDUCIARIES OF THE KINGDOM

When it was declared in the Word of God or when Jesus said that all authority has been given to Him in heaven and on earth, it was a revelation. This signified absolutely all authority. Nothing has been left out of his reach. Everything in heaven and everything on earth has been given to Jesus. Everything is completely at His disposal, and Jesus has placed His kingdom in our hands. The kingdom is within us. When you recognize this, then you realize that we are the fiduciaries of the kingdom. We are responsible for the enforcement of the responsibility bestowed on us by the Lord God Almighty.

Now, return to Jesus' authority for a moment. We realize when it says, "all authority in heaven and on earth" has been given to Jesus, it's not just over sickness, disease, death, hell, and the grave. We need to come to terms with the fact that this authority is also over wealth, economy, goods trading, and all the things that you can possibly have on earth. This is a powerful concept, considering the fact that *Jesus, especially in the natural setting of this world, superseded and still supersedes riches and wealth.* Jesus owns wealth and all the riches of this world because He's the master of them. What a magnificent revelation.

Jesus is the source and the author of all we know. The Bible says He's the author and finisher of our faith (see Heb. 12:2). We know that God, through the Word and Jesus, created the worlds according to Proverbs

8. This reveals, right from the beginning, God had always placed a premium on Jesus' authority. However, after His death on the cross, God made it official and handed over all authority to Jesus.

HERE AND THERE—EARTH AND HEAVEN

Jesus' economy is powerful, especially when it engages here in the natural. This is something we really need to dwell on for a moment. Jesus supersedes riches and wealth. He is above the natural economy, and He also has power over sin, sickness, death, and the grave. Even the supernatural side of the economy is not left out. An example of this was given in Hebrews 7:8, which says, "Here mortal men receive tithes, but there he receives them, of whom it is witnessed that he lives." This Scripture is distinctly talking about Jesus the Lord of heaven and earth. *There* means "heaven" and *here* signifies "the earth," where mortal men receive tithes. What a powerful concept.

JESUS, LORD OF ALL

Jesus is Lord over all these things. Currently, I expect that you're beginning to understand how this is playing out in several ways. Jesus superseded riches and wealth in just about every area you can experience it. He superseded it not only in every single area of the economy that you can imagine, but also in the functionality and mastering of a trade. As a matter of fact, because of Jesus' gifts, when we look at what He did and how He did it, He could've had an instant return in an economic fashion from the miracles He worked. This is how Jesus superseded riches and wealth in the natural world.

Have You Any Food?

In John 21:4-5 it says, "But when the morning had now come, Jesus stood on the shore; yet the disciples did not know that it was Jesus. Then Jesus said to them, 'Children, have you any food?'" Remember, there is a circumstance coming up and it's the second time He will be doing this same thing. In that verse, Jesus says to them, "Children, have you any food?" They answered Him, "No." It's very fascinating that Jesus is doing this same thing for the second time in the Scripture. The first time, He went to them after they returned from fruitlessly combing the ocean for fish all night and coming up empty handed. Then He said, "Throw your nets out on the other side of the boat." If you recall the story, the fish filled up the net so much that their boat began to sink and their nets almost broke.

Way Too Many Fish

What you're looking at here is Jesus living up to the same narrative, but this time it was just to state their hunger and point out a current need. There's a lesson in this for us that reflects my point: Jesus is above wealth. Jesus supersedes wealth and He supersedes natural means. John 21:6-14 says:

> And He said to them, "Cast the net on the right side of the boat, and you will find some." So, they cast, and now they were not able to draw it in because of the multitude of fish. Therefore that disciple whom Jesus loved [John] said to Peter, "It is the Lord!" Now when Simon Peter heard that it was the Lord, he put on his outer garment (for he had removed

it), and plunged into the sea. But the other disciples came in the little boat (for they were not far from land, but about two hundred cubits), dragging the net with fish. Then, as soon as they had come to land, they saw a fire of coals there, and fish laid on it, and bread. Jesus said to them, "Bring some of the fish which you have just caught." Simon Peter went up and dragged the net to land, full of large fish, one hundred and fifty-three; and although there were so many, the net was not broken. Jesus said to them, "Come and eat breakfast." Yet none of the disciples dared ask Him, "Who are You?"—knowing that it was the Lord. Jesus then came and took the bread and gave it to them, and likewise the fish. This is now the third time Jesus showed Himself to the disciples after He was raised from the dead.

Jesus asked them to cast their net outside the boat, which they did. Peter, out of faith and zeal, swam to the shore, then dragged the fish-filled net of 153 ashore. After Peter got to the shore, Jesus made food for them with the fish. Jesus satisfied their hunger. I find it fascinating when it says, "Then Jesus said to them, 'Children, have you any food?'" (John 21:5). I don't know if you're like me, but I love the way Jesus functions. He says, "Do you have any food?" They respond, "No." He replies, "Cast your net on the other side." They did and they caught, once again, way too many fish.

The first miracle is that He fed them or gave them 150 extra fish. The second miracle is that the net didn't break. I believe this shows that Jesus superseded riches and wealth and He had command over whatever He needed. In this passage, we see it with the fish incident, just like we see it in many other instances. Jesus provided for Peter, John, and the other disciples. He asked a simple question, and after knowing their needs He acted. It's little wonder He enjoins us to always make our requests and supplications known to Him. He has said, after all, ask and ye shall receive. What a wonderful Savior we have!

To sum it up, Jesus gave His disciples excess food just because they said, "We don't have any food." Our God, the Provider, wants to give so much to His people out of abundance that there's not enough room to contain it. He desires to give us more, even to the point that you'll need supernatural help to keep your bins from breaking, your barns from bursting, and your nets from tearing.

Jesus gave His boys one hundred and fifty-three fish for breakfast. Come on, if that isn't wealth, then I don't know what is! If He were to catch that many fish in respect to the location and the volume of the catch, it would make any future trader in the New York stock exchange an absolute millionaire in a few days, especially if they knew where to cast their net to catch that many fish and predict it the way Jesus did. Jesus supersedes riches and wealth by His ability to do miraculous things. He causes the economy to turn and change just through a word from Him.

MIRACLE TAX MONEY

Let's talk about Matthew 17:24-25, which says:

> *When they had come to Capernaum, those who received the temple tax came to Peter and said, "Does your Teacher not pay the temple tax?" He said, "Yes."*

I imagine Peter would, of course, have answered "yes." He probably would have replied with the first thing that entered his mind. Matthew 17:25-27 says:

*And when he had come into the house, Jesus anticipated him, saying, "What do you think, Simon? From whom do the kings of the earth take customs or taxes, from their sons or from strangers?" Peter said to Him, "From strangers." Jesus said to him, "**Then the sons are free.** Nevertheless, lest we offend them, go to the sea, cast in a hook, and take the fish that comes up first. And when you have opened its mouth, you will find a piece of money; take that and give it to them for Me and you."*

I like how the Amplified Bible says, "Then the sons are exempt." Here is the powerful thing about this passage: Jesus is saying, "Hey, do people need to pay taxes or pay for certain things? Do they take it from strangers or from their sons?" Peter replies, "From strangers," then Jesus says, "So the sons are exempt." Once again, we see Jesus establishing His authority as God's Son in a subtle way.

I don't know about you, but I find this very fascinating because an argument could be made that Jesus should've said, "I don't have to pay taxes. I don't have to obey the rules of the land because I am the Son of God," but that is not what Jesus taught us. He didn't want to offend them, and it really didn't cost Him much to be at peace with them. In other words, you want to allow men to have their way as long as it's in accordance with the biblical standard so you can win them over. Jesus was clearly stating here, "Are we exempted from this? Yes, we are, but to avoid offending them unnecessarily through what we're trying to accomplish, let's go ahead and do this." Once again, we see Jesus exhibit His abundant resources by retrieving money from the mouth of a fish. Yes! A fish! Powerful, isn't it?

The scenario above is yet another clear indication that Jesus supersedes riches and wealth. I've tried to wrap my head around this incident, and every time I keep wondering, *How did He do it?* He was able to get money from a fish. I know some of us may want to argue and even develop theories to prove how the money got into the fish. I imagine you might hear people say, "Well, maybe somebody threw it into the sea and the fish swallowed it."

All I know is that we serve a living God! If Philip the evangelist could teleport from one place to another, then it's safe for us to assume God can do anything. This includes moving money from anywhere, be it lost money, money that fell into a lake or canyon, or was left on a mountain, and then transferred it into a fish's mouth. God's awesomeness is astounding!

MIRACLE PROVISION

I believe there are arbitrary resources that God can transfer to people. I've heard of miracles where God filled up bank accounts for people. I've also heard of supernatural debt forgiveness. I don't believe that God would take something from someone and give it to another person, but I do think there are lots of arbitrary places where resources can come from—places where only God can lay claim to them. Things that are unaccounted for, like a lost diamond ring or a gold coin in a lake. I believe God can transfer things like this to anyone He so desires; after all, all wealth is His to command.

When you follow Jesus, you have all of this too; but so many people don't know it and because they don't know it, they're not able to exercise it. There are a lot of people looking for a financial miracle. There's no better financial miracle you could ever experience than being in the wealth of Jesus and realizing that He was never broke. He's the Son of God. The magi brought Him wealth beyond comparison when He was a child—wealth He could have used in any way He desired—but Jesus became poor so we might become rich. He did this by putting down not only His heavenly glory, but the natural wealth the magi brought Him. He lived in the supernatural and showed us how we ought to live and generate something from nothing as we sow, follow biblical principles, and obey the voice of God. Obeying the voice of God can push you into the wealth of Jesus.

THE GREATEST PHYSICIAN

Let's take this even higher, shall we? We reviewed Jesus' potential commerce and fishing industry where He could have made millions using His gift and talent. We also looked at Jesus' ability to pay taxes and how He paid them. He superseded wealth and riches and He was also able to pay taxes. Now, let's look at Jesus' healthcare program and how that keeps Him above money and riches. If we turn our Bibles to Luke 5:12, it says, "And it happened when He was in a certain city, that behold, a man who was full of leprosy saw Jesus; and he fell on his face and implored Him, saying, 'Lord, if You are willing, You can make me clean.'" Oh, I love this Scripture. There's so much in it. "Then He put out His hand and touched him, saying, 'I am willing; be cleansed'" (Luke 5:13). This is one of the "I am" statements of Jesus. I encourage you to study all the "I am" statements of Jesus, such as: "I am the vine," "I am the Prince of life," "I am the way, the truth, and the life," "I am that I am," or "I am He," in John 18:5. Set aside some time to study all of them, if you can.

We recognize that saying, "I am willing; be cleansed." When this leper reached out and said, "Lord, if You're willing," Jesus' reply wasn't for him alone, but also for you, in every area of your life, including your finances. God is saying, through His Son, "I am willing." Jesus is willing to heal and make you whole and strengthened in all areas. If we read Luke 5:14, it says, "And He charged him to tell no one, 'But go and show yourself to the priest, and make an offering for your cleansing, as a testimony to them, just as Moses commanded.'" Just look at all that power in action. Jesus put out His hand, touched him, and said, "I am willing," and the leprosy left him immediately. With this, we can say that Jesus was above the healthcare industry. Imagine this—if Jesus could heal then, He still can today. This also applies to the body of Christ. We can heal incurable diseases of this day with just a touch—a touch of His hand. There's no need for laboratories or years and decades of research that costs millions of dollars.

Think about the wealth Jesus would've generated if He were a healthcare provider. Think about the wealth He would have garnered if He charged everyone He healed for His services; but He didn't, because His wealth supersedes the wealth in the healthcare industry. When you acknowledge that this power is also available for you, then you can start to think of all the wealth and riches you can save in the absence of medical bills.

JESUS SUPERSEDES TRANSPORTATION

Let's talk about the transportation of Jesus. A lot of people have invented several things in recent times. We have space craft that travel to space, trains that travel through underground railways, hyperloops, electric cars, and many other amazing inventions. The transportation industry just keeps advancing; however, Jesus already had the best transportation program around then. In every example, we keep seeing that Jesus superseded wealth and riches because He could easily call up whatever He needed. We also see another fine example when Jesus sent two of His disciples to get a donkey. Matthew 21:2-3 reads:

Saying to them, "Go into the village opposite you, and immediately you will find a donkey tied, and a colt with her. Loose them and bring them to Me. And if anyone says anything to you, you shall say, 'The Lord has need of them,' and immediately he will send them."

I believe that either something had happened or God, through an angel, had told the owner of that donkey that someone was coming for it. That is why Jesus told the disciples the exact words to say.

"The Lord has need of them." Sounds like a fancy password, secret knock, or even some code, doesn't it? I imagine this scene was something from the movies like *Mission Impossible* where the actors communicated in code words. Both parties were able to identify themselves, and it's almost as if the Lord had programmed these folks through His voice to understand that the Messiah needed the donkey. Let's take a moment to read this passage starting at Matthew 21:4-9. It says:

All this was done that it might be fulfilled which was spoken by the prophet, saying: "Tell the daughter of Zion, 'Behold, your King is coming to you, lowly, and sitting on a donkey, a colt, the foal of a donkey.'" So the disciples went and did as Jesus commanded them. They brought the donkey and the colt, laid their clothes on them, and set Him on them. And a very great multitude spread their clothes on the road; others cut down branches from the trees and spread them on the road. Then the multitudes who went before and those who followed cried out, saying: "Hosanna to the son of David! 'Blessed is He who comes in the name of the Lord!' Hosanna in the highest!"

This is awesome!

Here's the point I'm making. Jesus at any given moment had the ability to transport Himself wherever He needed to. This means that Jesus had authority over transportation. At this point, I'm sure you're beginning to see a trend here. Jesus supersedes every industry or area we can think of, and He's able to go beyond them. Why, you may ask? It's because He is above it all. Thus, He's able to command it and do whatever He wills with it.

I want to emphasize how powerful this is for us as Christians. Did you know that you had that much power at your disposal? You can do the same thing Jesus did if you're in Him. The problem is many of us are not tapping into Jesus. With Jesus, you have the necessary authority because all authority in heaven and on earth has been given to Jesus. We are joint heirs with Him. What this means is, you also have the same authority to do the kind of things that Jesus did. It's this way because Jesus has made it so.

Chapter Eleven

SEED WARS

Taking Your Territory Is a Battle

Let's start by talking about something very important in Christendom. Whenever you take or seize what belongs to you in the kingdom of God, whenever you lay hold of what's yours in the kingdom of God, a war breaks out. I don't mean that hypothetically, mind you. I mean a full-blown war erupts in the spirit!

A challenge breaks out, difficulty breaks out, and that's why so many times I talk about the term *seed wars*. Let me simplify this concept for you. When you sow seeds in the ground, or when you put resources in the kingdom of God, you're putting God's economy to work. The devil will do anything to destroy that process.

The war is over the seed. The war is over your returns because if you can win once, you can win twice; if you can win twice, you can as well do it three times. Now, imagine if you won every single time. You will begin to create a momentum that Satan cannot deal with, and he knows this. So what can he do? He does all it takes to stop you from winning; he starts a seed war.

In Genesis 26:12-13, it says, "Then Isaac sowed in that land, and reaped in the same year a hundredfold; and the Lord blessed him. The man began to prosper, and continued prospering until he became very prosperous." I believe this passage explicitly portrays the law of sowing and reaping.

This law applies to all people, even if they don't have any faith in the Word of God. When a giver gives, he receives; it's a natural law. As Christians, we can certainly take this a step further by tapping into Jesus' authority, because all authority has been given to Him in heaven and on earth. Jesus exercises this authority in areas of commerce and in parts of our daily lives. This is the key that can help us unlock our true potential in Christ Jesus. You've got to get this in your heart, because when you begin to see this, only then can winning be achieved. Sowing and reaping is one thing, but the blessing that causes an ongoing linear prosperity is unlocked only when you begin to tap into the wealth of Jesus. There is a difference between sowing and reaping and tapping into the wealth of Jesus. Jesus has infinite knowledge, just as He has infinite resources.

John 7:14-15 reads, "Now about the middle of the feast Jesus went up into the temple and taught. And the Jews marveled, saying, 'How does this Man know letters, having never studied?'" Remember, we're talking about the wealth of Jesus and how it supersedes natural abilities. It is not just about money. When you get into the wealth of Jesus, you will supersede natural money and wealth. But you must seek first the kingdom of God, and afterward all these things will be added unto you. It applies to every area of your life and experience, not just your bank account.

Look with me at Psalm 119:32. It says, "I run in the path of your commands, for you have broadened my understanding" (NIV). This is one of my favorite Scriptures. Psalm 119:97 says, "Oh, how I love Your law! It is my meditation all the day." You might as well call the word *law* the Word of God. Oh, how I love Your Word! Oh, how I love Your commandments. Oh, how I love these things. Jesus and His Word are inseparable. Jesus is the Word made flesh. When you say, "Oh! I love Your law," or, "Oh! I love Your Word," you're indirectly saying, "Oh! How I love Jesus!" He is my meditation all day. Psalm 119:98 says,

"You, through Your commandments, make me wiser than my enemies; for they are ever with me." This is the psalmist talking to God, and he goes on to say in Psalm 119:99, "I have more understanding than all my teachers, for Your testimonies are my meditation." What confidence he had! Here's what I wanted to bring home through this passage—the psalmist loved the law and meditated on it all day long.

MEDITATE LIKE A COW

A good way to understand meditation of the Word is by likening it to how a cow eats. Cows have four compartments in their stomach. What a cow eats is cycled through the four compartments, first by chewing, then swallowing, and then regurgitation. This process then repeats itself until it becomes nourishment for the cow. This paints a picture of what meditation is. Meditating on the law of God means that you devour the law, swallow it, and then regurgitate it. This also involves repeating the process until you're able to derive its essence, just like a cow derives nutrients from its food. This is what it means to meditate. The by-product of someone who meditates on the Word is Jesus' wisdom, which supersedes that of your teachers. Psalm 119:99 says, "I have more understanding than all my teachers." This is amazing, to say the least; Jesus doesn't promise us knowledge alone—He pairs it up with divine understanding!

Have you ever crammed for an exam? You studied or crammed all night for a test and aced it, but the next day you couldn't remember anything from what you studied. That's not understanding but rather knowledge for the moment. It is called memorization. Understanding means that you have a grasp of what you have read, or you have a firm grasp of what's being talked about. When it says, "I have more understanding than all my teachers," it means when your teachers are showing you something you actually understand what they're talking about, even if they don't. This is because of revelation knowledge and divine understanding through the Word of God. Let's keep going. Psalm 119:100 really brings it home. It says, "I understand more than the ancients, because I keep Your precepts."

STUDYING VERSUS MEDITATING

We know a lot of people study ancient philosophy. Everything from Homer to Shakespeare, Plato, Socrates, and others—people study their works. However, the Word of God tells us that if you meditate on the Word day and night, you'll get a hold of it. As a byproduct you'll step into the wealth of Jesus that supersedes man's knowledge and wisdom. You'll have more understanding than all your teachers, which means that you'll be able to understand everything you're taught, irrespective of where it comes from. According to Psalm 119:100, "I understand more than the ancients, because I keep Your precepts." You have access to a wealth of knowledge and understanding far greater than those of the ancient times because you keep God's precepts.

Moving on to Psalm 119:104, we see that it says, "Through Your precepts I get understanding; therefore I hate every false way." A person with supernatural knowledge will hate falsehood. I mean, if you truly carry understanding, you'll hate falsehood in its entirety. This is because the nature of God will grow within you. You will begin to love what He loves, but there's a hatred attached to that as well. You'll hate the things that are inaccurate and incorrect, and because the devil is a liar and his native tongue is lying, by extension you won't like any of his traits either.

Once again, we've seen how the wealth of Jesus gives knowledge. Do you remember the Jews' astonishment in John 7:15? "And the Jews marveled, saying, 'How does this Man know letters, having never studied?'" How, you ask? It is because He had understanding. He is the Word made flesh and nobody can know more than Jesus because He created all that there is in this world. The point I'm trying to make here is that through this wealth of knowledge, Jesus could have accumulated wealth more than every other person because He knew all things. He could shut down an argument with just a few words because He always presented a superior argument whenever He was engaged. Jesus was amazing, even though the religious leaders liked to deny it.

ETERNAL RESPONSIBILITY

Do you want to talk about wealth? Do you want to talk about someone who possesses all things? Then let's look at Mark 8:36. These words came from Jesus. He said, "For what will it profit a man if he gains the whole world, and loses his own soul?" It doesn't matter if you're the richest man on earth with land, airspace, or the moon bound legally to your name. It doesn't matter if you're the happiest person on earth or the most delightful. Even if the wealth of Solomon cannot be compared to yours, your wealth does not count if you lose your soul! Again, Mark 8:36 says, "For what will it profit a man if he gains the whole world, and loses his own soul?" Like David would say, selah!

Again, I ask, what does it profit a man if he gains the whole world and loses his soul? Well, Jesus gained the whole world back from the devil. He created the whole world, and the world is His. Jesus lost His soul when He died on the cross but regained it upon His resurrection. Jesus has the world and His soul. As a matter of fact, He's the only being anywhere who has both. There's not a man alive right now who owns the entire world.

A believer can own large portions of land. A believer can do a lot of things if he believes in God, but I've got to tell you, there will be a day when God will put us in charge of some things in eternity. In this age, we are called to occupy. We're called to take over territories, but no one person owns the whole earth except God, and Jesus redeemed it back to God. The earth is under a lease program and mankind is enforcing the kingdom of God on this earth. Acts 13:35 says, "You will not allow Your Holy One to see corruption." Jesus is at the right hand of God, the Father, and they own heaven and earth. Jesus supersedes that statement in Mark 8:36 because He conquered death and He also owns the whole world. He is the Lord of heaven, the Lord of the earth, the Spirit, and the Soul.

I believe in the age to come; a lot of things will be revealed about Jesus' ownership of the world and the universe at large. We often say the word *universe* like it's just an ordinary word without noting its magnitude. The universe is extremely vast; yet it is God's playground. I must say this—the wealth of Jesus supersedes this planet and the universe at large. It supersedes the power and energy used to fuel several suns. Science tells us that the sun is just a giant star and that there are more stars than grains of sand in the universe.

ONLY LIMITED BY THE TEMPLATE OF YOUR MIND

People sometimes zone out when confronted with these facts because they can't comprehend how wide and how magnificent the breadth, depth, and height of God's love is. They can't take in the far-reaching expansiveness of who God is and how much Jesus supersedes wealth and riches. The only limitation we have to the wealth and riches in this world is the doctrinal template called the "mind," which is where things are built and constructed. When you get into the Word of God and start to understand the wealth of Jesus, that template will be renewed. Eventually, you'll begin to get a hold of who Jesus is and what He possesses.

When He said, "I'm going to prepare a mansion for you," you must know that He's been preparing it for the past 2,000 years. He said, "I go to build a place for you, if it were not so I would not have told you." When the living Son of God says, "Anyone who has given up houses, lands, mothers, brothers, or family for My sake and the gospel will now, in this time, receive a hundred times as much," you better believe it! A hundred times as much on the human mathematical scale reads *infinity and beyond* in the spiritual world. Our thoughts do not even scratch the surface of what God has made available for us through Jesus, the Son, because Jesus supersedes all wealth and riches.

IF YOU BELIEVE

When we're in Him, the only thing limiting us is our belief system, giving, and our lifestyle. I must let you know that Jesus wants you to expand. He wants you to grow and inherit His possessions. He's looking for someone daring enough to take Him at His Word and receive a hundredfold in return. If you don't believe what Jesus said, I do. I believe it, even though it doesn't make logical sense to me. I outright believe everything Jesus says even if it contradicts my doctrine. If Jesus, whose knowledge supersedes natural knowledge—this same Jesus who owns the universe—promises to compensate you for your loss by a hundredfold, then you can be sure that He will fulfill it. You can and will have a hundredfold return for your losses, if only you believe. Indeed, sweet are His promises.

Why Water into Wine?

In John 2:1-11, Jesus performed His very first miracle by turning water into wine. I've heard people argue that for Him to make that much wine, the water must've been a non-alcoholic version much like Kool-Aid or regular grape juice. The Bible mentions nothing in that manner. In fact, we know from the biblical narration that the master of the wedding said, "This wine is the best!" Sometimes the things that Jesus does will *offend your mind to reveal your heart.*

Do you know why Jesus performed this miracle? It's because:

1. His mother asked Him to.

Jesus was reluctant to do it at first because His time was yet to come. In verse 4 of that passage, Jesus said, "Woman, what does your concern have to do with Me?" His mother didn't give up when she heard this; instead, she put a little pressure on Him by saying to the servants, "Whatever He says to you, do it." I believe Jesus was still somewhat under her auspices at that moment because Jesus honored her by performing the miracle.

2. I believe Jesus really enjoyed watching people celebrate.

This should be a lesson for everyone that the Lord cares about what you're involved with. He cared about this wedding. I really do believe this because the wealth of Jesus supersedes human ideologies. It supersedes different things that people consider cultural norms and values. He knew it was a wedding feast—a typical fun Jewish wedding and celebration according to their culture. I think Jesus looked at the scenario and said, "You know what? Yes, I'll do it. I like watching people celebrate the joys of life and being happy." Now please understand, when it comes to alcohol and believers, I believe the best practice is to abstain. Regarding the full meaning of Jesus turning water into wine, this has more layers to it than what is just presented. Honestly, I think Jesus is probably not as different from us as we think. He is, after all, going to be celebrating with us at the marriage supper of the Lamb!

God Is Not as Religious as We Think

I think God is not as religious as we sometimes think Him to be. People say, "Have fun but not too much fun; do everything in moderation." Yes and amen to that. In this scenario, I think Jesus just said, "Hey guys, we're celebrating, but something is missing; I can help provide it." It was that simple. Just another day in the life of the Savior seeing to the needs and even enjoyment of His children at that time.

God wants you to prosper on every level. He wants you to increase and acquire God's knowledge, which would help you understand that Jesus wants what's best for you. Jesus is the kind of person who provided healthcare services to people and paid His taxes. He's the type who makes sure you're fed spiritually and physically. He can provide you excess breakfast until you say, "Lord Jesus, this is way too much; I don't know what to do with this excess." Jesus is the King of abundance.

Malachi 3:10 says that God will pour out such a blessing on you that you will not have enough room to contain it. He can do this because He owns the entire universe. He owns everything. When will the body of Christ awaken to that understanding that He's the creator of all things? The devil didn't invent money or the good things in life. He didn't invent provision. The devil has only ever come to steal, kill, and destroy. However, the Bible tells us that Jesus came that you might have life and have it more abundantly. He's the author of all good things.

People ask, "Who's the richest person to have ever lived?" I'd say Jesus. Jesus was and still is the wealthiest man who ever lived, and amazingly, you're joint heirs with Him. When you begin to recognize this, you're going to begin to see the wealth of Jesus that was provided for Him from the beginning of His time on the earth.

Let's reinforce our point with a few Scriptures. Ecclesiastes 5:19 says, "As for every man to whom God has given riches and wealth, and given him power to eat of it, to receive his heritage and rejoice in his labor—this is the gift of God." God richly gives you gifts and power to eat and enjoy. He allows you to enjoy the work of your hands. God is good! Deuteronomy 8:18 says, "And you shall remember the Lord your God, for it is He who gives you power to get wealth, that He may establish His covenant which He swore to your fathers, as it is this day."

YOU CAN'T GIVE WHAT YOU DON'T HAVE

When we begin to increase in the wealth of Jesus, let's not forget that it's God who gives us the power to make wealth *for the purpose of establishing His covenant around the world.* The gospel needs to be established all over the world and you should contribute to this establishment. Hence, while enjoying your wealth, remember to establish God's covenant. It's a Christ-centered prosperity. It's a Christ-centered increase.

Jesus knows you can't give what you don't have; that is why He has made you wealthy out of His abundance. Jesus had everything, but He gave it all away for you and me, only to take it up again and receive us back to Him. He sowed Himself and received a new name—a name that is above all names. This is why at the mention of the name Jesus every knee must bow, and every tongue must confess that Jesus Christ is Lord. He received us as brothers and sisters, making Him the firstborn among all brethren. The wealth of Jesus is yours for the taking, brother and sister.

As you engage Him through His promises, I encourage you to start sowing with that in mind. I encourage you to be a giver. Not just any kind of giver but the type that obeys Jesus, and from it you will begin to experience the wealth of Jesus. Believe it, engage it, and step into it. I know this is helping you right now, as I believe somebody's coming alive as they're reading this truth.

Jesus wants to celebrate your increase right now. I bless you in the name of the Lord. I'll say this also—there are two things to keep in mind when you give to God. Make sure that you're sowing into "good ground," and make sure you're listening to good, healthy gospel preaching on giving and receiving that celebrates the wealth of Jesus.

Chapter Twelve

JESUS AND
THE WISE MEN

In this chapter, I want to explore something that is often overlooked or misunderstood. I'm pretty sure you're going to find this topic quite interesting. It begins with a question. If Jesus had real physical wealth on the earth, where did it come from? We are going to answer that question.

Jesus was given gifts at birth. These gifts were fit for a king, and not just any king—the King of the world. Let's talk about the story of the wise men in Scripture. The wise men are mostly recognized by their depiction during the Christmas season. Much of what we know of them is an image formed by tradition, not a true historical representation.

THE ORIGIN OF THE WISE MEN

Matthew 2 tells us the story of these wise men and their connection to Jesus. Historically, the wise men were called *magoi* in Greek, or *magi*, which means "powerful or great one." They were known for magic and mystical arts. The name *magi* found its way into Persian culture, which was part of the Parthian dynasty under these magi's governance. The office of the magi was equivalent to our current parliamentary houses or branches of government.

KINGMAKERS

The Bible additionally describes them as astrologers. Ancient history's description of these men from the east places an emphasis on their ability to read the stars; however, they also had authority to validate kings. These "kingmakers," magi, or wise men were involved with far more than the image depicting three kings on camels in the desert.

In the Bible, these kingmakers were mystical individuals from the order of the Chaldeans. There were way more than three of them. They would arrive with the authority of an army when they came to a location. In addition to being astrologers, they were labeled magicians and were highly influential in the culture. These wise men were influential with extraordinary capabilities and a commanding authority equivalent to that of the government. They possessed power, prestige, and were capable of actions that were nearly paramilitary.

From biblical and historical points of view, they were astrologers, kingmakers, government officials, and magicians. Modern-day history might label them "magicians," as they were shrouded in mysticism. They observed the sky, the stars, and other heavenly bodies. Their governmental influence would be similar to the likes of Merlin, the magician or the country's wizard who endorsed King Arthur in legend. Another similarity, you could say, would be like the relationship between King Aragorn and Gandalf, the wizard in *Lord of the Rings*. Stories such as these transcend history.

Star Gazers

The magi, through their ability to read the stars, knew the time and season when an event of historical significance was taking place. They were able to ascertain when a king was going to be born. Not just any king, the King of the world. These kingmakers came from a far country looking for baby Jesus with a star leading their way. In Matthew 2, we learn that they came from the East of Judea. This eastern part refers to the Persian Empire.

The Silk Road

The Persian Empire is known today as Iran, and it was formerly part of the Parthian Dynasty. This empire controlled the ancient Silk Route or the Silk Road. Today, we live in a civilized world where we instantly are able to connect with anyone in the world through a global communication network. In those early days, travel systems and trade routes were the only form of communication. The Silk Road was a marvel in its time, connecting everyone who had access to it and to the rest of the world. They traded everything including precious metals, gems, rugs, spices, silks, incense, and many other precious commodities.

Now, one of the things about the Silk Road is that it is largely responsible for the beginning of modern history. Its network of roads started small and over time began to traverse the entire ancient world. It connected everyone inland to civilizations on the coast. The Silk Road changed the world by connecting everyone together. Some of the precious things hauled on the Silk Road's commercial landscape were gold, frankincense, and myrrh. These items were some of the most valuable items the world trade could offer, and those who traded them were held in high esteem.

Daniel's Influence

The story of Daniel brings more clarity to the story of the magi and Jesus. The life of Daniel as described in Daniel 1:20 reads, "And in all matters of wisdom and understanding about which the king examined them, he found them ten times better than all the magicians and astrologers who were in all his realm." This passage is talking about Daniel and his three comrades. It says that they were ten times better than all the magicians and astrologers in their realm.

The magicians and astrologers mentioned in that passage were Chaldeans. If you take a critical look at it, you'll see that the wise men who were searching for Jesus were descendants of the Chaldeans in Daniel 1. These Chaldeans studied the stars and mystical arts, yet the Bible tells us that Daniel was ten times better than them and was eventually given charge over them because of his excellent spirit. Daniel oversaw the magicians and astrologers in Babylon and other places, including Persia. Daniel's influence over these individuals reset their course, and by reading the stars, they looked to a future day when something big was to come.

Zodiac and the Gospel

Now, if you've ever done a study on the stars, you'd know that there's something called the zodiac. The zodiac is a counterfeit of something God initially put into order. If you study the zodiac, you will come across God's story. *History* is simply HIS-story. Mystical groups usurped the true purpose of studying the stars. They perverted the meaning of something that God put in the heavens for humanity to see—His handiwork. God's plan for star charts was to learn *History* through a biblical lens, not some mystical demonic lens. God wrote His covenants in the heavens and the story of Jesus in the stars.

The prophet Daniel came into the country and was made to oversee the ancestors of these Chaldeans. Under his authority, they transitioned from primarily magicians to the level of government officials. Even kingmakers, who fulfilled a similar role to what prophets are supposed to do, could anoint or declare a person a king. Kingmakers also had astrological knowledge.

The Magi Troubled Herod and the City

Matthew 2:1-2 says, "Now after Jesus was born in Bethlehem of Judea in the days of Herod the king, behold, wise men from the East came to Jerusalem, saying, 'Where is He who has been born King of the Jews? For we have seen His Star in the East and have come to worship Him.'" Again, these are wise men or astrologers from the order of the Chaldeans. Because they were now under Daniel's influence, they came in search of the Messiah. They came looking for the King of the world.

Matthew 2:3 says, "When Herod the king heard this, he was troubled, and all Jerusalem with him." In other words, he was greatly disturbed or terrified. The magi's presence troubled Herod and all of Jerusalem. Why was their message such a big deal to these people? It is because they knew the magi's history and reputation of being kingmakers. This understanding terrified Herod. He must have asked them, "Are you here for peace, or are you here to put the city in a siege?" He must have also inquired if they came bearing a message or came to inform him that he was no longer king.

There must be a significant reason for them to come because these guys did not travel from a far country to Jerusalem for nothing. They didn't just show up as three people on a camel! I believe they came in like an army on a mission. They came bearing gifts for a king, and this is what gave them away. Their coming made Herod and the whole of Jerusalem know that a new king was about to be anointed. They knew this because the magi came in "kingmaker mode." If three guys showed up to town, I don't think it would shake up the city or scare them. However, the case would be different if a well-known army came into town, and you recognized their logo. Then, without needing an introduction, you'd quickly realize what their purpose for coming was.

They automatically might easily conclude that this "army" came to do something serious—like anointing a new king.

Chapter Thirteen

WORSHIP THE KING

The magi had traveled 750 kilometers, or 466 miles, from the Persian Empire to Roman territory. Accompanied by an army of elite forces, these magi were without fear while passing through Roman territory. They arrived to ask Herod where the King of the Jews was because they were there to worship the Messiah. Herod saw these men with their army and considered their question a major threat to his reign as king. He knew at that moment that he had a contender for the throne, which had been given to him by Caesar Augustus. These magi were not afraid of anything; they were the most elite special force in the world and a force to be reckoned with.

Now, the entourage that came with them had a history in Rome. When you study history, you realize these guys already had run-ins with Rome. Some commentators even suggest that the magi had once temporarily removed Herod from office before and then reinstated him.

The people of Jerusalem probably felt like citizens in the movie *Independence Day,* when in the movie they woke up to fifteen-mile-wide alien saucers over their significant cities and were highly terrified. They knew who this military entourage was, which possibly numbered in the hundreds or even thousands. I discovered something important about their visitation—the gifts they brought were part of what shook Herod and the whole of Jerusalem at large. Let's talk about these items they brought for the Messiah.

Befitting Gifts for the King

Typically, the king's culture demands that when kingmakers visit a new king, they don't just go to worship him. They also must come bearing gifts. I want to emphasize something before we proceed. I told you about the ancient world's Silk Road trade system and the precious commodities they traded. As a rational person, what kind of gifts do you think they would bring to honor and anoint a king whom they believed was the King of the world? Bear in mind, they aimed to impress and stand out like real kingmakers, who came to anoint the greatest king they've ever heard of or met. Think about it—do you think they would travel that far from home, pass through military zones with their awestruck army, in order to present a substandard gift to the King of the world? I don't think so. Remember we said the most valuable commodities on the Silk Road were gold, frankincense, and myrrh. The Bible tells us that this was precisely what the magi, being led by a star, brought to baby Jesus while He was in the manger.

Jesus was given gifts beyond comprehension. Do you realize that these gifts were given directly to Jesus and not His parents? Yes, that was the case. Jesus entered this world rich. It means that He probably had more money than everyone in that region because of the kind of gifts He received as a baby. These gifts presented to Jesus became His royal property as a king.

Gifts Equal to the Recipient

The wise men brought gifts that were equivalent to the recipient. Jesus is a King, Lord, and ruler over the world; they could see it through the prophecies of Daniel and through the reading of the stars. When you recognize how significant this is, that is when you realize that these astronomers, jurors, and biblical people knew that the King of the world was coming. So they prepared gifts that were equal to His kingship. This behavior shows how great Jesus was in their sight. This point is crucial because it helps us understand the fact that Jesus had everything—not just in heaven, but also here on earth. These gifts were massive, yet He poured them out for us. He laid them down for you. He became poor so you could be rich.

SOLOMON'S WEALTH

I want to drive home a point about Jesus and His wealth. All the kings in the Bible were just minor men, including Solomon. The Word of God says that Solomon was the wealthiest man who ever lived. His story is kind of like an allegory; it's exciting. Solomon was the richest man who lived, but did you realize that David took the land, paid for everything, and made Solomon wealthy? Solomon inherited his father's throne. You could shadow this to Jesus inheriting the earth.

Let's talk about Solomon for a minute. The Bible says that there was none wealthier than him. He had so much wealth that during his reign the streets had gold and silver strewn on them. This must have been overwhelming for the community. Think of it—silver and gold lying around like rocks. Kings also brought gifts to Solomon, who was just a mere human king, yet he basked in the glory of his opulent wealth. Solomon's experience was luxuriant and over-the-top extravagant. He possessed an overwhelming amount of wealth.

I want you to pay very close attention to Matthew 12:42, which says, "The queen of the South will rise up in the judgment with this generation and condemn it, for she came from the ends of the earth to hear the wisdom of Solomon." Solomon was the wealthiest man ever. He was loaded with lots of stuff, including wisdom. But without a doubt, his understanding was without comparison. Solomon's greatness was in his wisdom and wealth.

GREATER THAN SOLOMON

> *The queen of the south shall rise up in the judgment with this generation, and shall condemn it: for she came from the uttermost parts of the earth to hear the wisdom of Solomon; and, behold, a greater than Solomon is here.*

—**Matthew 12:42, KJV**

Yet, wonderfully, we have someone who is greater than Solomon available for us. If we think about the scenario in the Garden of Gethsemane in Matthew 26:47-55, Jesus could've decided to exercise His power by resisting arrest. He could have said, "You can't do anything to Me because I'm the reason you're alive." Instead, He said, "You're allowed to put Me in shackles and take Me into captivity, because it's been given to you to do so. However, you should know that I could at any moment call on more than twelve legions of angels to come down and destroy the earth." If you've ever done a study on that, you'd know that He could have destroyed the world several times over by saying, "God, I refuse to do it. I don't want to die on the cross." So what we must understand is that Jesus had all of heaven at His fingertips, just like He had all the earth, and at birth He received an unbelievable amount of wealth. I believe He never accessed this wealth to the level He could have. Neither did He access all of heaven's armies when He was going to be crucified. Remember, Jesus, who was rich both materially and supernaturally, became poor for your sake. Why? So that through Him you can have access to that supernatural ability. You can also have access to natural wealth through Him because He paid a gruesome price to give you this access.

THE STAR

There has been a lot of controversy over the star. When the Bible talks about how they followed the star—and it landed over the stable—some people have said it was the North Star, while others believe it was an angel. Others talk about it being Planet X; these magi studied the stars just like sailors study the sky, which led to using compasses to navigate their way through the sea. When the magi finally identified the star they were looking for, they rejoiced.

The truth is, we don't really know exactly what the star was. It appeared along the way and over the house Jesus was in. It could have been that God illuminated one star above the others to serve as a GPS for them. He is the same God who sent fire to burn Elijah's sacrifice; thus, anything is possible with Him. What makes this whole narrative regarding the star fascinating is the magi, who were experts in their field, could read the stars. So often, we over complicate the simple things that are right in front of us. These guys were astrologers; it was their job to read the sky. The addition of this unknown, supernatural shining star must have thrilled them!

Again, there is precedent for these types of miracles. A pillar of fire led Moses and the children of Israel by night and a cloud by day; fire came from the heavens to burn Elijah's sacrifice. Yes, all these things happened. Nonetheless, what was the star? Where was the star? Can we still find the star today? Well, maybe you can, but it is likely that this was a supernatural manifestation guiding them. As astrologers, they knew how to read the sky and they had prophecies concerning the coming of the King of the world, given by Daniel. The prophet Daniel would have trained the forefathers of these wise men and mentored them in the practice of reading the heavens without involving diabolism. According to the Scripture, they followed their charts and, upon the miracle of the star appearing, they found exactly where Jesus was laid.

> *When they saw the star, they rejoiced with exceedingly great joy.*
>
> —**Matthew 2:10**

When the Bible says, "they rejoiced with exceeding joy," it means they began to go wild with excitement! All the military convoy along with the magi began to shout and jump up and down at the appearance of this star. We can only imagine the volume and power of this entire group of remarkable people shouting in the desert. It would be like a Superbowl score-winning moment.

Chapter Fourteen

DELIVERY OF A FORTUNE

There was an allusion to this in Psalm 72. I believe these wise men or Chaldeans knew they were fulfilling Psalm 72:1-10. Psalm 72:10-13 says, "The kings of Tarshish and of the isles will bring presents; the kings of Sheba and Seba will offer gifts." These verses contain the prophecy of Jesus being presented with precious gifts. "Yes, all kings shall fall down before Him; all nations shall serve Him." This is a prophecy of the magi coming to worship Jesus. "For He will deliver the needy when he cries, the poor also, and him who has no helper. He will spare the poor and needy, and will save the souls of the needy." This Scripture makes two references to the poor and needy, which I find fascinating; one says He will spare the poor.

Isaiah 61 says that He preaches the gospel to the poor, and the gospel means good news. What is good news to the poor? It's not just salvation but also the realization that you don't have to be poor anymore. So, the good news to a poor person is that they don't have to be poor anymore. That Scripture also mentions the needy. It says that He will save the souls of the needy. So He spares the poor by saying you should not be poor anymore, and then He begins to save the souls of the needy. It's talking about Jesus.

Earlier, we talked about how Herod and the whole of Israel were terrified; Isaiah 60:6 paints a picture of this scenario. It says, "The multitude of camels shall cover your land." People used a multitude of camels in those days to carry loads while traveling. In our context, they brought gold, frankincense, and myrrh to Jesus, which is in accordance with the Scripture that continues in verse 6, "The dromedaries and Midian and Ephah; all those from Sheba shall come; they shall bring gold and incense, and they shall proclaim the praises of the Lord." They followed a star or star charts in search of Jesus, and when they got to Jerusalem, the Bible says a multitude of camels covered the land. You can see why Herod was afraid—not only were these kingmakers in town, whom he had already had encounters with, but they brought with them an enormous and unbelievable amount of wealth. The treasure they carried under military protection was vast. The sheer amount of personnel and soldiers could have ranged into the thousands. You can see why the people of Israel, or children of Jerusalem, were terrified or troubled. If the camels covered the land, that means a lot of them carried the gold, frankincense, and myrrh. Not to mention a variety of other items that were customary to bring to even a low-level king.

> *When they had heard the king, they departed; and, lo, the star, which they saw in the east, went before them, till it came and stood over where the young child was.*
>
> —Matthew 2:9, KJV

When the magi came to see Jesus, He was no longer in Bethlehem. He was now two years old and in a house. This house was located in Nazareth. Joseph, Mary, and Jesus were only in Bethlehem for 40 days. From there they traveled to Nazareth.

> *When they saw the star, they rejoiced with exceeding great joy. And when they were come into the house, they saw the young child with Mary his mother, and fell down, and worshipped him: and when they had opened their treasures, they presented unto him gifts; gold, and frankincense, and myrrh. And being*

warned of God in a dream that they should not return to Herod, they departed into their own country another way.

—Matthew 2:10-12, KJV

A Literal Fortune Was Delivered

Matthew 2:11 says, "And when they had come into the house, they saw the young Child with Mary His mother, and fell down and worshiped Him. And when they had opened their treasures, they presented gifts to Him: gold, frankincense, and myrrh." Note the plural word *treasures.* These guys gave Jesus a lot of treasures consisting of very precious items. This passage says that the magi presented *gifts,* another plural word. These were royal gifts. The cargo brought by the magi included a variety of treasure going beyond gold, frankincense, and myrrh.

As they "opened their treasures," the meaning of this goes far beyond a hand-sized box. By opening their treasures, it means to clear a way because they were carrying an enormous number of gifts into the house. History has left us with a lot of documentation and researchers have gathered data to know exactly what the Persians and magi would have brought.

In this Eastern culture, diplomatic gifts were in proportion to the size of the recipient. These magi knew that they were bringing treasure to the King of the world. If they did anything less than the most magnificent treasure available, it would have been insulting to the king. How much more to the King of the world!

It was customary to give even low-level kings gifts such as vases, lamps, plates, dishes, carpets, rugs, urns, and regal clothing along with a variety of exotic materials. The catalog of gifts would have amounted to an absolute fortune.

Diplomatically, if you were going to see a king at birth, or at any point, you would bring your very best gift even if you were not royalty yourself. Some Bible scholars believe that the offering of gold and precious spices does suggest that the magi, who had given these gifts, were wealthy themselves, as the items themselves were of great value.

First, the gold, frankincense, and myrrh were of great value. Second, it's just like how Jesus died on the cross. Some people don't see the fact that He died and was resurrected on the third day as being a huge deal.

The type of gold they brought was the highest quality of gold reserved for dignitaries, ambassadors, and heads of state. Frankincense was a difficult item to make and costly to transport due to how far it was from the area. It was known as the favorite fragrance of kings. Myrrh was an ointment to embalm the dead. This would be a strange gift to give a two-year-old king. This gift was prophetically speaking of Jesus' death.

Frankincense and myrrh alone were worth more than gold. These magi pulled out all the stops; they were, after all, giving to the King of the world! The estimated, cumulative value of all the gifts Jesus was given is staggering. For a low-level king, 110 kilos of gold were the standard gift; converting it into today's value, some estimate it would be valued at more than five million dollars. This is the lowest level a king would receive. It can be speculated that Jesus' fortune was the most any king had ever received from these kingmakers. Some speculate that it was likely upward of a billion dollars in today's value—possibly far more!

When you get this concept, you begin to understand that the magi were not just three kings riding along on donkeys, camels, horses, or whatever medium of transportation they employed, because it wouldn't have been safe for them. The road could have been filled with thieves who could have robbed them because of the gifts they carried. They were Chaldean and astrologers who were under Daniel's tutelage. I believe with Daniel's help they were able to interpret the

Scripture. When they coupled this knowledge with their astrological skills, they were able to see the coming of the King of the world, which was the coming of Jesus, the Messiah. Thereby, they felt a sense of shared responsibility to bring gifts to the King. When they came, their presence terrified Herod and the entire city, but they went further and sought the Lord God Almighty and found Him. When they did, I believe they fell and worshiped Him.

Please note that they didn't just present these gifts for the sake of it. Neither did they give them to Mary and Joseph, his parents; these gifts were meant for King Jesus. Since Jesus Himself was the recipient of these gifts, only He could be the one to give them away. This was an inheritance given to the firstborn Son of God. A firstborn child carries a significant meaning. In the Book of Deuteronomy 21, we learn that the firstborn gets everything or a double portion of what the parents leave behind. Only that firstborn child had the authority to receive such a gift and give it away.

The point is that the magi gave these gifts to Jesus, but Mary and Joseph had to be responsible for them because Jesus was a child. Realizing the extreme lengths God went through to get Jesus provision for His life on earth is a profound reality.

JESUS' GIFT TO THE WORLD

Oh, the depth, the height, the breadth, and the width of God's love. How measureless is the love of God for you! Jesus did this because He knows that you can't worship with what you don't have. You can't sacrifice something you don't have. You can't give away or deny something you don't have access to. Thus, Jesus became poor when the day came that He poured out the very wealth given to Him from birth.

Jesus received wealth as a child, yet He had no ability to spend it. His mother and His father, Joseph the carpenter, had to serve as fiduciaries for Him.

Chapter Fifteen

JOSEPH, THE FATHER OF JESUS

At the outset of this chapter, I would like to acknowledge Rick Renner. He is one of the finest teachers and authors in the body of Christ. Rick's insight and expertise inspired me to investigate the life of Joseph. Thank you, Rick.

Joseph, Jesus's earthly father, was handpicked by God to raise His Son on earth. Think of that responsibility! Not only was Mary a chosen vessel of the Lord but Joseph was a major part of that equation. Joseph had many attributes. First, he was a devout Jew. We know this because he always brought Jesus to the synagogue. Jesus frequented the synagogue on a weekly basis, and the Bible tells us that He learned this from His adoptive father, Joseph. Much of the terminology Jesus used was learned during His childhood while working alongside Joseph. Jesus might have been a carpenter's son, but his understanding of culture, society, and commerce came from the environments He was exposed to through His earthly father. This knowledge was exercised in His teachings as well as when speaking to the Pharisees.

Can Anything Good Come out of Nazareth?

It might sound puzzling. How is this possible when the Bible asked, "Can any good thing could come out of Nazareth?" Nazareth was a little town that was opposite another town named Sepphoris. The city stood on a hill, and it was a modern city at the time. When Jesus was still a young child, there was an uprising against Archelaus, Herod's son, who had to summon the Roman army. The Romans destroyed Sepphoris and crucified two thousand Jews in the process. It is this uprising that Gamaliel refers to in Acts 5:37.

Joseph was not a carpenter the way he has been portrayed. The gospels use the Greek word *tekton* to describe Jesus' profession. This word means "builder" rather than carpenter. From this we can conclude that Joseph was also a builder. He didn't whittle bowls or build tables; rather, he was a contractor—he used giant logs to build huge structures. Joseph had dignity. He was an ethical and hardworking man who provided for his family through his carpentry work.

After the destruction of Sepphoris, it was rebuilt and needed builders like Joseph to reconstruct the ruined city.

Working in the City on a Hill

Joseph was raising Jesus in Nazareth, which was about an hour's walk from Sepphoris, so Joseph, being a builder, would take Jesus with him to work there. It was during these trips that Jesus learned about business and money. He was exposed to the world of theater in this once-again booming town where entertainment was vibrant with people performing on stages along the roadsides. Actors on a stage were referred to as "hypocrites" while performing. This was terminology Jesus used while speaking to the Pharisees. Applying this cultural understanding, Jesus said, "You hypocrites!" or "You actors on a stage!" He was also able to craft lines such as, "A city on a hill that cannot be hidden" during His teachings. This came from seeing Sepphoris, the city on the hill with its lights and vibrancy, while living in Nazareth. Jesus had all these examples in mind due to helping His earthly father with his business.

Joseph taught Him his craft, including the business aspect of it. This is one reason Jesus talked about money more than hell. Jesus saw a lot of things at Sepphoris. Imagine Jesus as a young boy, potentially walking past those rebels who were crucified in town by the Romans. He likely saw the bodies of those rebels nailed on crosses, knowing deep within Himself that something similar awaited Him. History doesn't tell us much about the young life of Jesus; neither does the Bible. However, by combining historical narratives with the Bible, you can discover otherwise elusive information about the childhood of Jesus.

Sepphoris was an entertainment city. It was a booming metropolis in its time. This place also contributed to Jesus' entertainment and commercial knowledge. Jesus learned from His father as well as His childhood exposure to this society. Over the course of the many trips, people would have known Him and would have been shocked seeing Him preach in the synagogue. They said things such as, "Isn't that Jesus of Nazareth, the carpenter's son?" Others might have asked, "Is He not the one who constructed those buildings in Sepphoris over on the hillside with His father?" It must have been a very fascinating sight. The people who knew Him as a builder must have been astonished.

During that time, Jesus had all the wealth you can imagine, but He kept traveling to various places with Joseph. I believe it was all part of God's plan to have Joseph train Jesus in an earthly manner. It was most likely geared toward helping Jesus function seamlessly as a human being.

Jesus was not only a tradesman who was wealthy, but He was also industrious. This is a great lesson because He had to learn how to function as a man and as a leader. He needed to learn how to run a corporation, or you could call it a ministry. Joseph deserves credit for this.

LAWS OF INHERITANCE

The Word of God tells us the account of the time an angel appeared to Joseph in a dream telling him that it was safe to leave Egypt. I personally find it interesting that there was another dreamer named Joseph in Egypt. Joseph from the Book of Genesis was a dreamer who ended up in Egypt, and now we have another Joseph who was raising the Son of the living God. I find that quite fascinating.

There is a law of the firstborn son, which is labeled *primogeniture*. Primogeniture means that the firstborn son receives a double share of the inheritance. We can find this in Deuteronomy 21:17, which says, "But he shall acknowledge the son of the unloved wife as the firstborn by giving him a double portion of all that he has, for he is the beginning of his strength; the right of the firstborn is his." This Scripture says that the firstborn should be honored with a double portion of his father's inheritance; it's a principle. Therefore, as Jesus is the firstborn among His brethren (biblically), He is entitled to a double portion of whatever favor or gift is given to Him by anyone.

Usually, inheritances are passed from father to son, but in Jesus' case, the gifts came from royalty. These gifts came through prophecy and through leaders who were sensitive to the voice of God. They came from God, passed through Daniel to the magi, and then on to Jesus. This means that these gifts came from God to Jesus. His heavenly Father, through earthly means, gave Him the gifts. In other words, they were His inheritance.

Because Jesus was God's first and only Son, the principle in Deuteronomy 21:17 applied to Him as well. God used the magi to transfer His inheritance to Him. Jesus had a choice to pour it all out, which we will see He did for our sake, and it's something we must all recognize.

THE PROUD FATHER

God was obviously very pleased with Jesus. That's a statement I'm quite emphatic about. You may be wondering how I know this. When Jesus was being baptized by John the Baptist, I think God just couldn't take it anymore. He had to lay claim to Jesus and put a seal on Him that the whole world would not dispute. He saw Jesus getting baptized in the river and He came down from heaven suddenly with a shout, which was not characteristic of God. John the Baptist and the people who were there heard God say in Matthew 3:17, "This is My beloved Son, in whom I am well pleased." I think God was super proud of His Son and burst into shouting down from heaven. God, a proud Father, was in a sense saying, "My Boy, look at You, let's go mess up the devil's kingdom and make a disaster out of the devil's playground! That's My Boy right there!"

Can you imagine Jesus in that moment? It's quite humorous to think Jesus was a lot like a kid at a sports event in modern day, having His Dad going wild in the stands. He might have even said under His breath back to God, "Um, Father, Your people can hear You. You're talking out loud and might want to take it down a notch." In all of this, God was unconcerned with anything else other than just shouting from heaven, "You're My Boy! That's My beloved Son!" I think that is what happened in that scenario. When Jesus was born, God must have said to Himself, "You know what? No Son of Mine is coming into this natural world without getting every bit of wealth I can get to Him through natural means." God had to follow the laws of nature to get this to Jesus. It was a prophetic act. It was a prophetic assignment that He sent through the prophet Daniel, carried all the way to the magi, and finally to His first and only begotten Son. It was a Father's inheritance that was passed down to His Son. Isn't that wonderful? Glory to God!

What Happened to All of Jesus' Wealth?

God gave Him a double portion of all He had. The magi brought the Father's inheritance directly to Jesus. Jesus' earthly father, Joseph, was an honorable man who was given the responsibility to oversee all the wealth of Jesus. Even though the inheritance didn't come from Joseph, he was obligated to manage all Jesus had until He could possess it. That was the rule of *primogeniture*. The question then arises, what happened to all the wealth of Jesus? Where did it end up? History doesn't reveal every detail, yet there is enough information available to fill in the gaps.

The Uncle of Jesus

There came a point in history when Joseph, the earthly father of Jesus, died. He had trained Jesus in business and how to be a Man of character and honor. We know that Joseph was alive during the time when Jesus was twelve years of age. Beyond this, it is not known exactly when Joseph died. What is known is that upon Joseph's death, all of Jesus' wealth was placed into a trusteeship or into the possession of a guardian to oversee the family wealth. The person appointed for this responsibility was likely Jesus' uncle. Jesus' uncle, through this transition of wealth, would have become the wealthiest man in Israel at the time. Some suggest that Jesus' uncle was Joseph of Arimathea.

History suggests that Joseph of Arimathea was a merchant who would make trips to what would become Britain, where he had tin mines in Cornwall. Some even go as far as to say Jesus accompanied Joseph on these voyages during His childhood, but that is speculation.

> *For you know the grace of our Lord Jesus Christ, that though He was rich, yet for your sakes He became poor, that you through His poverty might become rich.*
>
> **—2 Corinthians 8:9**

Jesus emptied Himself, remember—He put down all His wealth in the natural for you. He became poor so we might become rich. Part of this was done when He left His earthly wealth in the care of His uncle, Joseph of Arimathea. Upon Jesus' burial, He was placed in His uncle's tomb.

> *When the even was come, there came a rich man of Arimathaea, named Joseph, who also himself was Jesus' disciple: He went to Pilate, and begged the body of Jesus. Then Pilate commanded the body to be delivered. And when Joseph had taken the body, he wrapped it in a clean linen cloth, And laid it in his own new tomb, which he had hewn out in the rock: and he rolled a great stone to the door of the sepulchre, and departed. And there was Mary Magdalene, and the other Mary, sitting over against the sepulchre.*
>
> **—Matthew 27:57-61, KJV**

Now with the realization and knowledge of what Jesus did to make a way of provision for you spiritually, physically, and financially, it becomes your responsibility to act on it. Understanding this truth does not mean an automatic manifestation of what Jesus paid for. Faith to step into it must be applied. Jesus gave up to go up on your behalf.

> *Let this mind be in you which was also in Christ Jesus, who, being in the form of God, did not consider it robbery to be equal with God, but made Himself of no reputation, taking the form of a bondservant, and coming in the likeness of men. And being found in appearance as a man, He humbled Himself and became obedient to the point of death, even the death of the cross.*
>
> **—Philippians 2:5-8**

> *For you know the grace of our Lord Jesus Christ, that though He was rich, yet for your sakes He became poor, that you through His poverty might become rich.*
>
> **—2 Corinthians 8:9**

> *So Jesus answered and said, "Assuredly, I say to you, there is no one who has left house or brothers or sisters or father or mother or wife or children or lands, for My sake and the gospel's, who shall not receive a hundredfold now in this time—houses and brothers and sisters and mothers and children and lands, with persecutions—and in the age to come, eternal life. But many who are first will be last, and the last first."*
>
> **—Mark 10:29-31**

Jesus gave up everything and worked as a Man. He built alongside His earthly father, Joseph. He never took control of the wealth His uncle managed. He did this as an offering for you. Jesus was believing for a hundredfold return, and He got it—your salvation (with benefits). The same salvation and ability to access the provision that will break hell's economy is available, right now, for anyone who calls on His Name.

Chapter Sixteen

THE MAGI BROKE HELL'S ECONOMY OVER JESUS

These magi are a tremendous example of individuals who broke hell's economy in their generation. Armed with a prophecy and the means to honor the King of the world, these individuals traveled great distances only to be met with the manipulation of a tyrant (Herod). It takes a Word from God and the strength to rise against the scheming plots brought on by the kingdom of darkness, and that they did! Mission accomplished, they broke hell's economy by fulfilling their assignment of equipping Jesus with the God-ordained resources from the heavenly Father to His one and only Son.

These magi have a place in all of history as a vital part in the greatest story of man's redemption! It is fascinating to recognize that the Lord used these magicians and astronomers for such a profound task. These mystics were truth seekers, not unlike Cornelius, whose alms and gifts to the poor came up before the Lord, resulting in the salvation of his household (see Acts 10). In every generation there are those who may be mystics or truth-seekers.

Generally, mystics are simply defined as those searching for truth through symbolic or spiritual interpretation. This can lead to occult and demonic practices; however, in a pure form, these are individuals like the magi searching for more than what the natural world has to offer.

They are some of those who are willing to accept the truth and believe in things that are outside of the box. These are the kind of people who say, "I just want to know what the truth is." These mystics were trying to honor God in all the light (knowledge) they had. It reminds me of the Scripture where Jesus instructed His disciples to not forbid others from attempting to cast out demons. Jesus said about these types of people, "He that is not against us is for us."

> *And John answered and said, Master, we saw one casting out devils in thy name; and we forbad him, because he followeth not with us. And Jesus said unto him, Forbid him not: for he that is not against us is for us.*

> —Luke 9:49-50, KJV

Their ancestors were under Daniel and the knowledge of prophetic Scripture was learned during this period and traveled down through the magi's generation. This is the reason they came to worship the King of the world with gifts. You might ask, "How in the world would God work with these kinds of people?" I think Matthew 2:12 sort of answers this question. It says, "Then, being divinely warned in a dream that they should not return to Herod, they departed for their own country another way." Why did God speak to these magi? For the same reason we mentioned earlier regarding Cornelius, whom God spoke to through an angel. God is a "heart" God; He is not as religious as we have been led to believe. God has spoken to many different types of people all throughout history. Consider King Abimelech in Genesis 20. God warned him in a dream not to touch Abraham's wife, Sarah, and the king obeyed. Let's consider the people of Nineveh. God sent Jonah to preach to them and they did not take offense at the judgment of God but rather had a contrite heart. They earnestly wanted to know what they were doing wrong and how they could amend their ways.

In Matthew 2:12, God additionally spoke to the magi about Herod in their dreams. It is possible He spoke to all of them simultaneously in their dreams. This greatly suggests that these men were spiritually centered on the Lord.

The time of these events was the intertestamental period in history. In each generation, there are those who are called upon by the Lord to break the plans of the devil. Breaking hell's system is the plan of God through whomever will listen. His highest desire is that all mankind be saved, and He will provide supernatural provision to those who want to help Him in His mission to see the world saved.

I believe when Jesus finally died at the age of 33, these wise men, if they were still alive, would have given their lives to Him. They would have made Jesus their Lord, accepted Him completely, repented of their sins, and would have become preachers of the gospel.

HEROD'S PLOT

Herod must have plotted something evil against them while he awaited their return. Somehow, even though these guys were a force to be reckoned with, there was probably a lot of trouble going on in the city during their absence. Their presence in Jerusalem must've caused quite a stir, and I speculate Herod would have manipulated the situation into his favor. The Lord warned them, saying, "Don't go back, you might get manipulated. Something could happen to you, or Herod could dig up a trail in your camp that might lead him to where Jesus is." The wise men went home another way and avoided Herod. They listened to God. Not only did God speak to them, but they listened to God's voice.

We've talked about this in previous chapters—these mystics from afar knew the Scriptures, which is a very powerful thing to realize. They were on a mission from God. I urge you today, my friend, do not hold back; let the Master use you to do His purpose. If God will work through individuals such as these magi, He will certainly work through your life.

God Wants to Use Your Life More Than You Realize

If the Lord would use those who did not know the salvation of Jesus, how much more will He use your life to rise up and break the powers of darkness off your generation? Do not say you are small, unable, weak, cannot speak, or offer any other excuse. God loves to take the unqualified and smash the evil plans of the qualified. He delights in using the foolish things of the world to shame that which is wise. He delights in beating the odds through the humble. God is not religious; He loves you and is thrilled at the opportunity to shock the lives of many through you. Get ready to be a sign and a wonder to your generation by simply saying yes!

Chapter Seventeen

JESUS' SOURCE OF INCOME

Not only did Jesus have a rich uncle, He also had other means of revenue. He paid the sacrifice for sin making salvation available as well as providing healing from sickness. For our sakes, He took to the cross everything that held you in bondage. I believe He took poverty to the cross as well for us to become rich.

JESUS HAD AT LEAST TWO SOURCES OF INCOME

First, He supported Himself with His carpentry work. He was called the carpenter's Son for a reason. As we saw earlier, history doesn't explain how Joseph died because the Bible does not mention him in the latter part of the story. Upon Joseph's death, it's very possible that Jesus took over the family business at an age as early in His teen years or into His early to mid-twenties; He ran this business till the age of 29 or 30. People have different ideas about what happened to Joseph. I believe that the Bible, based on God's design, intentionally omitted that information for a variety of reasons. It is possible that unhelpful doctrines may have developed around it and God didn't want that, decidedly omitting the information.

Jesus ran the family business and this gave Him personal income. Earlier we learned that Jesus had a home in Capernaum. It was probably a nice house; there is no record saying that Jesus abandoned His home after He began His ministry.

Jesus also ran His own personal ministry and was so successful He required a treasurer. You'd probably think it would've been any other person than Judas! It is mind-blowing that Jesus allowed Judas to oversee the money!

Partners in Ministry

Jesus never asked for one financial offering during the time of His earthly ministry. Now, He worked miracles when receiving what could be considered an offering of five loaves and two fish. There is a principle to be understood that requires giving all you have. Such was the case with the young man who gave all the food he possessed. The result was a miracle of epic proportions. It is also an amazing fact that there were baskets left over! Why? Because God is always the God of too much, if we will just let Him be!

Jesus may not have routinely asked for offerings, yet what He did have were partners and supporters, some of whom worked with Him. Who's to say He didn't also contribute to His ministry from His personal business? My wife and I have done that many times to support the people around us, because we really care about the ministry that God assigned us to. There have been many times that we have been the biggest givers in our ministry for the sake of our staff, team, and the vision God has called us to accomplish.

If you're running a ministry, you should have the mindset of being the biggest giver in that ministry for the sake of others and not yourself. Our experience with giving has resulted in us being surrounded by radical givers. There are two fundamental things you should know about giving and a third point that is an important life lesson. These are:

1. You can't out-give God.

2. You can't out-give a giver.

3. You can't out-give a taker.

We're blessed to be surrounded with so many generous givers in our ministry; we believe this is a direct result of being radical givers from the beginning of our marriage and ministry. I strongly believe Jesus might have taken some of His wealth and used it for the benefit of God's kingdom on earth.

The Importance of Partnership

And Joanna the wife of Chuza Herod's steward, and Susanna, and many others, which ministered unto him of their substance.

—Luke 8:3, KJV

Partnership was important to Jesus, and it should be the same for us in our ministry today. One of the ways Jesus must have given access for people to become rich through Him, even in His earthly ministry, was through partnership. Peter made his boat available to Jesus, and many others supported Him through their resources (see Luke 8:3). This means that people supported Him financially, including His uncle, Joseph of Arimathea, the richest man in the entire region, who surrendered His tomb for Jesus to be buried in.

Woman with the Alabaster Jar

One powerful example of giving to Jesus is found in the story of the woman with the alabaster jar (see Matt. 26). She broke it on His feet and poured perfume all over Him. Do you recollect how Judas rebuked the woman and said the oil could have been sold and the money given to the poor? Jesus responded against Judas' accusing, greedy nature by saying, "No, don't do that, because what she has done is a beautiful thing." He received a gift worth a year's wages from that woman. How much more do you think others would have given? Just think about it.

In today's world, this would be the equivalent of giving a one-time gift of twenty to one hundred thousand dollars, which is the average annual income, depending on someone's salary, industry, or the current economy. Jesus would say to that kind of gift, "Oh, it's beautiful." Consider the widow who gave her last mite. Though the Pharisees gave large sums of money and made sure to put on a show while doing so, Jesus considered her offering more than everyone else's due to her heart. I'd love to hear the end of the story about the woman with the perfume jar and the widow who gave her last mite. I'd like to know what they received after they sacrificed their extravagant gifts. I believe Jesus' partners entered God's economy even while Jesus was on earth.

Operating in God's Economy

Can you imagine giving directly to the Son of God? The same Jesus who walked on water. Think about the boy who brought Him five loaves and two fish—suddenly, He multiplied it all over the hillside! This is what it's like giving to Jesus; you become rich. He was a distribution center, a wealth exchange, and the prophet's reward. Allow me to illustrate the wealth of Jesus with an example. It is like bringing God a potato, and then God says, "How amazing!" It doesn't end there. God then goes on to say, "Hey Michael, give this precious child a truckload of gold for his obedient heart." That, my friend, is how you operate in God's economy. He'll exchange His truckload of gold for your potato, and all you've got to do is obey Him. Look what He did with the five loaves and two fish and other instances when He multiplied food. He even paid taxes from a fish's mouth. God's economy can accomplish far more than we can comprehend.

It is fascinating to consider that Jesus had financial giving partners to such a degree that He needed to have a treasurer. As mentioned above, Judas was the treasurer, who would sometimes leave late at night to give alms to the poor. There are only a few references to Jesus' partners; we can find this in Luke 8:3 where it says, "And Joanna the wife of Chuza, Herod's steward, and Susanna, and many others who provided for Him from their substance." Note, the Bible mentioned women like the wife of Herod's steward. This sounds like someone who was well-to-do.

Why did the Bible mention these women? It's probably because of their status, or even more so because of how much they gave. Joanna, Susanna, and many others assisted and gave a lot to Jesus' ministry. The word *many* as used in that passage means a lot of people sowed into "Jesus of Nazareth Ministries International."

Imagine the Return on Sowing into Jesus' Ministry

I bet everyone who partnered with Jesus had a wild, crazy biblical return, and I bet they were falling over each other to give into His ministry. When we give into ministries today that are filled with purity and the

Spirit of Jesus is on them, we can begin to receive in the same magnitude. It's a powerful concept.

The second reference to Jesus' partners is in Luke 23:55-56 where it says:

> *And the women who had come with Him from Galilee followed after, and they observed the tomb and how His body was laid. Then they returned and prepared spices and fragrant oils. And they rested on the Sabbath according to the commandment.*

This passage is talking about what happened after Jesus died; His partners were still doing things for Him. This is just a quick sidebar Scripture to show you that these partners, these friends of Jesus, stood by Him.

You need to know that Judas was Jesus' accountant or rather employee; we can find this in John 12:6 and John 13:29. This was to provide for the poor and keep the accounts for the entire ministry. In His early days, Jesus provided for Himself through His business, but He deliberately stepped away from this source of income after He called His disciples.

Jesus did not just give to the poor but also provided for His disciples and staff. Maybe this is just me, but when Jesus said in Mark 10 that it was difficult for a rich man to enter the kingdom of heaven, He meant two things. Remember the disciples asked, "Who then can be saved?" Peter then said, "We have left all to follow You!" Jesus replied to Him saying, "No one who has left lands, houses, mothers, brothers, or families to follow me will fail to receive a hundred times as much in this time."

Now it's possible that Peter made this statement because he still had some of his holdings, or could it be that Jesus just paid His staff so well that they were wealthy themselves? Something to further consider is that His uncle could have placed them all on payroll for their service to Jesus of Nazareth Ministries International. He may have paid them from the wealth given by the magi and watched over by His uncle, or it may have been that His financial partners were that generous, or both! Those partners mentioned in Luke 8:3 were so supportive that Jesus could take care of the poor and provide for His staff.

When you do your highest and best calling for the kingdom of God, you will be a money magnet as well! God wants to finance all His sons and daughters! Find out what God has called you to do; go after it with all your heart and you will not have to worry about the needs being met. He is looking for those who will take Him at His word and perform their high calling.

Section 3

WEAPONIZING YOUR FAITH

D ear reader, you are called to destroy hell's economy over your family and as a service to your generation. This does not mean you must make money and become rich to do so. Rather, it means you are called to do what you can, where you can, whenever you can—it's that simple.

Your life matters far more than you might realize. The role you play in this generation is vital. You might be a single mother, a wife, a business-person, or an individual in public service. Your "yes" is what is required; from that point, a teachable heart will take you places you never imagined. God is looking for those who will step forward in their generation to break the antichrist spirit that is rapidly increasing in every nation.

In this next section, we are going to focus on what it takes for you to break hell's economy both practically and through raw determination mixed with obedience to the Lord.

Remember, the kingdom of darkness has no answer to a believer who has faith in their heart, speaking it from their mouth, and displaying corresponding actions to back up what they are professing. The person I am talking about is you!

Chapter Eighteen

BURN THE SHIPS AND DON'T LOOK BACK

I love those who love me, and those who seek me diligently
will find me. Riches and honor are with me, enduring
riches and righteousness. My fruit is better than gold,
yes, than fine gold, and my revenue than choice silver.
I traverse the way of righteousness, in the midst of the
paths of justice, that I may cause those who love me
to inherit wealth, that I may fill their treasuries.

—**Proverbs 8:17-21**

There is a phrase associated with Spanish Conquistador Hernando Cortés from 1519: "Burn the ships." This phrase encompassed his single objective—capturing the treasures of the Aztecs. History's view of Cortés has differing points of view. However, the phrase "burn the ships" was made famous in his order to sink his own ships as an open display of resolve to finish what he started. There comes a point in attaining that requires a mindset of *"no return."* This same principle applies to breaking out of hell's economy. It is a mindset of faith and endurance, to endure hardship like a good soldier (see 2 Tim. 2:3-4). By enduring hardship, you should be ready to persist against opposition until you receive what you are contending for.

The Mindset of a Finisher

It seems many people enjoy the beginning of a journey; however, half-way through they want to exit or turn back. My wife, Heather, and I were recently reminiscing about the many sincere individuals along our journey who have started with us to reach massive amounts of people around the world through media to make a global impact with the gospel. Nearly two decades later, most of these excited beginners are long gone. However, we will continue on in our calling. It takes more than a starter mentality. You must develop the mindset of a finisher.

I recall the day my associate pastor used a phrase during the time of a great decision; he said, "I think we burn the ships and don't look back!" He was making a statement about a tremendous move we were contemplating for our organization. We were deciding on relocating; the result would be churches planted, Bible schools raised up, and overseas outreach would become far more effective. His words of faith and boldness provided the final push to step out fearlessly and do what we all sensed was right.

Each of us, including myself, has experienced the "tough it out," "suck it up," and the "grin and bear it" mentality, combined with the "what doesn't kill you makes you stronger" speeches. Although these phrases aren't incorrect, they are, by God's standards, incomplete. What they do not take into consideration is a loving Father who loves to bless His children, not only for their sake but also for His divine purposes.

RELIGION IS A "BREAKTHROUGH" KILLER

Religion may cause us to forget the absolute loving favor of our Father, but relationship does not. Someone once said, "Metaphors reign where mysteries reside." This simple saying is a great example of religion's way of thinking. It bases its point of view on the experiences of others rather than an encounter of your own. When you try to live off of someone else's experience, good or bad, you will never own it.

Therefore, metaphors come into use. Tragedy happens and the response so often is, "Well, you just never know what God is going to do." Or someone becomes ill and succumbs to death, and religion gives well-meaning but hollow answers. "It must not have been God's will to heal them." Or the ever-sad comment, "God just needed another angel in heaven." None of these sayings are biblical. However, due to lack of revelation on what God's Word actually says on specific topics, religion is forced to come up with well-intended answers. This applies to a variety of issues.

First, we must understand what a breakthrough is. One way of describing it is "to step into a *more than enough* blessing." *Webster's Dictionary* defines a breakthrough as *an act or instance of moving through or beyond an obstacle.* In order to receive a breakthrough, you must be obedient to the Lord and then be positioned in the appointed place or at the appointed time, according to God's will, to receive it.

What is required for a breakthrough or to maintain a breakthrough is a revelation of what God has said in His Word; it must become rock solid inside you and applied to the situation you are confronting. The most potent force of any breakthrough is when you know or recall information contained in the Word of God for your situation, and it seemingly becomes illuminated or revealed at just the "right" time. This becomes a revelation or supernaturally "revealed truth" and knowledge for you! Peter had this encounter when Jesus asked the disciples, "Who do you say I am?" Peter was able to respond (because of a revelation), "You are the Christ!"

REVELATION IS REQUIRED FOR BREAKTHROUGH

Many of our spiritual forefathers once stood exactly where you are—on the edge of something they could not see. We know about the powerful ways God used them because we know the end of their story, but they couldn't see it coming when they were living it. Instead, they chose to stand in hopeful expectation. Another way of saying *hopeful expectation* is using the term "faith." When you take your revelation or "revealed truth" and apply it with hopeful expectation/faith, the outcome is a breakthrough!

Let's look at three of our spiritual forefathers and their stories.

King David

David, the greatest king Israel would ever know, was once a mere shepherd boy. Even his own father considered him insignificant. In 1 Samuel 16, God told Samuel the next king would be the son of Jesse. But when Jesse learned this, he showed Samuel all of his sons—except David. It took Samuel specifically asking, "Are all the young men here?" before Jesse finally called David to meet Samuel. On that day, Samuel anointed David as the next king of Israel, and the Spirit of the Lord came upon David from that day forward (see 1 Sam. 16:13). One day he was a shepherd, the next day he was the future king.

Do you remember the story of David's cave days? The days when all the promises were made, he had killed Goliath, completed exploits, and yet his father-in-law was hunting him. These were very difficult days for

David. What we call his "cave days," David would have called those his "last days." However, he stood through it all and took his rightful place. His day came, he broke through, and he overcame the plans of darkness.

Abraham

The man often referred to as the father of our faith was once childless. It looked as if Abraham and his wife, Sarah, would never have children. Their time had passed, and Sarah remained barren. Then, God blessed them with a child, Isaac. *This appeared to be their day of increase.* However, God had one more major blessing in store, but first came obedience. Abraham was to take his blessed son and sacrifice him on an altar. Looking into the history of this story, you will discover that Isaac was between the ages of 23 and 30 years old. He was a willing participant in this scenario. Now that is faith!

From Abraham's perspective, this could have been the end of his dream, but he faithfully obeyed anyway. God rewarded that obedience by sparing Isaac and promising to multiply Abraham's descendants. In Genesis 22:16-18, God promised Abraham that He would make his "descendants as the stars of the heaven and as the sand which is on the seashore." Abraham was once childless, but God blessed "all nations on earth" through Abraham's offspring. His day came, he broke through, and he overcame the plans of darkness.

Joseph

The journey to a day of increase for Joseph came after many hardships. First, he found himself in a pit (see Gen. 37), then in a palace (see Gen. 39). That was short-lived before this innocent man of God was thrown into prison (see Gen. 39-40). Joseph went from disappointment to disappointment, from waiting to waiting, until his day of increase came when he interpreted Pharaoh's dream (see Gen. 41). In one day, Joseph went from the dungeon to second in command over all the land of Egypt. There is great insight into Joseph's journey as written for us in the psalms.

> *He sent a man before them—Joseph—who was sold as a slave. They hurt his feet with fetters, he was laid in irons. Until the time that his word came to pass, the word of the Lord tested him.*

> —Psalm 105:17-19

The Word of the Lord tested Joseph. How? Because Joseph knew he had a vision. God showed him his future, but everything he experienced leading up to the "Word" coming to pass was contrary. It must have been hard for Joseph not to throw in the towel. Thankfully he didn't, and his day came, he broke through, and he overcame the plans of darkness.

For each of these spiritual forefathers, their day came *after* God took them through a *season of preparation*. God had a calling on their life, but they needed to be ready to rise to the occasion when that breakthrough or day of increase came.

Maybe you are in a *season of preparation* too. Would you recognize it if you were? Are you struggling with feeling insignificant like David? Or waiting on a heart's desire like Abraham? Or overwhelmed with trials and setbacks like Joseph? Maybe it's time to look at it differently; maybe it's your season of preparation.

God has a day of breakthrough for you and age has nothing to do with it. Just like David, Abraham, and Joseph, your calling is at the door of your heart and crying out to come forth.

You may not see it yet. You may question your circumstances and your struggles, but never doubt God has a call and a plan for your life. He is working through all these seemingly unplanned events and dreary days to position you for His moment of blessing.

Your season of preparation will bring with it opportunity if you do not give up. Choose today to stay the course. Like our spiritual forefathers, your day of increase will change everything. Your day will come, you will break through, and you will overcome the plans of darkness. This could be coming sooner than you think!

Chapter Nineteen

IT TAKES VISION

Then the Lord answered me and said: "Write the vision and make it plain on tablets, that he may run who reads it. For the vision is yet for an appointed time; but at the end it will speak, and it will not lie. Though it tarries, wait for it; because it will surely come, it will not tarry. Behold the proud, his soul is not upright in him; but the just shall live by his faith."

—Habakkuk 2:2-4

WRITE YOUR VISION AND MAKE IT CLEAR

Your day of breakthrough has a purpose: to help you accomplish your life assignment. That's what you have from God. A job to do. He's assigned you work to be completed, and you're going to need help getting it done. For any assignment, task, or responsibility, you need certain tools. Your day of breakthrough is that tool. But how do you know what that job is? How do you find it? When you do find it, what do you do when your day of increase hasn't yet come?

Habakkuk had questions, too. He sought an answer from God. Here is how God answered in Habakkuk 2:2: "Write the vision and make it plain on tablets, that he may run who reads it."

God is giving us direction. He's giving us a formula for how to approach our task when we're unsure what to do next. He continues in verse 3, "Though it tarries, wait for it; because it will surely come, it will not tarry."

WRITE THE VISION DOWN

God has placed a dream in your heart, and you owe it to Jesus to pursue it. You also owe it to yourself to write it down. Habakkuk 2:2 shows us that there is power attached to writing your vision down. It is a spiritual statement as well as a heightened clarity of that vision. Writing it down is a powerful and necessary tool. The act of writing your vision down also allows you to visually see your deepest desires written out before you.

God wants you to have your desires. The key is to first place a priority on His desires. "But seek first the kingdom of God and His righteousness, and all these things shall be added to you" (Matt. 6:33). This is the proper order for receiving your desires the kingdom way.

Remember, the kingdom of God is a system, and the kingdom of heaven is a place. To receive your desires, you must first understand that God made you. He knows what makes you tick, or as one dear friend of mine used to say, *"God knows how to give you a buzz!"* The kingdom system approach is by seeking His ways of doing things first and His righteousness. His ways of doing things are clearly laid out for us in the Scripture. If you desire His kingdom economy to begin working dramatically in your life, then you must follow the kingdom "rules of engagement."

Rules of Engagement

Simply put, you must be into the business of sowing and reaping. This is what creates a rhythm in God's economy that brings continuous prosperity. It is, however, the hidden vein of gold that you encounter when you seek first His kingdom through His way of doing things. Second, His righteousness is what you must also seek. This simply means knowing Jesus paid it all for you, and as you grow in the revelation of what He did and how righteous you really are in Him—then all these other things are added unto you! These things are the vein of gold—the things only God knows you truly desire. There are things you desire that you don't even know about! But God does—He wants to give you everything you never knew you wanted.

Once you have written your known desires and vision down, there is a process to pursue what you have written. In Psalm 37:3-5, it reveals a process of receiving the desires of your heart.

> *Trust in the Lord, and do good; so shalt thou dwell in the land, and verily thou shalt be fed. Delight thyself also in the Lord: and he shall give thee the desires of thine heart. Commit thy way unto the Lord; trust also in him; and he shall bring it to pass.*
>
> —**Psalm 37:3-5, KJV**

Verse 3 broken down reads: trust in the Lord, do good, dwell in the land, and *feed on His faithfulness!*

It Is Better to Do Good...Than to Not

The first thing you must do is to trust in the Lord! God has this thing about being believed! He really wants you to develop your trust in Him completely. Second, do good. That's an interesting thought, isn't it? To simply do good. It makes me think of Steve Martin's quote from the movie *Dirty Rotten Scoundrels*.

> "My gram-gram is the one who taught me it is better to be truthful and good...than to not."
>
> —Steve Martin, **Dirty Rotten Scoundrels**

That quote makes me laugh every time for being hilariously obvious. In all actuality, this is the truth—one of the ways we approach the desires of our heart is through doing good!

Your Presence Should Demand an Explanation

Psalm 37:3 goes on to say, "Dwell in the land." Another way of saying this would be "take dominion where you are"! Wherever you are, be there! I like to say it this way, "Your presence should demand an explanation!"

You taking your dominion is a way of enforcing the kingdom of God on this earth. Let's continue reading verse 3: "feed on His faithfulness." Knowing God is always going to come through for you and will show up every time is equivalent to you not feeding worries and doubt. Instead, you are feeding on His consistency. Know it and meditate on His consistency.

"Delight yourself also in the Lord, and He shall give you the desires of your heart" (Ps. 37:4). In this verse, we begin to see the words "delight yourself in the Lord." *Delight*, as *Webster's Dictionary* defines it, is "a more permanent pleasure than joy." Make God the most permanent pleasure in your life. Place more pleasure in God than in the things that make you happy. If you do this, suddenly the things that give you joy, or the desires of your heart, are given to you. "Commit your way to the Lord, trust also in Him, and He shall bring it to pass" (Ps. 37:5).

But wait, there's more! Part of delighting in the Lord and receiving the desires of your heart is to give them staying power and longevity. This comes from committing your way. All the above including a focused commitment to the Lord will cause Him to bring the fullness of your desires and purpose to pass. If you lean in, so will God. Pretty awesome if you think about it.

Examine Your Heart

This process gives you focus for the journey ahead. Start this process by first examining your heart. When God begins speaking to you, you might not immediately understand what He's saying. Take the time to hear all that God is doing inside you.

Don't feel overwhelmed. If you don't know what your life's about or where you're going, simply start with your desires. Write down your thoughts. For example, "God, I would like to see my life doing this," and "I would like to do that." Ask Him for understanding of what your life is about.

Anything with More Than One Head Is a Freak!

This is crucial because you need a one-mind, one-heart, one-head vision to lead you in one direction. You can't be double minded about your vision. If you want to defeat a man's vision, give him two. When you have more than one vision, you will not only see the potential of division, but it will cause diversion. You need clarity, focus, and oneness. Anything with more than one head is considered a freak. Be single minded!

If you are washed in the Word of God, you will see your desires line up with His commands. His words will provide clarity and direction, so your heart's desires become clear and in agreement with His plans for your life.

Years ago, as I dove more into the Scriptures, the Lord challenged me to write down the answers to these questions: What do I want out of life? Where do I want to go? As I sought out His direction for my life according to the Word of God, my vision found clarity. Yours will, too. Your desires will come more into focus and develop further as you stay in His Word. Then, when opportunity meets preparation, you'll recognize that God has developed your heart and placed you in your lane.

Elevator Speech

Remember to keep it simple. We need to write down our vision and keep it simple. God directed Habakkuk to "make it plain" so it would be understandable.

In earlier times, messages were written down and passed between villages. Simplicity was key. A simple message could easily be understood with one look to a rider passing by quickly and simply retold.

That's how you need to view your vision. It must be simple. Easily understood. Quickly comprehended. If you can't write a simple vision, then your plans are too complicated. You should be able to put your vision on a placard, hold it up, and anyone passing by can understand what you're all about. My placard would read, "Building lives by the Word of God." That's my vision. Simple, uncomplicated, and easy to understand.

The placard then creates the foundation for your elevator pitch. In other words, if you had 60 seconds in an elevator to explain your vision, what would be your answer? You should be able to explain what you do, who you are, and what you're about in simple bullet points or a quick explanation. My elevator speech is, "To build lives by the Word of God. I accomplish this through discipleship and media so the Word of God can run swiftly and be glorified."

Ultimately, you need one thing that clearly identifies your life.

JACK OF ALL TRADES, MASTER OF ONE

Have you ever heard the expression "jack of all trades but master of none"? A better rendition of the expression would be "jack of all trades but *master of one*." This basically means you should know a little bit about everything, but know everything you possibly can about one thing. Excel at something! When you give focus and training to the area you want to develop, your "elevator speech" about who, what, where, and why becomes simplified.

You Must Stand

In Habakkuk 2:3, God followed His first two instructions by assuring Habakkuk that the vision is for an appointed time: "For the revelation awaits an appointed time; it speaks of the end and will not prove false. Though it lingers, wait for it; it will certainly come and will not delay" (NIV).

Let's say you've written your vision down. You kept it simple. You've waited, but nothing seems to be happening. This desire is so strong and it's burning a hole in your heart, but it still hasn't come to pass. So what's going on?

What God is telling Habakkuk here is that His plans have an "appointed time." That time simply hasn't come yet. But it will. Notice God's command here: "Though it linger, wait for it; it will certainly come."

The fulfillment of your vision is coming, even though it hasn't yet arrived. God's direction for us in this moment is to wait. You've prayed, you've written it down, now you stand.

See Yourself Victorious with the Prize

Ephesians 6:10-17 gives clarity on what it actually means to stand.

> *Finally, my brethren, be strong in the Lord, and in the power of his might. Put on the whole armour of God, that ye may be able to stand against the wiles of the devil. For we wrestle not against flesh and blood, but against principalities, against powers, against the rulers of the darkness of this world, against*

spiritual wickedness in high places. Wherefore take unto you the whole armour of God, that ye may be able to withstand in the evil day, and having done all, to stand. Stand therefore, having your loins girt about with truth, and having on the breastplate of righteousness; and your feet shod with the preparation of the gospel of peace; above all, taking the shield of faith, wherewith ye shall be able to quench all the fiery darts of the wicked. And take the helmet of salvation, and the sword of the Spirit, which is the word of God.

—Ephesians 6:10-17, KJV

The word *stand* in this passage is mentioned three times and carries the contextual meaning of "seeing yourself victorious" and "receiving the prize." This passage is all about the full armor of God, preparing, and going to battle. *Stand* means to stand as if receiving the trophy or reward for beating the opposition in the gladiator arena.

Stand—it doesn't mean just endure and take the punishment and at some undetermined time in the future you might get through it. *No!* That is not what *stand* means. It means to see yourself victorious going into the fight. When going into the process of attaining those desires of your heart, you stand seeing yourself victorious until you step into that reality.

There is something supernatural that happens when a man or woman writes down their vision and stands on it. You wait with expectancy. You wait with confidence. You wait, knowing the appointed hour may not be here at this moment; however, in faith, you have it and in the natural it's coming.

Do not faint. Stand on the Word of God and mix it with your faith and see yourself receiving the prize. There's an appointed time for you. Even though it lingers, wait! It will certainly come!

Chapter Twenty

DELAY IS NOT DENIAL

For the vision is yet for an appointed time; but at the end it will speak, and it will not lie. Though it tarries, wait for it; because it will surely come, it will not tarry.

—Habakkuk 2:3

TARRYING CAN BE PART OF THE VISION

Tarrying is something that can be part of the journey. However, you are not called to stay there always! This can manifest in the form of a trial or just becoming weary in well doing. This is where you lean in. Trials don't last always; they are not able to last forever. Do you know what is designed to last forever? You! God designed you to never experience that kind of difficulty and delay. It was the "fall of man" that allowed this type of disappointment to reign in the earth. It is through the blood and victory of Jesus that we are called to stand up in defiance of this fallen world. Don't be fooled; don't give in to the mirage of this world. If you do not faint, you will absolutely see victory.

The Battle Isn't Over Until You Win!

Taking a thought from the previous chapter, there is a quote I often use while speaking: "The battle isn't over until you win!" Arm yourself with the mindset that you know the battle isn't over because you haven't seen the victory yet. With this mindset, you will begin to take more ground both in your heart and in the natural. God never designed you to fail or fall into despair. Be armed with the Word of God and put some intensity into your believing. The enemy of your soul and the spirit of this age has no response for a believer who mixes their faith with the Word of God and speaks it out!

Sometimes people misidentify what they are going through. These ones might as well call *denial* a river in Egypt! (Pun intended.)

During those "in between" times, it is important you keep yourself encouraged. If the enemy can get you discouraged or into a place of disbelief, you will begin to lose the momentum on what you are believing for. It is a form of "abortion" to the seed that has been placed in you by the Holy Spirit to be birthed in this world. It reminds me of an article I once read regarding the common surviving traits of those lost in the wilderness. Among several traits, the one that stood out to me most was that many people who make it after being terribly lost in the wilderness end up with a good sense of humor.

Have a Sense of Humor

Someone may ask, "A good sense of humor! Are you kidding me?" Well, think about it. It makes sense to me on several levels. The best one of the traits, in my estimation, is while suffering through the worst conditions you start laughing in faith! You should give joy a voice! Imagine the kingdom of darkness throwing everything they have at you and your response is to laugh. It would confuse them! It would make them question their tactics. So—*ha ha ha!*

THE ART OF FAITH AND PATIENCE

> *And we desire that each one of you show the same diligence to the full assurance of hope until the end, that you do not become sluggish, but imitate those who through faith and patience inherit the promises.*

> **—Hebrews 6:11-12**

I firmly believe you can limit the time you have to wait. You have far more authority than you may realize. Let's discuss the power of patience.

Patience, in so many words, means to remain consistently the same no matter what is happening in the world around you. Circumstances may change, but regarding the promise of God you will not be changed. Faith is the substance of things hoped for, the evidence of things not seen. Once you have substance and evidence of what you cannot yet grasp with your hands, this is where stubborn patience is employed. I promise you, the man or woman of God who refuses to step away from the promise and stays consistently the same while using the standard principle of seeing yourself receiving the prize will in no way lose. It's not possible.

Now let's add some hot sauce to the mix of what we just talked about. Combine all the above with the intensity of prayer! The intensity of prayer will force obstacles out of the way.

The path of the righteous is supposed to be brighter and brighter until the full light of day, meaning you are meant to go from glory to glory in your journey. The issue is most people never develop the practices nor incorporate the combination of principles listed above in order to create "staying power" in their life. Staying power is applying consistent pressure and not letting up to attain what you first began to believe for. You must stay encouraged even when you don't see your circumstances changing. You may be on a road headed toward your destination, but you can't see the destination yet. Even though the landscape looks the same as when you left and doesn't seem to change, you know if you keep going you *are* getting closer, and soon the destination will appear in the distance until you arrive!

A praying believer is a dangerous thing to the plans of the devil. It makes the weak strong and the foolish wise. It gives impossible breakthroughs to the average person, if they will give themselves over to the intensity of prayer. I like to say it this way, "On a bad day, you're called to be the best there is!" The praying believer is the best there is.

Binding Yourself to the Lord

What we're called to do during this time of tarrying is to stand and *wait well*. Psalm 27:14 says, "Wait on the Lord; be of good courage, and He shall strengthen your heart; wait, I say, on the Lord!" We see the importance of waiting on God throughout Scripture. In Isaiah 40:31, it says, "But those who wait on the Lord shall renew their strength; they shall mount up with wings like eagles, they shall run and not be weary, they shall walk and not faint." This is an active, purposeful waiting. It binds us with God's will.

In Hebrew, the phrase *waiting on the Lord* means "to bind together with the twisting as with wire." When you wait on the Lord, you're taking your life, desires, and heart, then binding yourself with the Lord. When you're at the point in the process where you don't see your vision manifesting, you must twist your life tightly to God. You bind yourself to Him. "A cord of three strands is not quickly broken" (Eccles. 4:12 AMP).

As you bind yourself to the Lord, you move closer to Him. In this process, you become one with the Lord in your thinking. Your heart, mind, emotions, and calling become intertwined with God's will. This isn't a time of sitting around until God moves. It's a time of moving closer to Him.

In the middle of Habakkuk 2:3 it says, "Though it tarries, wait for it; because it will surely come." God cannot lie. His words are always true. If He says it's coming, it's coming. It doesn't matter what happens in the meantime; whether we're amid the apocalypse or hell freezes over, the Word of God never lies. The vision is coming. It is not dependent on your family situation, your financial situation, your successes or failures, your mistakes or regrets. God's promise remains unaffected if you do not quit and if you continue to bind yourself with the Lord. Do not be discouraged. Trust God's process and stay faithful. Your appointed time, your day of increase is coming.

PROSPERITY THROUGHOUT SCRIPTURE

A pastor once told me that prosperity and increase are not in the gospel. I told him I could prove it from Genesis to Revelation—that God wants His people to have abundance.

We can start with Abraham. In Genesis 12:2-3, God tells Abraham, "I will make you into a great nation; I will bless you and make your name great; and you shall be a blessing. I will bless those who bless you, and

I will curse him who curses you; and in you all the families of the earth shall be blessed."

We could also start with the very first man, Adam. In Genesis 1:28, God tells Adam, "Be fruitful and multiply; fill the earth and subdue it; have dominion over the fish of the sea, over the birds of the air, and over every living thing that moves upon the earth."

God wants His people to be prosperous, to multiply, to subdue the earth, and spread His teachings. You are not supposed to be broke or in poverty. He wants you to experience your day of increase. If you meditate on the Word of God both day and night, Psalm 1:3 says you will be like a "tree planted by streams of water that yields its fruit in its season, and its leaf does not wither. In all that he does, he prospers" (ESV). Your due season is your day of increase.

Do Not Listen to Anything That Limits You

Creation is going to continue roaring, shaking, and quaking because the manifest sons and daughters of God are too broke to complete the Great Commission. We've got to send people. We've got to go. We've got to increase financially to spread the gospel in Jesus' name.

We move toward our day of increase by following the guidelines in Joshua 1:8. We keep the Word of God in our mouth, then our mind, and finally our actions. Break the mindset that believes poverty is good. Jesus came "that they may have life, and that they [you] may have it more abundantly" (John 10:10).

God's Abundant Nature Brings Prosperity

Do we fully understand the word *abundantly*? It means to have too much. It means you have more than you can hold. An abundant basket overflows. That is God. He's a God of too much. If you disagree, look at the universe. How many stars are in the sky? Can you count them? He made them before He made us. That's where He started. He made the universe so big we cannot fathom the size. You are also His creation. You are His masterpiece. He wants you to increase more than the vastness of the universe!

In 2 Chronicles 20:20, it says, "Believe in the Lord your God, and you shall be established; believe His prophets, and you shall prosper." In other words, when you believe God, you're established.

It doesn't end there. In 2 Chronicles 26:5 it says, "He sought God in the days of Zechariah, who had understanding in the visions of God; and as long as he sought the Lord, God made him prosper." Seek the Lord as you write your vision and make it plain. Then, stand on that vision, wait in faith, bind yourself to the Lord, and you will prosper.

In 2 Chronicles 31:21, Scripture adds, "And in every work that he began in the service of the house of God, in the law and in the commandment, to seek his God, he did it with all his heart. So he prospered."

This is a vital point. When we do what God has called us to do with all our heart, we prosper. We can't do it half-heartedly, apathetically, or despondently. We commit with all our heart to the Word of God. At whatever level we give or commit to, we prosper up to that level.

Hear the voice of God prophesying to you right now: believe and prosper. God wants you to increase. Believe the Lord, your God, and you shall be established. Believe His prophetic voice, and you shall prosper. In the name of Jesus, I break the yoke of bondage, poverty, lack of vision, and no provision for your vision. Believe this and put your faith in it. You are destined to increase. You are destined to prosper. You are destined to multiply

Chapter Twenty-One

GOD WANTS YOU TO INCREASE

Are you questioning if God wants you to increase? Believers often do question this when they become entangled in religion instead of relationship. Prosperity is then viewed through carnal eyes. It becomes about you, your pleasure, your lifestyle, and ceases to be about God's goals.

I'm here to tell you, right here, right now, God wants you to increase. He needs you to increase. Fulfilling your calling is the highest form of spiritual warfare, and you need to increase to do that. When you set your heart, mind, and affection on Jesus, you'll seek increase to accomplish God's plan for your life. This is how we impact the world. It's how we share the Word of God globally.

When your increase comes and your vision is put into action, the increase God placed in your life for this very purpose becomes a testimony for Jesus. First, however, we must remove any mental or spiritual obstacle to receiving that blessing.

Holding on Until Transition Comes

Many who argue against prosperity do not argue with the Word of God. They base their view on opinion. Scripture, however, repeatedly speaks of increase. Decrease is never God's desire for mankind, only increase. We find one of many examples regarding increase after Elijah was taken into heaven and Elisha stepped into his full calling. In 2 Kings 2:14 Elisha said, "Where is the Lord God of Elijah?" Then, he struck the water with the mantle, and it parted. His day of transition had come.

Like Elisha, are you hanging on until your day of transition comes? To move away from religion and move toward a relationship with God, we must get into the Word of God. Scripture says that is when "good success" comes. "This Book of the Law shall not depart from your mouth, but you shall meditate in it day and night, that you may observe to do according to all that is written in it. For then you will make your way prosperous, and then you will have good success" (Josh. 1:8).

When you meditate on the Word of God day and night and mix it with your faith, the byproduct is not poverty or weakness. The byproduct will cause you to be a wrecking ball to the gates of hell.

Removing the Carnal Mind

The reason people struggle with the concept of increase is because they're carnal. If your success is viewed from a carnal perspective, it will be seen as all about self and a lust of the flesh. That is wrong thinking. "For the love of money is a root of all kinds of evil" (1 Tim. 6:10).

If you view increase as wrong, you probably are experiencing the love of money. That is what motivates people to judge other preachers and people with increase. That anger at others for having more is because they want what others have. They get upset at ministers teaching increase, people having increase, and how people and ministries give, because they have a worldly perspective.

They are agreeing with Judas. He believed the expensive alabaster jar Mary poured over Jesus' head should have been sold and the money given to the poor (see John 12:4-6). Agreeing with that mindset is agreeing with Judas.

If you hear anyone saying God doesn't want you to have too much, that is a lie of the devil. By choking the people of God and keeping them in poverty, they are unable to fulfill the Great Commission (see Matt. 28:19-20). If you've believed that lie, I bind that demonic, lying, poverty spirit in Jesus' name. God wants you to increase, and increase is based on the Word of God.

What are the steps to increase? You bind yourself to the Lord. You do what God's called you to do. Write down your vision, make it plain, and meditate on the Word of God day and night. The byproduct of that, according to Joshua 1:8, is "good success."

Defining Good Success

You need to define what good success looks like to you. For me, it's the ability to pay all my bills and help whomever God places on my heart. That means when I hear about someone in need, I can help them. When I see missions that need help, I can assist in meeting their budget. No wonder the devil doesn't want us to believe in the blessing of increase. If you believe in prosperity, increase, and abundance, he will hate you for it.

It's time for you to stand up. Mark 10:30 says, "Who shall not receive a hundredfold now in this time—houses and brothers and sisters and mothers and children and lands, with persecutions—and in the age to come, eternal life." People will persecute you more for the message of prosperity than for any other message. Scripture says increase will come "with persecutions" because the devil cannot stand by passively while you increase to fulfill your God-designed calling. If he doesn't intervene, he knows you'll take over the world through the preaching of the gospel.

When you know your value in Jesus, you will have a sense of worthiness for all God's increase to come into your life. Say it out loud right now, "Thank You, Jesus, for making me worthy of Your increase. I receive Your increase today!"

INCREASE ISN'T ABOUT YOU

What God gives, He gives to be used for His glory and His gospel. This may be the biggest misunderstanding religion has caused around the concept of prosperity. God wants us to increase, but many don't believe it because they see increase as carnal. They view wanting and having financial stability as greed or evil.

The hard reality is if this sounds selfish to you it's because you're selfish. It's time for you to stop thinking about you and start thinking about amplifying the Word of God around the world.

Is it wrong to want more so you can give more? Is it wrong to want the ability to share God's message further and wider and louder? That's what your increase enables you to do when you're in the Word of God and following His vision for your life.

Ask yourself—what could you accomplish for the kingdom of God without the stress of finances?

Change your thinking around finances from self-focused to others-focused. Instead of your finances being about meeting your needs, think of how they could meet the needs of others and share the gospel message. Think of yourself as a giver, a producer, and a distribution center of wealth for the gospel.

Sowing Is a Magnet for Increase

When you start thinking that way, you've turned your eyes away from self-focused motives and become selfless. It is the prosperity critics—priding themselves for never sowing to get—who have been blinded by their carnal thinking. According to God's Word, you must always give to get.

Every time my wife, Heather, and I give, we say, "I'm sowing this, and we command it to go and come back with friends, in the name of Jesus." We send our resources so more will return. We want our resources to multiply because then we can give more, do more, and impact more for God.

I continue to challenge myself in this area and test this principle. When God stirs my heart to give, I give. When God doesn't necessarily stir my heart to give, I still give because I want to be a giver. When I do, I say, "God, I have needs here. I'm giving and now it's Your problem." You should never claim that it's your problem once you've sowed. When you have a need, you know it's time to sow a seed. Give that responsibility to God. Not as a threat. You come to God with a heart that says, "God, I acted on Your Word, and I love You." Tell Him, "I have this problem and I'm sowing because I don't have enough to take care of it." When you do that, the worry, stress, and pressure is moved off you and onto God, who wants you to have abundance. He has this thing about being believed! When you radically believe Him, He will radically come through for you!

In Proverbs 19:17, Scripture says, "He who has pity on the poor lends to the Lord, and He will pay back what he has given." If you sow into good ground, you get a multiplied increase. We are called to give to the poor, but most of the body of Christ is too broke compared to the need. That's because our giving is happening backwards.

GIVING IN THE RIGHT ORDER

Here's what I mean. Many ministries build to a bigger scale by holding fundraisers for starving people. They'll show pictures of desperate children, bloated bellies, horrible poverty, then ask for money to buy them food. Scripture, however, says when we give to the poor, we aren't to let our right hand know what our left hand is doing (see Matt. 6:3). First and foremost, our giving is to go toward preaching the gospel. Donating to help the poor is called alms and should always be done in secret. That's how Jesus ordered giving to be done.

Many people are not prospering because they're giving to the poor out of their soulish anguish to help. They give generously but never see their increase. That's because the Lord says to support the house of God first. Giving into the storehouses of God is where your increase and abundance comes. Then, from that abundance, you can meet the needs of the poor.

We always want to be open to the needs of others and seek ways we can help, but we must keep it in the right order. Our first responsibility is to stand with the gospel.

This was an issue that arose among the disciples, too. When the woman with the alabaster jar broke it over Jesus' head, Judas reprimanded the act as wasteful. It was worth an entire year's salary. Judas believed the oil should have been sold and the money given to the poor. The other disciples didn't share Judas' view. He was a thief who loved money and betrayed Jesus for a few pieces of silver. When people say money should be given to the poor instead of God's work, they are lining up with Judas.

Your First Fruits Belong to Jesus

That may sound terrible to a carnal person who thinks, *But the poor need it*. No, the poor need your abundance, not your scraps. Sow into the Word of God for your abundance and give that abundance to the poor. Your first fruits, however, go to Jesus. The woman with the alabaster jar did. She sowed into Jesus, and Jesus is the Word of God. When she did, Jesus said her act would be remembered forever, and here we are thousands of years later talking about her.

Am I saying not to give to the poor? Absolutely not. I'm saying we give in the order God intended. We sow into His Word. We receive abundance. We give from that abundance. Instead of giving the poor our scraps, we give them our best. God absolutely cares about the dignity of the poor, and so should we.

Their needs should not be broadcast and exploited. Instead, we should be in a place of abundance where we can meet all their needs—privately.

Pray this with me: "Lord, please show me how to walk shamelessly, believing that You want to increase me in every area of my life. Lead me in a greater capacity of sowing and reaping. Thank You, Lord. I receive all You have for me in this area of sowing and supernatural return, amen."

Chapter Twenty-Two

YOUR BEGINNING WAS SMALL

Though your beginning was small, yet your latter end would increase abundantly.

—Job 8:7

When Heather and I first married, God told me our beginning would be small, but my latter days would be abundant. It echoed the Scripture above in Job 8:7.

The small part we saw right away. For the first several years of our marriage, we were super broke. Even though I had a talent for ministry, it didn't bring us any financial success. I could pack rooms and create million-dollar conferences for others while my wife and I lived on government assistance. It wasn't working.

One day, Heather told me she got a word from God to sow a single dollar into the richest ministry we knew. One dollar. It was a small start, but we were obedient. We started small, and we didn't stop. More and more, we found other successful ministries and sowed our one dollar.

We didn't do it to receive but to faithfully follow God's direction. It was after years of sowing that I had my revelation about Mark 10:30, which I shared in Chapter 6. As we discussed earlier, the Scripture says,

"Who shall not receive a hundredfold now in this time—houses and brothers and sisters and mothers and children and lands, with persecutions—and in the age to come, eternal life." Giving into the kingdom of God gives back a hundred times more.

As Heather and I activated that promise, we broke hell's economy over our life. Now, out of our abundance, we're able to bless others through financial assistance, cars, even houses, and we are impacting the world with the gospel.

Your beginning might seem small, too. You may not feel prosperous or see the blessings overflowing. You're looking for it to be overwhelming, and it's underwhelming. After a while, you can be tempted to doubt things are going to happen. But don't give up! Even though your beginning might have been small it doesn't mean your latter won't increase. If you maintain faithfulness in all God has called you to do, you will see hell's economy broken in your life.

Engage Your Calling

In Nehemiah 2:20, it says, "So I answered them, and said to them, 'The God of heaven Himself will prosper us; therefore we His servants will arise and build, but you have no heritage or right or memorial in Jerusalem.'" This verse is saying we've got to get up, work, and do what God has called us to do. We must engage our calling. When we do, the God of heaven meets our needs and prospers us with our day of increase.

For David, the day of increase came when he killed Goliath. For Jesus, His day of increase came when He was raised from the dead. For Moses, his day of increase came when he met God on the mountain and returned with his face glowing. These are all examples of engaging their calling and seeing their day of increase.

For us, engaging our calling is by writing our vision, making it plain, mixing the Word of God with faith, and keeping the vision in our mouth, mind, and actions. Then, the God of heaven will prosper us. It starts with sowing aggressively. Even if that start is as small as a single dollar.

CALLED TO ENJOY INCREASE

Throughout Scripture, we read that God wants to richly bless His children, and He wants His children to enjoy those blessings. What does that look like? Let's look at several Scriptures and break down what God is telling us about our day of increase.

> *He shall be like a tree planted by the rivers of water, that brings forth its fruit in its season, whose leaf also shall not wither; and whatever he does shall prosper.*
>
> —Psalm 1:3

When your season comes, you will bring forth your fruit. He's calling you to prosper, to increase, and to sow seed. Step out. Don't step back. Lean forward. Don't lean back. God has called you to multiply and increase in Jesus' name.

> *Wealth and riches will be in his house, and his righteousness endures forever.*
>
> —Psalm 112:3

God wants wealth and riches in your house. Praise God!

Pray for the peace of Jerusalem: "May they prosper who love you."

—**Psalm 122:6**

That I may cause those who love me to inherit wealth, that I may fill their treasuries.

—**Proverb 8:21**

The byproduct of asking for wisdom is inheriting wealth. When you seek wisdom, God fills your treasury, also.

The blessing of the Lord makes one rich, and He adds no sorrow with it.

—**Proverbs 10:22**

You can gain riches through your own efforts, labors, and even through manipulation and deception. In the end, you'll be full of sorrow. When you sow into the Word of God, you will be blessed superfluously.

But seek first the kingdom of God and His righteousness, and all these things shall be added to you.

—**Matthew 6:33**

Seeking God first means putting His Word in your mouth, mind, and actions. By putting Jesus first, the blessings are added. Although some say this only refers to spiritual things, this verse does not say "spiritual" things. It only says "things." That can include whatever you need to fulfill your calling and fulfill your desires.

Delight yourself also in the Lord, and He shall give you the desires of your heart.

—**Psalm 37:4**

If your desire is to seek Him, the byproduct is blessings that will overflow. Then you will be able to do whatever God has called you to do.

> *They shall build houses and inhabit them; they shall plant vineyards and eat their fruit.*
>
> —**Isaiah 65:21**

The verse says they shall build houses, not one house, and inhabit them. In other words, they will be at their homes, planting vineyards, and eating the fruit of their labor.

All these Scriptures are God pointing to His desire to bless His children and for His children to delight in those blessings. You are meant to increase and to enjoy that increase.

GOD WANTS YOU TO LOVE LIFE

Some of you aren't having enough fun. Many ministers and Christians become absorbed in striving and condemnation. What eventually happens is that people spend their time with mindless entertainment because they feel they can't do anything anyway.

God has given you all things to richly enjoy. He wants you to have fun. He wants you to enjoy your life. If you're exhausted, I understand that. I lived life hard for more than twenty years, and it nearly took me out. I felt old, sick, and tired all the time. It nearly ran my family into the ground.

That is not God's plan for our life. We are called to enjoy life. That doesn't mean we shouldn't work hard, but we should also be taking time to smell the roses. You must stop every now and then to take time off for your kids and yourself. Don't just take time, make time. There will always be times to fight and war against evil, but in normal times we need to make enjoyment part of our journey.

Chapter Twenty-Three

A DIFFERENT VIEW
OF WEALTH

There has been a lot of bad teaching on the topic of wealth, which is why I want to approach it differently. Hopefully, this will help bring understanding. We've got to develop a belief system with a corresponding faith that says, "God wants me wealthy."

Not in a self-indulgent way. Not in a worldly way. It is Christ-centered prosperity. The ultimate end is to spread the gospel around the world through the preaching of His Word, whether that's through the airwaves or by missionaries. Although God has given His people all things to richly enjoy, His ultimate purpose for wealth is to establish His covenant around the world.

THE 30, 60, 100 PRINCIPLE

To understand His purpose behind wealth, let's look at the parable of the sower. In Mark 4:3 Scripture says, "Behold, a sower went out to sow." As Jesus tells the story, we learn in Mark 4:8, "But other seed fell on good ground and yielded a crop that sprang up, increased and produced: some thirtyfold, some sixty, and some a hundred." As seeds were sown, different results happened to different seeds. Some fell on stony ground, some were choked by thorns, others fell on good ground. The seed which fell on good ground thrived by thirty, sixty, and a hundred times more.

In this parable, Jesus is talking about preaching the Word of God, not money. He's speaking of the gospel being sown into the hearts of men and women, but He's also introducing the principle of thirty, sixty, and hundred. More than one thing can happen with the Word of God.

The principle of thirty, sixty, and one hundred also refers to your development, discipleship, and conversion, while establishing the principle of sowing and reaping. What type of ground you sow into will determine the outcome of your harvest and the level of your growth from that ground. In other words, if you sow resources into shallow, thorny ground that doesn't put Jesus first, you will not have the kind of increase you hope to gain.

God wants His people to have thirty, sixty, and one hundredfold increase. To see that increase, we begin by sowing the Word of God into the hearts of men and women.

Find Good Ground

The principle of sowing and reaping means two things: sowing with the right heart and sowing into good ground. Many will sow with a good heart and get a good return from the Lord. God multiplies them because they're sowing into the kingdom. However, if you do not sow into good ground, there are limitations on your return.

Good ground is where the preaching of the Word is paramount. You want to sow into ministries that yearn to share the gospel, burn for the gospel, stand for the gospel, and teach the gospel of Jesus Christ. You'll know them by their fruit as people grow and mature in the Word of God.

When you sow into the Word of God, the seed returns in good measure, pressed down, shaken together, and running over (see Luke 6:38).

Giving to the poor is good. That's lending to the Lord. The woman with the alabaster jar came in with a year's wages, broke the jar of precious oil, put it on Jesus' feet, and washed it with her hair. She was sowing into the Word made flesh. When you sow into the Word, you will have a potent return. The purpose of your giving is to sow into good ground, and there's no better ground than the Word of God.

Remember, you are a distribution center for God's economy to the world. He is calling you right now to receive the responsibility of becoming a distributor of His kind of increase! Amen.

In God's Economy Faith Is the Currency

God is not moved by your need. He's moved by your faith. He's not motivated by needs because God has already paid for everything through the life of His Son, Jesus Christ. If He was moved by need, third world countries suffering horrific starvation would have their needs supernaturally met. The poorest countries in the world would become the most prosperous, all based on the level of their dramatic need.

What moves God and activates what He has for you is your belief and trust in who He is and what He has promised to do. In God's economy, faith is the currency of action and receiving.

Start with Faith and Apply Action

Faith, however, must come with works. Without works, faith is dead (see James 2:26). To sow wealth in the kingdom, you start with faith and apply action by sowing seeds into good soil. Our example is the woman with the alabaster jar, who sowed a year's salary by pouring the oil on Jesus' head and washing His feet with her hair. That small act, performed thousands of years ago, is still talked about today. That is the power of sowing our faith in good soil.

Does that mean we should not help the poor? God forbid! As we've discussed in previous chapters, never misunderstand the principle of faith and sowing to mean we can ignore those in need. James 1:27 says, "Pure and undefiled religion before God and the Father is this: to visit orphans and widows in their trouble, and to keep oneself unspotted from the world." What we want to give the poor is our overflow, not our scraps.

We want to give from our abundance. We do that through first sowing into the preaching of the Word of God.

When you are struggling to see the thirty, sixty, and one hundredfold breakthrough, it's because you are sowing in the wrong order. You need to stop sowing into yourself and the things you want. Start sowing into where you are fed by the Word of God.

Years ago, I saw this principle playing out in my own life. I had heard a preacher whose message touched my life, but the only thing I owned was a savings bond given to me by my family. I told Heather I wanted to give him that savings bond. It may not have been much to some, but it was all we had. We took our everything and sowed into the ministry with pure faith. We sowed completely into Jesus.

At that moment, things exploded around us. Checks began arriving in the mail. Random, supernatural blessings started happening. There was a complete shift in our life and the journey began from struggling to thriving.

Sadly, many in the body of Christ have received unhealthy teaching on wealth and increase. They've been taught it's selfish instead of being taught God's purpose for your increase is for others. When you have increase, you can not only meet your needs but also the needs of others around you. That is wealth!

In Mark 4:8, we learn that different types of ground produce different types of return. If you're sowing into soil that's not preaching the Word of God, you will not receive the potency you seek. When you sow into the gospel, you're sowing into the advancement of the gospel of Jesus Christ. That is when life comes your way with increase that cannot be hidden.

Chapter Twenty-Four

SACRIFICIAL GIVING CREATES RADICAL RETURNS

S omething special happens when you give sacrificially for the gospel. The returns become radical.

In Mark 10:23, Scripture says, "Then Jesus looked around and said to His disciples, 'How hard it is for those who have riches to enter the kingdom of God!'" In the previous verses, Jesus told the rich young ruler he lacked one thing—to give to the poor and then follow Him. For this young, wealthy man, that was a soul punch. So he walked away.

Afterward, Jesus told His disciples it is hard for the rich to enter the kingdom of God. Scripture records in Mark 10:24 that the disciples were astonished at His words.

For those whose riches come from their own efforts and not the blessings of God, giving up everything on the altar becomes abhorrent. With that mindset, you cannot enter the kingdom of God. You cannot enter the righteousness, peace, and joy of God. However, when your riches come from God, no sorrow is added. Being wealthy, rich, and blessed by God is joyful.

Notice the difference between verses 23 and 24. In Mark 10:23, Jesus says, "How hard is it for those who *have riches* to enter the kingdom of God!" In Mark 10:24 Jesus says, "Children, how hard it is for those who *trust in riches* to enter the kingdom of God!" Do not miss the difference. In verse 23, He's speaking of those who possess riches from their own efforts. In verse 24, He's speaking of those who trust in riches to enter the kingdom of God. He is saying that people who trust their riches before they trust in God cannot enter heaven. Riches become their god.

In the next verse, Jesus expounds on the struggle for the rich. In Mark 10:25, He says, "It is easier for a camel to go through the eye of a needle than for a rich man to enter the kingdom of God." As said earlier, some have surmised that this "eye of the needle" refers to a small gate in Jerusalem that a camel cannot get through while carrying its load. This is not true. There is no such gate. Jesus was creating a shocking image in the minds of His disciples. He is referring to an actual needle and a real camel going through it. His point was, getting to God by trying harder isn't difficult—it's impossible!

People who trust in riches instead of God cannot enter the kingdom of God. First, they must lay it all down and surrender to Jesus, then they will have access to the Father.

TRUST JESUS, NOT RICHES

This may sound shocking. It shocked the disciples, too. In Mark 10:26, Scripture says the disciples "were greatly astonished, saying among themselves, 'Who then can be saved?'" Why were they so concerned? Because they had financial means. They were fishermen and a tax collector.

They were businessmen who owned companies and assets, like boats. They probably worried that they couldn't be saved either. They were misunderstanding Jesus' words. He was emphasizing the difficulty for those who trust in riches, not those who possess them. "But Jesus looked at them and said, 'With men it is impossible, but not with God; for with God all things are possible'" (Mark 10:27). Here in verse 27, Jesus is telling us not to trust in our own strength or our own wealth, but to trust in Him. Upon hearing this, Peter pointed out to Jesus that he and the disciples had "left all and followed You." Jesus put their sacrifice into a different perspective. In verse 29, He answered Peter saying, "Assuredly, I say to you, there is no one who has left house or brothers or sisters or father or mother or wife or children or lands, for My sake and the gospel's."

There is something powerful that happens for those who sacrifice everything for the sake of the gospel. If the rich young man had been willing to trust Jesus, he would have experienced it. He would have received back a hundred times what he gave. If he'd given up everything to serve and trust Jesus by seeking the kingdom first, then all these things would have been added.

GIVE UP EVERYTHING FOR AND TO GOD

That's the secret to the hundredfold increase, which Scripture mentions in Mark 10:30, "Who shall not receive a hundredfold now in this time—houses and brothers and sisters and mothers and children and lands, with persecutions—and in the age to come, eternal life." It's about letting go of what we're holding on to and embracing the gospel with both hands. We release the wealth we've acquired in order to receive the wealth God has planned. We must come to God with a pure heart and tell Him, "I'm leaving everything behind to serve You. I don't care what it costs me." That's when something supernatural happens.

Sadly, the rich young ruler never grasped what Jesus was saying. He wanted to give this young man more than he could possibly imagine, but he first had to willingly give it all up for Christ. Instead of Jesus telling him this, He tested him. When he turned around and walked away, he walked away from Jesus and the hundredfold blessings that were awaiting him.

Sacrificial giving for the sake of the gospel is one of the highest acts of worship, while creating one of the highest forms of return. That level of giving is a level of trust that cannot be faked. It is precious to the Lord, who has placed such a valuable reward for those who practice this type of selflessness. Are you ready to give everything up for the gospel and follow Jesus?

BELIEVE GOD OVER YOUR EXPERIENCES

God wants you to win. Yes, there are sacrificial times in your life, times when you must be willing to pour yourself out for the gospel. However, when you pour out and don't see a return, what should you do?

You stand on the Word of God. You say, "Your Word is true. My heart might lie, people's wisdom might lie, but God's Word does not. Your Word will perform and will, absolutely, come back to me." I've personally stood here, on this statement, and I've seen the overflow. He who began a good work in us is faithful to see it until the end. You hold on to that promise, and you refuse to let go.

This is the mindset we must grasp. We believe the Word of God over our experiences, because persecution will come to steal the Word of God out of us. For me, that means holding on to a billion-dollar vision to spread the gospel around the world. People say I sound crazy for such a dream, but I think they're crazy for not accomplishing everything God's called them to do. They're wasting their existence. We're going to live for eternity, but what we do here is what we'll be measured by there. We need to grab hold of the Word of God and start living for eternity.

Find Your Bigger Vision

In many churches where I minister, I see people with good hearts who are pacified with their gospel outreach. I love the body of Christ, but many members view their church and community as all there is. We need a bigger vision. If you want to prosper, think globally. You can't be "locally owned and globally minded" as many of my friends in business say. You've got to think about the greater body of Christ and how you can use your gifts to serve. We're not an island. Focusing inward is a sign of selfishness.

Over the years, I've had more people attack me over this message than anything else. But if you don't believe for increase in your life or seek to become a distribution center for the Word of God, you're insulting Jesus. It isn't until God stirs your heart and you start radically giving that you'll see the hundredfold increase in your calling.

I have a crazy level of favor on me because I've paid a high price for the sake of the gospel. I've followed God no matter what anyone says, including my family. Many people prioritize other things more than seeking the kingdom of God first—like family, things they own, their jobs, etc. Instead, put your effort into the kingdom of God and watch your life multiply forward.

Take That Faith Leap

What about you? What's hindering your dream? The only thing that can hold you back is your mindset. You've got to take a leap of faith. Unless you do, nothing will change.

This isn't about works. It's about encouraging you to step forward. If you struggle with the thought God wants you to increase, you've either been mentored by poor teaching or you're carnally minded. Receiving abundance is not about getting. It's about increasing the kingdom of God. You are the body of Christ, and God wants His body prosperous. He wants the message of Jesus to go around the world. He needs you wealthy to achieve His goal.

Chapter Twenty-Five

THE PERSECUTION
OF INCREASE

*No one who has left home or brothers or sisters or mother
or father or children or fields for me and the gospel will
fail to receive a hundred times as much in this present age:
homes, brothers, sisters, mothers, children and fields—along
with persecutions—and in the age to come eternal life.*

—Mark 10:29-30, NIV

When you begin to break the grip of hell's economy off your life, you would think others would celebrate. Sadly, the opposite happens. A spirit of criticism very often will rise with a desire to persecute the righteous; these individuals who "gave up to go up" become the target of accusation.

Envy and slander are the go-to's of those under the influence of hell's economy. Born-again believers who are on their way to heaven can allow the spirit of the world to speak through them, causing difficulty for those who have left it all to follow Jesus.

Amazingly, those who gave up everything to follow Jesus have an uncommon, supernatural grace that induces the promise Jesus predicted—a hundred times as much now, in this time!

PERSECUTION IS THE THUG SIDE
OF HELL'S ECONOMY

To the carnal it can appear that those who gave up everything to follow Jesus didn't attain what they later possess through proper means. Looking for wrongdoing or being willing to slander someone else steps into the influence of hell's economy, which will always suggest the worst. It will cause those who have not given up to criticize the blessed. The critical view toward the righteous is only a reflection of how they themselves would attain increase—meaning they feel any form of illogical abundance must be from doing something wrong. When someone is trapped in hell's economy, they display criticism of the blessed. They are compelled to speak through envy, accusation, and suspicion based on their own limitations. These individuals have caused great damage to good people.

Maybe you have been critical of another's increase. Let God be their judge. Remember, Jesus is head of the church, not anyone else. If something is glaringly wrong and must be dealt with, then let leadership do so. Remember, no one, and I mean no one, gets away with anything! If something is truly wrong, there must be repentance and correction. Otherwise, eventually what is wrong shows up somewhere! Certainly, it will be on full display the day each one of us gives an account before the Lord.

VICTIMS OF CRITICISM

Speculation and accusation are a slippery slope littered with many victims. Those who desired to follow God at all costs and became offended from intense criticism received it from other believers. Offended believers abound in the church, and it's often those who started out strong but did not have the maturity or faith to navigate through persecution. Favor and increase can destroy an immature believer. When the principle of increase begins to happen in the life of a new believer or someone not accustomed to dealing with criticism, it can be so toxic for them that they completely quit. Offenses are a strategy of hell's economy and can be so incredibly challenging that the immature believer can be permanently stopped.

Not only does criticism and persecution hurt believers and potentially destroy immature believers, but those doing the persecution are in danger of experiencing tremendous damage to their walk with the Lord. They are allowing the accusing spirit to work through them, but they will reap a terrible harvest eventually and become casualties of their own compliance with hell's economy.

THE NATIVE TONGUE OF THE UNINSPIRED IS CRITICISM

I often say while speaking, "The native tongue of the uninspired is criticism."

Those with an ideology but no revelation, trained in religion's ways with no genuine love for their brothers and sisters, can easily be weaponized by hell's economy against you. A sad reality comes into view in which many are unwilling to go the distance with Jesus when life gets hard from misplaced expectations. Proverbs refers to it as, "hope deferred makes the heart sick." They cease developing; they plateau. These who experience persecution in the middle of the battlefield are not willing to hold on to God's promises during the attack. Satan knows this. He knows when you give something up for Jesus and pour it out as a drink offering before the Lord, you are destined to receive a hundred-fold return.

Satan knows, if you sacrifice, that your increase will allow you to dominate in this life for Jesus. He recognizes the precious harvest you have coming, and he does not want that to happen. When you sacrificially give, expect the devil to fight you tooth and nail with persecution. This is how he fights believers to stop them from receiving their wealth.

He will discourage. He will offend. He will keep you off focus. Expect persecution, believer. That means people will talk against you and lie about you or worse, but know these attacks are demonic and designed to stop you from receiving your increase. Do not get offended—you are not wrestling against flesh and blood, just those who are cooperating with hell's economy. Instead, look at it as a stamp of approval that God is with you. If you have sown, then stand. You have precious harvest coming your way if you do not give up.

If you knew what was on the other side of your battle you would never quit!

> "If you knew what was on the other side of your mountain you would move it!"
>
> **—Mark Hankins**

Move your mountain! Don't give up now—what's on the other side of your mountain is better than you can imagine. I've said God wants you to prosper more than you do, but I'm going to say something even bolder—God needs you to prosper. If you aren't prospering, you are ineffective with your calling. Therefore, you can never give up your harvest. You've sown too much to give up now. Whatever you've given up for the sake of the gospel is your precious seed, and from that seed is coming a precious harvest.

In Mark 10:29-30 Jesus said that "no one who has left home or brothers or sisters or mother or father or children or fields for me and the gospel will fail to receive a hundred times as much in this present age: homes, brothers, sisters, mothers, children and fields—along with persecutions—and in the age to come eternal life" (NIV). These are words written in red.

In verse 31 it goes on to say, "But many who are first will be last, and the last first" (NIV). Notice the principle. We've read how our beginnings may be small, but our latter end has great abundance (see Job 8:7). There is a day of increase coming for you.

If you feel unprepared and unqualified, congratulations. You qualify! God loves to use the foolish things to shame the wise (see 1 Cor. 1:27). Even when you feel weak and incapable, be radically engaged with God by sowing, being obedient, and standing on the Word of God. This is how you qualify for what God wants done through your life. Stand on God's ability, not your own. If you knew what was on the other side of your battle you would never quit! The victory will outshine the battle of the seed war. Sow and contend in faith until you receive.

NEVER LIMIT GOD'S GLORY

When it comes to our increase, we must get out of the flesh and stop loving money. Instead, seek the kingdom first. Then, as Ephesians 3:20 tells us, there will be more waiting for us than we could ever think or imagine, all according to the grace of God.

You are called to increase and glorify God. He doesn't want you to limit anything that brings Him glory. In John 15:8 it says, "By this My Father is glorified, that you bear much fruit; so you will be My disciples."

God is glorified when we bear fruit because He's a fruit-bearing God, and we're made in His image and likeness.

God is not broke; Jesus wasn't broke. Paul the apostle wasn't broke. The disciples weren't broke. As it is in heaven, so be it on earth (see Matt. 6:10). You will work harder than you've ever worked, be more faithful than you've ever been, and produce more than you've ever produced when you apply the grace of God and mix it with your faith.

When you pray Ephesians 1:3, "I am blessed with all spiritual blessings in heavenly places," that manifests in the natural. You are praying in the covenant of Abraham, Isaac, and Jacob through the seed of Abraham, which is Jesus. When we speak God's Word, the angels hear it and move. We are not commanding angels. We're not authorized to do that. We're praying the Word of God. They hear it and go to work. Hebrews 1:14 speaks of these ministering spirits. It says, "Are they not all ministering spirits sent forth to minister for those who will inherit salvation?" When we, the heirs of salvation, speak and confess the Word of God, we're sowing in faith and *spiritual responses* are released and able to flow.

DON'T BE AFRAID TO FALL IN FAITH

God has spoken to you. He's already released blessings for you, as long as you set your heart, mind, and faith on what God has provided for you. For me, I'd rather stretch out in faith and fail but rise again, like Proverbs 24:16, which describes the righteous man. This verse is not speaking of a sinful man, but a righteous man who falls seven times. That means he was trying to do what God told him. He was working toward his destination, and even though he didn't make it during those times, he never gave up.

I'd rather fall in faith than succeed in unbelief. When you fall in faith, God touches you and takes you further than you could have ever gone. He wants you blessed beyond your imagination so you can spread the Word of God around the world.

Even though increase comes with persecution, never let persecution stop your sowing. Whenever I feel persecuted, I sow more. I lean into it. God has called His ministry to overcome dead religion and help people break through by mediating on the Word of God. I declare over you today that precious harvest.

THE BLESSING OF THE LORD IS YOURS!

In Proverbs 10:22 we read that, "The blessing of the Lord makes one rich, and He adds no sorrow with it." When many read that verse, their first thought is, *How does the blessing work?* They see the blessing as something to own, like a vehicle, or something that happens to them, like a friendship. That is not the blessing.

The blessing of the Lord is the spoken Word of God. It is the favor of God spoken over you, which empowers you to prosper, to increase, to experience favor and abundance in your life. The blessing is the empowerment of God in your life.

If you think the blessing of the Lord is money or things, it's time for a revelation. All those things may be byproducts, but they are not the blessing. Matthew 6:33 says, "But seek first the kingdom of God and His righteousness, and all these things shall be added to you." Those added things are the byproducts, but they are not the blessing.

Seeking the kingdom first means seeking understanding of what Jesus did for you. The blessing of the Lord is the spoken Word of God over mankind. In the beginning, God told Adam to be fruitful, to multiply, and to take dominion over the earth. When He spoke, things happened. Adam took dominion over everything—land, sea, and animals. God also blessed Abraham with a covenant promising multiplication.

That Word was spoken over Jesus, Noah, and David, among many others. When Christians say, "Oh, our new car is such a blessing," I agree! You were blessed, but that is not the blessing of Proverbs 10:22.

When Jesus gave His life on the cross, He released a supernatural covenant blessing over you. We now have access to that blessing every day. We can possess that blessing and see it work.

Proverbs 10:22 clearly shows us, "The blessing of the Lord makes one rich, and He adds no sorrow with it." However, many people have abused this topic and made it all about riches. In Matthew 6:33, we see a progression to the blessings. First, we seek the kingdom of God. Then, all these things are added.

IN THE MIDDLE OF PERSECUTION, CONTEND!

You are not called to be passive! You have permission here and now to contend for the manifestation of what Jesus provided for you. Contend by not being offended. Contend by rising in faith and speaking out loud what God's Word says about you and what He has promised! Become fully persuaded that what He promised you He is able to perform, and if there is delay, it is not denial; you will outlast the storm, the persecution, or any other thing that tries to separate you from the love of God

There's a way to continuously access the blessing God has released over you. First and foremost, we seek the kingdom of God by seeking His righteousness. What is the righteousness of God? It's Jesus.

In Christ Jesus, we have become the righteousness of God, according to 2 Corinthians 5:21. We have all the rights Jesus has. Let's look at Galatians 3:14, which says, "That the blessing of Abraham might come upon the Gentiles in Christ Jesus, that we might receive the promise of the Spirit through faith." Those of faith are the seed of Abraham, which means you have access to the covenant between him and God.

When you can understand this, you can operate in the blessing. That's how the blessing of the Lord makes you rich. The blessing has a financial and healing aspect. According to the Word of God, we have the right to abundance in our life because of Jesus' sacrifice. Because of the cross, we are saved and have the right to access our healing, increase, purpose, plan, calling, and gifts.

The Word of God teaches that the kingdom of God is not eating or drinking; it's righteousness, peace, and joy. What makes you rich is God's blessing. Spend time with God seeking out your honest motive for wanting an increase. Is it selfish, or is it out of a desire to be a blessing? You will know whether you're operating under the blessing or in fruitless toiling based on your motive. Have a heart to seek the kingdom of God first, and you'll see your increase.

Do not grow weary in well doing, do not faint, stay in faith, and you will see the goodness of the Lord in the land of the living. Do not fear or be intimidated by persecution or the spirit of the culture. You have every right in Jesus to break hell's economy off your life, be it now or if the entire world collapses. His covenant with you stands, period!

POSITIONED TO BREAK HELL'S ECONOMY

Chapter Twenty-Six

DELIVERED OF HELL'S ECONOMICS

God's supernatural kingdom operates on a supernatural system to impact our world. That system includes economics. It has always been the goal of the devil to run this world completely. It seems to me that the devil did not fully understand what Jesus came to do. More significantly, the devil certainly never intended for the church to run it! The church was a surprise, as it was a concept that was concealed or hidden in the Old Testament. Jesus hit the kingdom of darkness with something it was not equipped to handle—you! You're God's ultimate plan to bust up hell's system; you are the enforcement to Jesus's mission. As He is in this world, so are we, and so are you.

God has a plan to finance the gospel around the globe. He is looking for anyone and everyone who is passionate about getting His message to every lost child of His.

> *And you shall remember the Lord your God, for it is He who gives you power to get wealth, that He may establish His covenant which He swore to your fathers, as it is this day.*
>
> **—Deuteronomy 8:18**

The ultimate covenant promise is the gospel! He wants the gospel to be established. When combining this promise with the great commission, we see that He wants His covenant to be established around the world until everyone has heard. This is something God will empower and give supernatural favor and finance to do.

God's economic plan for the gospel is often misunderstood. If viewed as a way to simply have more money, you've fallen into a trap created by the devil. God blessed Adam and instructed him to be fruitful and multiply and to take dominion over the earth. Satan hijacked that blessing and counterfeited it with mammon, but Jesus won it back on the cross.

Hell's economy is simply money, power, and the influence of an antichrist agenda—that's it. Wealth and power just for wealth and power's sake. It is an indulgence into selfishness, which is to cooperate with a Luciferian system. Hell's economy is absent of the Spirit of God and knows no other abundance but the accumulating of more for self. No joy, no satisfaction from the inside out, and no answers to the fight inside. That is why lust is so tormenting. Its desire is never resolved. It is a striving that has no solution. It is the chorus to the U2 song that says, "I still haven't found what I'm looking for." Lust is a selfish desire without resolve. Lust and mammon go hand in hand. Lust will pollute the idea of God's economy and supernatural increase through the cloak of mammon—which, again, is man's striving for the sole purpose of possessing money, power, and all the other counterfeits making up hell's economy.

No one can serve two masters; for either he will hate the one and love the other, or else he will be loyal to the one and despise the other. You cannot serve God and mammon.

—Matthew 6:24

Mammon Is Not Money, It's the Love of Money

Mammon isn't money. Mammon is the worship of money. It's placing all your faith in money and removing that reliance on God. It's a counterfeit blessing. It's fake. Mammon is the devil's economy, which strives in the flesh for wealth and resources, designed to prevent you from functioning in your blessing.

Teachings on poverty are often far more extreme than teachings on prosperity, because the idea of poverty aligns with hell's economy. This is carnal and logical to the world. It is the opposite of God's economy.

Those outside the church also do not believe Christians or ministers should ever have money. When we teach this, it's believed we're in agreement with hell's economy, because the world also believes churches should be broke. This carnal viewpoint reflects the desire of the devil, who does not want to see churches prospering and sharing the gospel.

For Christians, we often find it more comfortable to believe God does not desire us to have wealth than it is to accept God wants us financially blessed. We're mixing up two different concepts—prosperity and mammon.

Mammon and the Spirit of Humanism

Mammon is the love and worship of money. It's humanistic, striving after the flesh with no regard for God. It's going after money and never seeking first the kingdom of God. Mammon is having one desire only— to possess wealth and power, meeting one's own needs without the help of God or His economy. The purpose of mammon is not to use it for God's plan and purpose, but to use it for oneself.

This is the Babylonian system of selfish gain. It is not, however, Bible prosperity. Even though you may appear to be increasing, as you spend money on new cars, things, and possessions, there is no sweetness of the blessing from the Lord in it. It's the pursuit and pleasure of money without being kingdom minded.

We must always dismiss mammon, knowing that the Word of God says we cannot serve two masters. It will be God, or it will be mammon. It will not be both.

Instead, we seek first the kingdom and His righteousness, which are only found in Jesus. When you seek righteousness, peace, and joy through Jesus, He becomes your desire. Then, you will be filled with righteousness, peace, and joy, with no sorrow added.

How to Reap Your Blessing

The body of Christ has been misled to believe you can't have money. That's not true. When you seek the kingdom of God first, there is a supernatural blessing God releases for you. In the Old Testament, He spoke blessings over Adam, Abraham, Jacob, and David, who wanted to build a house for God, but God instead built a house for David.

You engage your blessing with your faith through giving, standing up, confessing over it, studying it, and not allowing yourself to love money.

Here's how it worked in our life: Heather and I were painfully broke. Instead of living in fear, we chose to live out our faith by radically giving. We gave to a ridiculous level; and although we had our ups and downs, the blessing of the Lord brought life and abundance.

Many argue that tithing is not a New Testament principle. Well, Hebrews 7 is in the New Testament, and it mentions tithing. Tithing explained here is revelatory! It dawned on me that tithing, or sowing, is not for the purpose of lining the offering bucket of a church or minister's personal vision. Quite the opposite! When you are sowing in the natural realm, the Bible says He (Jesus) receives it in the spiritual! This set me free, and it can set you free also. Anytime you give with a heart toward God, even if the place you gave to does something wrong or ends up being a disappointment, you can rejoice because it went straight to Jesus anyway! I encourage you to adopt this Bible truth; it will set you free.

THE PRINCIPLE OF HERE AND THERE

> *Here mortal men receive tithes, but there he **receives them**, of whom it is witnessed that he lives.*
>
> **—Hebrews 7:8**

First in the natural, then in the spiritual. We must activate our faith in the natural, which leads to a supernatural reaction. There are two areas involving your giving that apply to the "here and there" principle.

> *Howbeit that was not first which is spiritual, but that which is natural; and afterward that which is spiritual.*
>
> **—1 Corinthians 15:46, KJV**

Simply put, it is anything you sow into the kingdom, whether it be the tithe, an offering, or anything of value. Not only does it go into the "storehouse," but it's supernaturally received by Jesus! Giving is a faith action that has a supernatural response attached to it.

The Power of Tithing

Grace is powerful. It teaches us who Christ is and who we are in Him. Tithing, although not required to obtain grace, does unlock and protect what you possess.

Tithing should not be based on a fear of judgment. Some teaching today says believers who do not tithe will be cursed. Scripture, however, does not support that. Galatians 3:13 says, "Christ has redeemed us from the curse of the law." The only thing remaining is blessing, which on the topic of God's economy we activate through tithing.

Tithing is about being obedient to God's commands. We already have everything in the Spirit due to Jesus' sacrifice on the cross, but we activate blessings in the natural by acts of faith. You are loaded with supernatural horsepower and favor when you act on what you have already received through the kingdom of God. So often, people make this so complicated when it is so simple. Give and you shall receive!

Three Steps to Begin

You might be wanting to increase and multiply forward but are asking how to get there.

First, change your mentality. In 3 John 1:2, Scripture says, "Beloved, I pray that you may prosper in all things and be in health, just as your soul prospers." This soul prosperity includes your mind, will, and emotions. You can never receive beyond your level of believing. The way you believe the Word of God is the way you receive your blessing. If you do not understand how to believe and receive from the Word of God, your blessing is limited.

Second, you live out your belief. When you believe the Word of God, you begin to receive the Word of God. When you can stand in faith and believe God's will is to bless and prosper you, this releases God's spoken Word over you. We know that God activates what you believe, so believe God wants to give you abundance.

Third, once you've made this firm foundation of faith, you stand on it by giving radically. Remember, *if it doesn't mean much to you, it might not mean much to God.* If you are looking for big returns, you must consider sowing big seed. Big seed by your standards. You will know if you've sown "big" because many days after you've sown you will remember it vividly! It will get your attention!

Additionally, there are wise ways to budget and manage your finances. However, when you sow into God's economy, you sow to the level of your faith. That means you believe God wants to prosper you. You believe God's blessing is spoken over you. You are deciding to bust up hell's economy.

After your decision followed by action, then comes the seed war.

Prepare Your Heart for Battle

When your faith rises and you give radically, your blessing begins working for you and life flows freely and often superfluously. This outpouring of blessing, however, often comes with persecution. The devil doesn't want you to have blessings. When those blessings come, prepare yourself for challenges and trials.

Without this heart preparation, as we previously said, the persecution will shock you. As you multiply and receive blessings, you cannot expect people to celebrate. People with the *spirit of mammon* will be upset.

This spirit is demonic, anti-prosperity, anti-blessing, and ultimately it is powering hell's economy. It will compel people with carnal minds to attack you and your increase, or just attack you. You must be prepared to be attacked by the kingdom of darkness when your increase comes.

CELEBRATED, NOT TOLERATED

Imagine if people saw the body of Christ standing in faith, confessing, and sowing into a ministry, then reaping increase. Now imagine the joy that would be spread if only others in the body of Christ could celebrate and applaud those who received their breakthrough. Together we would break hell's economy on a global level.

When I see people increasing beyond my level, I sow into their ministry. I sow into them because I want that same momentum on me. I also don't want envy or jealousy in my heart. Envy is of the devil. What we should have is a sweetness and love for our brothers and sisters who increase. We should sow seed into their blessing and celebrate their victory with God. Sowing into others and celebrating their increase will place a spirit on you that joyfully says, "I'm next. I'm next. I'm next. Praise God."

YOUR TRIBE

Eventually, it is God's desire that you find yourself surrounded by people who celebrate each other's blessings, which leads to a corporate anointing. When I see good friends win, I'm so overwhelmed with emotion because I know that's my win, too. They are overcoming, and

I'm thrilled. Developing a heart that rejoices at the blessings of others is what Jesus longs to see in us.

You need to understand that God is no respecter of persons. If He'll do this for another person, He'll do it for you. Your time is coming.

YOUR ENTRY POINT INTO GOD'S ECONOMY

In the kingdom of God, there is no other avenue to step into God's economy than to turn from the love of money. That is a powerful truth! The love of money has a death grip on the world and is the basis for hell's economy. Hell's economy, based on the love of money or mammon, is the root of all evil. Once again, mammon is man's way of providing for themselves without God.

The love of money causes people to sin—all in hopes of having more for themselves. It's based on selfishness. However, we get rid of that carnal mind by loving Jesus and seeking His kingdom first. The byproduct of that action is accessing the kingdom of heaven.

When you turn from the love of money and toward the love of Jesus, you get excited about who He is. The Word of God comes alive in you, and you engage your mouth and God's written Word to weaponize your faith. You use God's system of praying, believing, standing in faith, accessing the kingdom of heaven, and drawing heaven's culture into the natural.

Remember, turn away from the love of money. That is the road to making mammon your master instead of God. To break the hold of mammon over your life, you begin by giving radically. This places money in its proper place—servant to the righteous. Set your heart to giving more than ever, and stretch yourself. This will never allow a love of money to overtake you.

Chapter Twenty-Seven

BREAKING HELL'S ECONOMY FOR YOUR FAMILY

God is a *heart* God. He is not as religious as we might think. He is, after all the one who showed David favor after he committed adultery, murder, and breaking the law by taking the showbread from the alter. David is the one who declared, "It is not sacrifices You desire, or I would bring them." What God desires is a contrite heart—God is a *heart* God!

> *For You do not desire sacrifice, or else I would give it; You do not delight in burnt offering. The sacrifices of God are a broken spirit, a broken and a contrite heart—these, O God, You will not despise.*
>
> **—Psalm 51:16-17**

Remember the story of the tax collector and the Pharisee? The tax collector was beating his chest, feeling unworthy, while the Pharisee said, "At least I'm not like that tax collector." God was pleased with the genuine heart connection from the tax collector rather than the law keeper. That story given by Jesus must have really angered the Pharisees when they heard it! This again is an example of our God being a heart God. He cares more about legitimate connection with you than all the law keeping you do.

Also He spoke this parable to some who trusted in themselves that they were righteous, and despised others: "Two men went up to the temple to pray, one a Pharisee and the other a tax collector. The Pharisee stood and prayed thus with himself, 'God, I thank You that I am not like other men— extortioners, unjust, adulterers, or even as this tax collector. I fast twice a week; I give tithes of all that I possess.' And the tax collector, standing afar off, would not so much as raise his eyes to heaven, but beat his breast, saying, 'God, be merciful to me a sinner!' I tell you, this man went down to his house justified rather than the other; for everyone who exalts himself will be humbled, and he who humbles himself will be exalted."

—Luke 18:9-14

Earlier we looked at the life of Cornelius. His desire to use his resources to please God got the attention of heaven, and Peter was sent to him and his household.

There was a certain man in Caesarea called Cornelius, a centurion of what was called the Italian Regiment, a devout man and one who feared God with all his household, who gave alms generously to the people, and prayed to God always.

—Acts 10:1-2

And when he observed him, he was afraid, and said, "What is it, lord?" So he said to him, "Your prayers and your alms have come up for a memorial before God."

—Acts 10:4

Cornelius' alms and generosity induced a move of God leading to his entire household being saved and filled with the Holy Spirit!

When the heads of any household give themselves completely over to the Lord and engage a corresponding action of giving, there is something supernatural that happens in the life of their entire household. I had the privilege of taking my first year of Bible school together with my grandfather. He was a godly man, a successful business leader, and a giver. I recall many times thinking to myself, *Why would anyone give their money away to that level?* Well, after being with him and seeing his example—which took some years—eventually, the seeds sown into my heart from his example caused me to rise and meet the opportunity to give little by little, until my wife and I became aggressive, radical givers. Giving to that level will change your life. It has ours.

IF YOU GET ADDICTED TO GIVING, GOD WILL SUPPORT YOUR HABIT

Mark Hankins and Jesse Duplantis both use a phrase I really like and have adopted: "If you get addicted to giving, God will support your habit!" We have discovered this to be true for decades. It will work for you. In today's world, the safest investment is to sow into the kingdom. After all, you're giving into your future. God doesn't need your money; He set up the kingdom's economic system for you to have a bright future. It's God's legal reason to provide His resources to His kids. He can't just do it automatically. He made His economy available through Jesus. Your part is to engage it and act on it. The level at which you give—in good measure, pressed down, and shaken together—will be given back to you!

Generational Purpose Leads to Generational Wealth

A good man leaves an inheritance to his children's children,
but the wealth of the sinner is stored up for the righteous.

—Proverbs 13:22

A powerful result to a patriarch or matriarch who surrenders to God's economy is effectively breaking hell's economy off their household. Through this, it will put them in a position to leave a two-generation inheritance after them. Psalm 128:3 says, "Your wife shall be like a fruitful vine in the very heart of your house, your children like olive plants all around your table." This verse outlines your right in God's economy to break hell's economy off your family, finances, mind, emotions, and anything coming against you. You should write this one down and pray it out loud over your family.

When hell's economy is broken, heaven's economy manifests in the natural. It attracts physical and tangible things, which you are to own and not allow them to own you.

Briefly, let's return to Malachi 3:11 again. When it speaks of not allowing the devourer to destroy the fruit of your ground, one interpretation suggests that the fruit and vine are protection for your family. God will protect your family and break whatever comes against them. The fruitful vine and olive plant mentioned in Psalm 128:3 refers to your spouse and children. If you're single, it's referring to your family and those in covenant with you. In other words, whatever matters to you, God will protect.

Psalm 128:4 goes on to say, "Behold, thus shall the man be blessed who fears the Lord." This verse means you're in God's economy, which destroys hell's economy. Fearing the Lord in the New Testament means you are walking in the kingdom of God, in God's system, and you are tapping into the kingdom of heaven.

The kingdom of heaven, as we discussed earlier, isn't a feeling. It's a place that is based on a system of obedience. When you obey the voice of God, you tap into the supernatural anointing that exists in the kingdom of heaven, and natural things are added to you.

As we continue, Psalm 128:5-6 says, "The Lord bless you out of Zion, and may you see the good of Jerusalem all the days of your life. Yes, may you see your children's children. Peace be upon Israel!" When you seek first the kingdom of God and His righteousness, blessings are added to you, specifically the blessing of a long life.

If we return to Malachi 3:12, it says, "And all nations will call you blessed, for you will be a delightful land." Imagine this: a delightful land where your children and you prosper. A place where the kingdom of God advances in your life. Where the blessings of the Lord are evident on you. Where happiness abounds in your life.

THE PROMISE OF HAPPINESS

When you eat the labor of your hands, you shall be happy, and it shall be well with you.

—**Psalm 128:2**

Many believe God's Word doesn't promise happiness. That's a lie. God promises that "you shall be happy, and it shall be well with you." In the Word of God, you can read that God wants you happy. Happiness is promised in God's economy in the kingdom of heaven. Do you

---

think there is sorrow in heaven? No. God not only wants you happy, but He also wants you so full of joy your emotions are overwhelmed. When your blessing comes, God will bring a breakthrough where happiness will be poured out on you, which is a result of trusting God and His economy.

When you tap into the anointing where the wealth of the wicked is stored up for the righteous, the hidden treasures of darkness will be given to you (see Isa. 45:3). Later in Isaiah 60:3 we read, "The Gentiles shall come to your light." Picture that light as a delightful land flowing with the favor of God. This is the land God has called you to possess, occupy, and go forward in.

God Wants You to Rest

Another way to activate your blessing comes through resting. When you rest, you are showing you know who you are in Christ. Resting does not mean ceasing to work. It doesn't mean a lack of passion and diligence in whatever God has called you to do.

It's about being comfortable and confident in your identity in Christ. You can find your identity in Christ through His finished works; then you can add corresponding actions like seeking first the kingdom of God, tithing, and resting.

Today, I declare over your life a yoke-breaking horsepower that will break hell's economy off your children and your marketplace. So many suffer from marketplace strife either through the trials of work or seeking more or different work. You wrestle with controversy, chaos, and lack of direction. Right now, God is going to bring you forward. Study the Word of God and believe what it says.

In our culture, we desperately need a revival of the Bible. We need to take the Word of God and mix it with our faith. Instead of believing a favorite Bible teacher, we need to be reading and believing the Word of God for ourselves. This is how we break the yokes over us.

In many cases, people are stuck and frustrated because they're listening to teaching that is not showing you a way forward. You need to be unstuck and to see a breakthrough in Jesus' name.

To see those blessings and breakthroughs manifested in our life, we must have corresponding actions of faith and belief in the Word of God. Activate the blessings in your life today by acting on what God is asking you to do. He's seeking your obedience. Out of that obedience, you will begin reaping the fullness of the blessings He has planned for you.

PLAN FOR YOUR INCREASE AND HARVEST

It's time to adjust your mindset and act like you know God is bringing you forward. It's time to walk out what you believe and believe God for the impossible.

Many fail here because they attempt to move forward in their own strength. If you want breakthrough, if you want abundance, you must see your life and your future through the lens of God's system. When you do, you will be preparing your heart and mind for your season of breakthrough.

You have dreams, visions, desires, and business concepts inside you. If you believe the Word of God, He's going to do the impossible for you. He is looking for people who will take Him at His Word. Are you that person?

Prepare and Believe for Your Blessing

So many don't believe God will bless them. They're ashamed to believe the promises in God's Word. God, however, isn't ashamed. He said it. He wrote it. It is there for you to read and believe. Don't ever let what you believe get in the way of the Bible. Instead, let the Bible get in your way as you prepare for increase.

Luke 14:28 says, "For which of you, intending to build a tower, does not sit down first and count the cost, whether he has enough to finish it." No matter what happens around you, you need to sit down first and count the cost. Do you believe God enough to stick it out and go the distance? Can you finish what God has for you?

Anyone who launches out in faith shouldn't shrink back (see Heb. 10:38). Doing so will cause you to lose your sense of pleasure in God. Instead, develop the ability to keep moving forward.

Understanding Is Coming

The Word of God breaks the barriers of your mind and heart. It opens the eyes of your understanding.

There's a prophetic mandate coming to the people of God. In due season, the pride of man will fall, and the glory of the Lord will be revealed. Every valley will be raised, and every mountain made low as the glory of the Lord is revealed (see Isa. 40:4).

God is saying over you that the humble will be lifted. Humility means you're surrendered to God's system. You will have a breakthrough understanding when you realize God is breaking you through—by a system.

Stand on a God Idea, Not a Good Idea

Luke 14:29-30 says, "Lest, after he has laid the foundation, and is not able to finish, all who see it begin to mock him, saying, 'This man began to build and was not able to finish'?" Many people start visions with a good idea, but it is not a *God* idea.

My ministry is founded on a God idea. God called my wife and me. That's why it doesn't matter what anyone else says—we're doing what God told us to do. God anointed us, and He's anointed you. I moved forward. You can, too. In Luke 14:31-33 it says:

> *Or what king, going to make war against another king, does not sit down first and consider whether he is able with ten thousand to meet him who comes against him with twenty thousand? Or else, while the other is still a great way off, he sends a delegation and asks conditions of peace. So likewise, whoever of you does not forsake all that he has cannot be My disciple.*

To *forsake all* means everything but God's mandate for you is dead. Jesus reiterates this idea a few verses earlier in Luke 14:26. He said, "If anyone comes to Me and does not hate his father and mother, wife and children, brothers and sisters, yes, and his own life also, he cannot be My disciple." He isn't referring to actual hate but speaking in comparison to your dedication to Him. You should have no regard for anything except God's calling.

To Quote Rocky: "Ain't so Bad!"

You carry out this mandate by letting Jesus love others through you. However, when God tells you to do something, you never let anyone get in your way. You do what God has commanded you to do. You forsake all through obedience of accomplishing your assignments. You consider the cost and finish what you start.

There are many starters in life but few finishers. Most fall after the first hit and never get up again. In ministry, we get knocked down, but we always get back up.

Today, I declare an end to whatever is stopping you. If it knocks you down, get back up. Picture the scene from *Rocky III*. When Rocky was in the ring, his response to Clubber Lang hitting him hard was, "Ain't so bad, ain't so bad." Even though he got hammered in the face, he said with sarcasm, "My mother hits harder than that. Ain't so bad. Come on champ, you ain't so bad!" When you can get that mentality, you can boldly look at darkness and say, "You ain't so bad. You've got nothing." It's not about rising up in the flesh. It's about realizing breakthroughs are available to those who have staying power, count the cost, and never give up.

Mind, Mouth, and Actions

Never give ground to the devil. Press forward. Believe God's system. When you do, you'll have the kingdom of heaven manifest, and it will break hell's economy. In the middle of the battle, hell's economy may ask, "Did God really make that promise?" Satan came to Eve with a question to make her doubt God's Word, too. You need to prepare for this question by getting the Word of God in your mind, mouth, and actions.

It means preparing to seek first the kingdom of God. It means writing your vision and making it plain. It means speaking your vision and declaring, "I'm in God's system and God's economy."

When you do this, you'll feel confident in casting your care on Him. This breaks hell's economy and brings happiness into your daily routine. God's peace and joy bubble up inside you. You'll be overwhelmed by simply looking around your surroundings and seeing all that God has done for you.

DECLARATION OVER YOU

I proclaim that your mind and heart will agree and line up with the Word of God. I pray you will seek first the kingdom of God with boldness, pushing back the darkness at every turn, and pressing into the fullness of every blessing and form of happiness God has for you.

I declare God is bringing your breakthrough today in Jesus' name. I believe God is saying hell's economy is broken off of you and your family. All the attacks against you, your children, and your family are broken now. Whatever comes against you, God is breaking things through for you right now. You are seeking first the kingdom of God and manifesting the supernatural culture of heaven all around you. You are altering this world by speaking the kingdom of God and acting on His Word. You can do this!

Your family has a bright future in God's economy!

Chapter Twenty-Eight

BREAKING OUT
OF BABYLON

The culture we are living in has taken a turn. Much like the days and seasons of those who have gone before us, we too must rise to meet this hour. Everything has an origin, a point of beginning. We know rebellion and a perversion of God's system was caused by Lucifer. In an attempt to become like the Most High, he rebelled by building his own system, a Luciferian system. This was reinforced during the strange events that unfolded in the Genesis 11 narrative.

> *Now the whole earth had one language and one speech. And it came to pass, as they journeyed from the east, that they found a plain in the land of Shinar, and they dwelt there. Then they said to one another, "Come, let us make bricks and bake them thoroughly." They had brick for stone, and they had asphalt for mortar. And they said, "Come, let us build ourselves a city, and a tower whose top is in the heavens; let us make a name for ourselves, lest we be scattered abroad over the face of the whole earth." But the Lord came down to see the city and the tower which the sons of men had built. And the Lord said, "Indeed the people are one and they all have one language, and this is what they begin to do; now nothing that they propose to do will be withheld from them. Come, let Us go down and there confuse their language, that they may not understand*

one another's speech." So the Lord scattered them abroad from there over the face of all the earth, and they ceased building the city. Therefore its name is called Babel, because there the Lord confused the language of all the earth; and from there the Lord scattered them abroad over the face of all the earth.

—**Genesis 11:1-9**

WE REBEL

The Tower of Babel was built by a well-organized people united to build something in rebellion against God. A leader by the name Nimrod was at the head of this ancient project. His name means "we rebel"—how fitting considering what they were attempting to accomplish. Nimrod and his followers settled in an area named Shinar; it was a city, likely industrious and excelling as a world leader in their day. The decision to make this monstrosity was their way of saying, "We will be like the Most High; we don't need God, we are all sufficient in our own ability."

They set out to build a tower reaching to heaven. Now, this is a widely misunderstood image. By the term, tower, most think it was a modern marvel of their day and an engineering feat unlike anything the world had seen at that time, or even by today's standards.

UNAUTHORIZED ACCESS TO THE SPIRIT REALM

What they were creating was a tower for access to the supernatural. In the ancient world, flat topped pyramids were regularly utilized for worship of various gods and much more nefarious activities, including but not limited to human sacrifice. This is what the Bible refers to as "causing their children to pass through fire." "We rebel" defines the occult environment for the deed they were looking to perform. They were creating an access point to and from the spirit realm.

For rebellion is as the sin of witchcraft.

—1 Samuel 15:23

Rebellion being labeled as equal to witchcraft is a comparison. Just as rebellion in the natural is a defiance of authority, so is witchcraft a defiance by unauthorized access into the realm of the spirit. God forbids it, as it is a gateway of permission. The spirit realm works by laws, just like the natural realm does. Take gravity, for example—if you defy this law, it can harm or even kill. What was unfolding here was the creation of unauthorized access for the purpose of evil powers that began in Genesis 6 with the angels who rebelled, saw the daughters of man, and took them as wives. This is where the monster race of giants comes from; additionally, this was the point of pollution in mankind's bloodline. Why? To stop the Messiah from being born.

BAD BLOOD

Noah was pure in his generation; it means he was one of the only individuals left on the planet who wasn't polluted. God was preserving the blood line so Jesus could step onto the earth. Additionally, all the killing and wiping out of towns, along with its women, children, and sometimes even the animals, was due to the same issue of irredeemable people whose blood lines were corrupt. God was fighting to get Jesus on the scene, by a virgin, with a non-polluted bloodline.

ZIGGURAT

Towers such as the Tower of Babel were known as ziggurats. Each culture built them a little different, but they usually had stairs going straight up the front to the top, or in a zigzag configuration. They were not towers built high enough to reach heaven, but rather as a supernatural portal. Some speculate it was to visit another realm. In this realm, fallen angelic entities were awaiting permission from mankind to engage them for even more insidious behavior on the earth, beyond what had already been done.

> *But the Lord came down to see the city and the tower which the sons of men had built. And the Lord said, "Indeed the people are one and they all have one language, and this is what they begin to do; now nothing that they propose to do will be withheld from them."*
>
> **—Genesis 11:5-6**

God had to intervene. He struck them by confusing their language, stopping the entire affair.

Today, the world is again functioning in one language, through the internet, and is more of a global community than anytime in modern history. Culturally, God has been removed to a large degree. Humanism and self-reliance, boasting an independence from God or even denying the thought of God, is a growing trend on a global scale.

As alarming as this has proven to be for believers around the world, this is not new. Nothing is really new under the sun. It is new for this generation—the former days of reasonable ideas regarding God and a moral society are fading quickly. A new Babylonian system is here, and its ultimate aim is control. It wants to dictate what you think, what you say, how to spend, where you will go, and what you will do. If you violate the demands of this new school of thought, you will be punished. Memories of liberty and freedom will become a thing of the past at the rate society is going.

Now more than ever, it's your time. The battle raging is not with flesh and blood; the battle is with rulers of wickedness in high places—a fight that is waged through intimidation and guilt. When it comes to provision, a dependence on God is required to a very high level.

Remember how we started this book?

It Was Dark in Egypt, but It Was Light in Goshen

We are once again symbolically in the land of Egypt and the answer is the same—God shining light in darkness through you! Hell's system is seeking to have its day, but it has a real problem—you're still here. Hell's economy believes it can bankrupt the church. Although this may be true for the institutionalized sectors, it is not true for those who walk in the Spirit and have made the Lord Jesus Christ their source. These individuals will supernaturally outrun their enemies in the rain. These individuals will survive and thrive through everything the enemy has to throw at them.

Now is your time to step into complete surrender and become fully persuaded that nothing can separate you from the love of God. If nothing can separate you from His love, everything a Babylonian system can muster will not be enough. Here is why: Jesus, as your guide, will take you through every pitfall and trap that hell can throw at you.

Supernatural Guidance

In A.D. 70, Jerusalem was surrounded by her enemies. The city was sieged, taken, and ultimately razed to the ground. There was, however, a group of individuals who avoided the entire conflict. Do you know who it was? Believers who placed faith in the words of Jesus in Mark 13:14-15:

> *"So when you see the 'abomination of desolation,' spoken of by Daniel the prophet, standing where it ought not" (let the reader understand), "then let those who are in Judea flee to the mountains. Let him who is on the housetop not go down into the house, nor enter to take anything out of his house."*

This was a prophetic reference by Jesus stating the signs to look for, and when they saw them happening they should get out of town immediately!

Those who stand near the Lord will always have a way of escape. It was true for John the apostle, who was boiled alive in oil. Due to his persuasion that God loved him, he was not harmed and went on to write the Book of Revelation! Your time to draw near to the Lord is no longer optional; it is a necessity. Through drawing near in prayer, worship, and radical, Spirit-led giving, there will be a supernatural protection that comes upon your life. You and your household will experience deliverance after deliverance from the spirit of the age.

We are going to get into what I believe a *last-days* wealth transfer could look like. Not only do I believe it's possible, but I believe it's necessary. We will take a biblical approach to considering what you and the corporate body of Christ has the authority to receive.

By walking out your calling, positioning yourself, and following the high call of God on your life, you will break Babylon's system and hold over your future. If you are doing the will of God for your life, it won't matter what control and evil is placed in front of you, you'll overcome it! It doesn't matter if all the money fails; you're a giver and a tither. If necessary, a fish will cough up a coin, a raven may have to feed you, or five loaves and two fish might just have to multiply on your behalf. When you place God in the position of provider and truly rely on Him as your source, He will not be mocked—whatever you sow, you will reap.

You surrendering to God with your faith switched on, keeping fear far away, is an overwhelming force against the powers of darkness. God needs your belief! The antichrist and all the forces of darkness cannot withstand you with your power on. Do not be distracted; this is a prophetic message to you as you read this—prepare, make ready, stand on the promises, act accordingly, and be in the location you are called to be in. If you don't know, pray and seek the Lord until peace floods you enough until you do know. The combination of a surrendered believer will cause Babylon and hell's economy to crumble wherever you are.

God has called you—get serious, be disciplined, rest in the promises, and watch victory unfold for you and your loved ones. You can't be beaten.

Chapter Twenty-Nine

LAST-DAYS WEALTH TRANSFER

Arise, shine; For your light has come! And the glory of the Lord is risen upon you. For behold, the darkness shall cover the earth, And deep darkness the people; But the Lord will arise over you, And His glory will be seen upon you. The Gentiles shall come to your light, And kings to the brightness of your rising. Lift up your eyes all around, and see: They all gather together, they come to you; Your sons shall come from afar, And your daughters shall be nursed at your side. Then you shall see and become radiant, And your heart shall swell with joy; Because the abundance of the sea shall be turned to you, The wealth of the Gentiles shall come to you.

—Isaiah 60:1-5

TIMES OF CRISIS CREATE OPPORTUNITY

Crisis often creates opportunity, and the days we are living in only qualify for more opportunity. It is encouraging to know that there is a Bible trend for us to see victory while facing unbelievable odds. You are living out a Bible story right now whether you realize it or not. The question is, will you be positioned for your part in a corporate anointing to receive what God has made available? If you recall, we walked through the concept of a corporate anointing earlier, and it is a vital thing to understand as we step into the understanding of a *last-days* wealth transfer.

For years, the terminology of *wealth transfer* has been thrown around. It sounds profound yet has produced very little substance. Here is why I believe that is. We are collectively the body of Christ, and within the body of Christ there have been multi-millionaires and even billionaires. In recent decades came the rise of mega churches and congregations. Even para-church Christian organizations have had tremendous amounts of wealth and resources. This is nothing special—a lot of money has gone through the body of Christ. Yet the global impact of what "could be" has not yet matched what the Bible suggests—a worldwide shift in the axis of power. The components needed for this axis shift would be global crisis, and the righteous preemptively being positioned in the *grace lane* they are called to walk in. Elements of crisis and alignment would set things up for a transition of power. As far-fetched as something like this may sound, it is possible. History is no stranger to moments of regime changes and national restructuring.

Constantine's Model Didn't Work

National restructuring by force or a Christian regime is not the will of God. Emperor Constantine, among other historical figures, could be cited as a global leader who had so much power. To some degree, he began to legislate various aspects of Christianity. There are many who believe we should be taking over—if necessary, by force. Everything about taking over in a "dominion theology" or "kingdom now" mindset sounds great until you realize dominion has everything to do with taking territory, with the exception of the heart. Without the heart, it's just another crusade.

Religion that is forced is not what God wants, nor should any of His people. Rather, what is in order is for genuine believers to attain seats of influence through the church, government, marketplace, and every other seat of authority.

Not Through Force, but Through Influence

Influence is what is required to shine your light, but here is the issue—it requires God's people to seriously consider if they are where they are supposed to be. Questioning if you are where you are called to be is serious business and must be answered because it impacts nearly every part of your future. Many respond by saying, "I will do what God wants me to do, I just don't know how to find what that is or how to even begin." Solutions for this issue are very present but require being a disciplined follower of Jesus through His Word and prayer. It may require a season of focused separation with Him. Most people sadly don't take their walk with the Lord seriously enough to discover His will for their life. Every believer must intensely seek the Lord as if their whole life and destiny depend on it—because it does!

Purpose of a Wealth Transfer

There is an idea about wealth transfer that it's a currency amount so large that we will just buy our way into a new culture. A nice idea, but money alone doesn't solve the purpose of a wealth transfer. It must also be for a purpose and positioning. When you begin looking at generational purpose rather than generational wealth, the narrative changes. It's vital that "purpose" be what is transferred to the next generation. Without it, the financial substance will only last as long as their consumer habits allow.

For decades, my wife and I have preached all over the world. In those travels, we have experienced a variety of encounters with individuals who hold unique beliefs. It is not uncommon to hear a person tell us that they are going to be a billionaire or exceedingly wealthy. There is nothing wrong with this type of belief, but usually it is coming from a well-meaning person who is broke and struggling to survive. Now, I am certainly not casting judgment on anyone; for many years, Heather and I were impoverished to the point of embarrassment. We sowed our way out and have since proved God's economy works if you will work it! What I'm talking about is the believer who is living in the clouds; they are filled with wishful thinking. They are hoping for something toward which they have taken no steps of action, including no measurable steps to get into God's economy, such as tithing, sowing, or partnering with the preaching of the gospel. They don't do any of the necessary things, and they often don't have a steady job or any form of consistency to show their faithfulness. Yet they believe God is going to supernaturally hand them millions, billions, or even trillions worth of currency. That is crazy and is never going to happen!

For starters, that goes against the principles of God's Word regarding faithfulness and stewardship. The idea that one person will have trillions in currency, setting them up for whatever they want, is like a Holy Ghost lottery mentality. This is not to say a faithful person who sows and shows intense diligence can't experience wild increase, favor, abundance, and more. However, it is still not God's highest and best. It is vital to step away from pipe dreams about wealth transfer. Also, it's vital to understand that increase on a personal level is not all there is. It will take far more than this to see major change. The purpose of wealth transfer is to ultimately see the gospel go around the world through the corporate body of Christ. This is what God will supernaturally finance. This is His heartbeat; this is what makes God rich—souls.

INDIVIDUAL FAITHFULNESS LEADS TO CORPORATE VICTORY

And as they heard these things, he added and spake a parable, because he was nigh to Jerusalem, and because they thought that the kingdom of God should immediately appear. He said therefore, A certain nobleman went into a far country to receive for himself a kingdom, and to return. And he called his ten servants, and delivered them ten pounds, and said unto them, Occupy till I come. But his citizens hated him, and sent a message after him, saying, We will not have this man to reign over us. And it came to pass, that when he was returned, having received the kingdom, then he commanded these servants to be called unto him, to whom he had given the money, that he might know how much every man had gained by trading. Then came the first, saying, Lord, thy pound hath gained ten pounds. And he said unto him, Well, thou good servant: because thou hast been faithful in a very little, have thou authority over ten cities. And the second came, saying, Lord, thy pound hath gained five pounds. And he said likewise to him, Be thou also over five cities. And another came, saying, Lord, behold, here is thy pound, which I have kept laid up in a napkin: for I feared thee, because thou art an austere man: thou takest up that thou layedst not down, and reapest that thou didst not sow. And he saith unto him, Out of thine own mouth will I judge thee, thou wicked servant. Thou knewest that I was an austere man, taking up that I laid not down, and reaping that I did not sow: wherefore then gavest not thou my money into the bank, that at my coming I might have required mine own with usury? And he said unto them that stood by, Take from him the pound, and give it to him that hath ten pounds. (And they said unto him, Lord, he hath ten pounds.) For I say unto you, That unto every one which hath shall be given; and from him that hath not, even that he hath shall be taken away from him. But those mine enemies, which would not that I should reign over them, bring hither, and slay them before me.

—Luke 19:11-27, KJV

The above Scripture is the parable of the ten minas. A fascinating understanding is revealed in this passage. First, notice that the reward for being faithful with the portion given them was equal to what they would receive in return. It is also fascinating to understand that the nobleman wanted increase on what he invested and turned over to each of these individuals. The nobleman also sized them up according to what he knew they could handle and produce. He knew each one's capacity for responsibility. When one of them did not produce what the nobleman knew he could, this caused issues.

Points we can learn from this:

1. The nobleman invested into each one what he knew they could handle.

2. The nobleman wanted a return on his investment.

3. The reward for good stewardship was territory.

4. The one who failed the stewardship test had his financial holding given to the one with the most.

5. How the individual with only one mina viewed the nobleman was how he in return was treated by the nobleman. "Thou knewest that I was an austere man, taking up that I laid not down, and reaping that I did not sow. Take from him the pound, and give it to him that hath ten pounds."

What is the lesson here? The way you view God is how you may receive from Him. It is our responsibility to be a good steward of what we are given. This in turn leads to picking up the investment given to the unfaithful. The reward of good stewardship is territory and responsibility. How does this apply to a wealth transfer? When you become positioned and are a good steward, which means you increase what God gives you, a reward of territory and responsibility comes into your possession.

Here is the takeaway. If you do what is prescribed above, you will take territory by the hand of God. Now, unite this action of one individual with the actions of many who do the same thing. What will happen is major territory is taken corporately as the body of Christ. Ultimately, we will be positioned through good stewardship to reap territory, cities, and more. Biblically, this is how the fundamentals of a corporate anointing work. Many individuals today most likely would keep increasing for their own benefit and giving to this or that cause along the way. Although there is nothing wrong with this, and it is most likely how the vast majority would handle their increase, hell's economy would be destroyed and never recover if the corporate body of Christ applied the principles in Luke 19:11-27.

Faithfulness with what you have, and increase united with other like-minded believers who have the same experience, will destroy hell's economy. Let's cheer them on and together take massive amounts of territory until the corporate presence of the body of Christ demands an explanation by the world. This is what I believe is possible in a *last-days* wealth transfer.

God Desires a Unified Body

What is God looking for? He is looking for a unified body. As a matter of fact, it is my personal belief that a wealth transfer will only be to the magnitude of a unified body.

A unified body of believers on a large scale would by default release an unprecedented wealth transfer and a miraculous supernatural shift in the culture. In a time of crisis, with people coming unglued around the world, we are anointed to be the solid lighthouse people run to. We as the united body would offer hope and stability. The antichrist will come as a counterfeit to disrupt true global peace and stability. If there is a counterfeit, there must be the *real*. Ultimately, Jesus will become the legitimate world leader, correcting and healing the world during the millennial reign of Christ, referenced in the Book of Revelation and the prophets. However, we are in a time when everyone is looking for answers—when markets inevitably will crumble, institutions will fail, the world will go into complete turmoil. We the body of Christ will have an opportunity to be positioned and draw all those who are desperate to escape the chaos into a place of peace.

It is possible for this generation or a future generation to step into a position of influence and financial authority as a united global super-power. Every generation has this opportunity, but who will take it? Even if the body of Christ rises and it is not to be attained in our generation, that doesn't mean it's not possible. I believe the absolute will of God will come to pass no matter what. However, there is also the opportunity God gives us.

Jesus Marveled at Exceptional Faith

Remember, Jesus marveled at exceptional faith. For example, in Matthew 8:5-13 the centurion soldier said in verse 8, "But only speak a word, and my servant will be healed." He went on to say, "For I also am a man under authority, having soldiers under me. And I say to this one, 'Go,' and he goes; and to another, 'Come,' and he comes." Jesus marveled and said, "Assuredly, I say to you, I have not found such great faith, not even in Israel!"

What a statement by Jesus! This means to me that instances like the centurion or the woman with the issue of blood have meaning. The woman with the issue of blood, in Mark 5:25-34, reached out and took hold of Jesus' garment evoking a response from Him: "Who touched me?" She wasn't standing on a Scripture for this miracle; she said within herself, "If I can touch the hem of His garment, I will be made well." When you apply radical, fully persuaded faith toward anything from God, it will get His attention! You can make such a draw on what is available that even Jesus might be surprised.

Your Faith Can Interrupt God

One more example: Jesus had given up His Spirit on the cross, died, and went to take the captives captive. He went to Abraham's bosom, also known as *paradise*. From there, He led them out and was taking a parade to heaven. Psalm 24 tells us the story.

Lift up your heads, O ye gates; and be ye lift up, ye everlasting doors; and the King of glory shall come in. Who is this King of glory? The Lord strong and mighty, the Lord mighty in battle. Lift up your heads, O ye gates; even lift them up, ye everlasting doors; and the King of glory shall come in. Who is this King of glory? The Lord of hosts, he is the King of glory. Selah.

—Psalm 24:7-10, KJV

The volley of declarations regarding Jesus went back and forth. Following Jesus was not only angels, but those who were in Abraham's bosom; they followed along as well. This is after Jesus made an open display on the powers of darkness and took the keys of death, hell, and the grave!

Mary Interrupted Jesus' Parade

But Mary stood without at the sepulchre weeping: and as she wept, she stooped down, and looked into the sepulchre, and seeth two angels in white sitting, the one at the head, and the other at the feet, where the body of Jesus had lain. And they say unto her, Woman, why weepest thou? She saith unto them, Because they have taken away my Lord, and I know not where they have laid him. And when she had thus said, she turned herself back, and saw Jesus standing, and knew not that it was Jesus. Jesus saith unto her, Woman, why weepest thou? whom seekest thou? She, supposing him to be the gardener, saith unto him, Sir, if thou have borne him hence, tell me where thou hast laid him, and I will take him away. Jesus saith unto her, Mary. She turned herself, and saith unto him, Rabboni;

which is to say, Master. Jesus saith unto her, Touch me not; for
I am not yet ascended to my Father: but go to my brethren,
and say unto them, I ascend unto my Father, and your Father;
and to my God, and your God. Mary Magdalene came and
told the disciples that she had seen the Lord, and that he had
spoken these things unto her.

—John 20:11-18, KJV

Something fascinating happened during this spectacle. A woman found herself searching for the body of her Lord at the garden tomb. As she did, she saw someone she assumed was the gardener. "Please tell me where you laid Him." Finally, this individual said to her, "Mary." "Rabboni!" she responded. Why bring this story up? Well, Jesus was in the middle of the largest celebration in all of history up to that time. He was leading the parade to heaven! Suddenly, He must have had to stop everything. Someone who loved Him was pulling on Him. Mary desired to see Him so intensely that she interrupted His party by her longing faith. She pulled Him out of the realm of the Spirit and into the natural. How do we know? Because Jesus said, "Do not cling to me, for I haven't ascended to My Father." Wow! This proves she interrupted His planned ascension. A vital understanding can be gained through this—when we do things in faith that line up with God's Word, like taking Him at His promise, there is something special that happens.

Much like the story of Mary, or Peter getting out of the boat and walking on water, there are moments we can stretch our faith based on His Word. Through this, tremendous things can happen. I personally believe the Lord loves over-the-top, faith-filled actions demonstrated by us toward Him.

Along with faithfulness, sowing, and stewardship, this kind of faith is required to see the impossible happen! You will only receive to the level you believe. Wealth transfer is not a necessity or a commandment, much like the receiving of blessings, healings, or any other thing the Word of God says we can have. It is something that must be pursued by revelation. The key element is corporate unification. With that in place, I believe a *last-days* wealth transfer is possible.

JOSEPH AND HIS GENERATION'S WEALTH TRANSFER

> *So when the money failed in the land of Egypt and in the land of Canaan, all the Egyptians came to Joseph and said, "Give us bread, for why should we die in your presence? For the money has failed."*
>
> —**Genesis 47:15**

As we looked at Joseph early on, Joseph was prepared for the seven years of famine. He was positioned to make Egypt the most powerful nation in the world, but only for the purpose of taking what they had accumulated. The wealth of the wicked is stored up for the righteous. Joseph literally brought this prophetic Scripture to pass by his obedience to God. The seven years forced all the surrounding peoples and nations to give over their money, food, and finally themselves. This all changed the day God's people left Egypt with all the gold, silver, and precious things. The wealth of Egypt was stored up for the righteous—those who had covered their doors with blood and had survived the ten plagues. These individuals were the recipients of what was accumulated during the time of Joseph. Generational purpose was in place in order for the exodus of God's people to go into the land of promise.

The Word of the Lord Tested Joseph

Until the time that his word came to pass, the word of the Lord tested him.

—Psalm 105:19

Of the utmost importance, it is vital for you to remember that Joseph spent years of his life not seeing what he was promised. It was a test for him, carrying his God-given dream while he experienced the opposite of what the Lord promised. Due to his tenacity and resilience, Joseph spent years being positioned until finally his day came. This was a result of refusing to falter on what the Lord showed him in his dreams as a boy. The takeaway—do not faint. It will come to pass if you have the staying power and selflessness to see it through!

What a Wealth Transfer Looks Like

We are going to dissect this prophetic passage of Scripture in Isaiah 60 to get a glimpse of what a global wealth transfer might look like.

Arise, shine; for your light has come! And the glory of the Lord is risen upon you. For behold, the darkness shall cover the earth, and deep darkness the people; but the Lord will arise over you, and His glory will be seen upon you. The Gentiles shall come to your light, and kings to the brightness of your rising. Lift up your eyes all around, and see: they all gather together, they come to you; your sons shall come from afar, and your daughters shall be nursed at your side. Then you shall see and become radiant, and your heart shall swell with joy; because the abundance of the sea shall be turned to you, the wealth of the Gentiles shall come to you. The multitude of camels shall cover your land, the dromedaries of Midian and Ephah; all those from Sheba shall come; they shall bring gold and incense, and they shall proclaim the praises of the Lord. All the flocks of Kedar shall be gathered together to you, the rams of Nebaioth shall minister to you; they shall ascend with acceptance on My altar, and I will glorify the house of My glory.

—Isaiah 60:1-7

Global Darkness

Verse 2 of the above passage talks about darkness covering the earth and the people. This describes a time of crisis, and it is in times such as this when opportunity arises. This is likely the description of a global darkness, a crippling terror much like the darkness that covered Egypt for three days. During this time, the darkness is not only covering the earth! It covers the people and the earth. This darkness is twofold.

1. Darkness that covers the people is the removal of light or revelation. Romans 1:21 says, "Because, although they knew God, they did not glorify Him as God, nor were thankful, but became futile in their thoughts, and their foolish hearts were darkened." Psalm 27 also refers to the Lord as light. First John additionally says God is light. This reference to darkness is the removal of God from thinking, society, and in their believing. It is a complete perversion of the mind and culture.

2. This is a full manifestation of the gates of hell setting up its nefarious system on a global scale—a cultural darkness

unlike anything the world has seen before. It is possible that this refers to a literal darkness as well. What we can see is that this darkness impacts the entirety of the planet.

The Lord Will Arise

The Lord will counter the darkness by rising. How does God rise? Over you! By causing His glory to be seen upon you. What this may be describing is a literal glow on the people of God, like the face of Moses when he returned from the mountain. It will be a distinction from the darkness that prevails on the earth at that time. Pure light shining through the righteous on that day will cause a reaction. Gentiles will be drawn to this light, to the brightness of your rising, meaning the believers will be put on display. Now this is where things become epic.

It will be on both Gentiles and kings, average people all over the world (Gentiles) and those in authority (kings). A revelation comes upon the people of God in Isaiah 60:5, saying, "You shall see and become radiant, and your heart shall swell with joy; because...."

Global Wealth Transfer

Pay close attention to this part. "The abundance of the sea shall be turned toward you; the wealth of the Gentiles shall come to you." The term *abundance of the sea* is important. The "sea" throughout the Word of God is often a direct reference to the nations, all the different types of people and ethnic groups from around the world. *Sea* in this passage is a way of describing what someone could argue was the entire world population. At the very least, there are many nations represented. It goes on to say "the wealth of the Gentiles." Notice it doesn't say *Gentiles* in a general way, it uses the definite article twice: "*the* wealth of *the* Gentiles shall come to you." It doesn't leave a lot of room for thinking something other than the wealth of the Gentiles. "Gentiles" is a reference to everyone and every nation outside of God's kingdom. They will not only come to you but all the wealth they possess will come to you as well—whether they bring wealth or not.

Regardless of whether the unbelievers, wicked people, or those in darkness bring their wealth willingly or unwillingly, this picture paints the wealth of the world as coming to you. A transfer is happening here. When Isaiah 60:5 describes seeing this and becoming radiant and your heart swelling with joy, I'm reminded of Proverbs 10:22: "The blessing of the Lord makes one rich, and He adds no sorrow with it."

The blessing of the Lord is behind this wealth transfer because only the blessing causes a heart swelling with joy and radiance! God is behind this transfer. The statement "the wealth of the Gentiles shall come to you" is additionally a result of the blessing because the blessing "makes" one rich. The remaining verses, even into the rest of Isaiah 60, deal with what the belongings and ownership of the received wealth looks like.

HELL'S ECONOMY HAS PRIORITIES IN REVERSE

> *Therefore do not worry, saying, "What shall we eat?" or "What shall we drink?" or "What shall we wear?" For after all these things the Gentiles seek. For your heavenly Father knows that you need all these things.*
>
> **—Matthew 6:31-32**

Gentiles, unbelievers, those who are rooted in hell's economy seek certain things. They don't seek spiritual truth because they are not able to discern it. They are not seekers of God's kingdom as Matthew 6:33 says to be. Gentiles seek what they will eat, what they can drink, what they can wear. In other words, they are seeking "stuff"—physical needs and comforts. They desire monetary means that will provide them with the things they seek. As believers, we are not to seek these things; rather, we are to seek the kingdom of God and His righteousness, then all these "things" will be added unto us (see Matt. 6:33).

Again, this is a place of positioning. How do you seek first the "kingdom" to be positioned? Through being where God has called you to be and by sowing seed. In proper order with the kingdom of God, as first priority, you will supernaturally have all these other things added to you. Remember what we learned about the blessing—it makes one rich! The blessing makes these things—what you shall eat, what you shall drink, what you shall wear (and everything you desire in line with God's Word)—come to you.

GENTILES COME TO YOUR LIGHT

Isaiah 60 references the Gentiles coming to your light. Why? Because they come to what draws them—stuff, things, and monetary provision. These are the things they seek. Consider what this means. The Gentiles will one day come to God's people, both because they see a light on you in a world of darkness and because you possess all the things they seek. You will own all their stuff!

As I said before, the greatest wealth transfers always arrive during famine and crisis. As is the case in Isaiah 60, darkness shall cover the land and deep darkness the people. Yet it is God's economy that has surprising wealth hidden away for those who enter His system.

A good man leaves an inheritance to his children's children, but the wealth of the sinner is stored up for the righteous.

—**Proverbs 13:22**

I will give you the treasures of darkness and hidden riches of secret places, that you may know that I, the Lord, who call you by your name, am the God of Israel.

—**Isaiah 45:3**

For the earth will be filled with the knowledge of the glory of the Lord, as the waters cover the sea.

—**Habakkuk 2:14**

Once again, the sea is a reference to people from all over the world—every tribe, tongue, and nation. The above Scripture, Habakkuk 2:14, is an allusion to the knowledge of the glory of the Lord covering the earth as the waters cover the sea or all the people on earth. The end game for God is to have the gospel reach every person—that is what the knowledge of the glory of the Lord means.

If you get behind that, position yourself in the path God has called you into, then you are being prepared for a potential end time wealth transfer. The body of Christ is literally called to change the world! You are called to take your place in history by participating in the corporate body of Christ. Your life is needed now more than ever, and you mean more to the big picture than you might realize.

Chapter Thirty

ON A BAD DAY, YOU'RE THE BEST THERE IS!

It must be said, and you must hear it. In a world of darkness, in a culture gone rogue, creating a slope for evil to plunge deeper into its own mire—society will arrive at a place of chronic desperation. Surely God has a plan! Surely God has something prepared to spring on the world at the last moment! He must have a secret weapon; His very best, the last line of defense, the accumulation of generations who have paved the way to where we are in blood. The great God of heaven certainly must have His plan and response to launch against this onslaught of darkness!

He does! It's you!

GOD BELIEVES IN YOU

You are marked and called by God to stand in the blood of Jesus and take territory unlike any other time in history. This is it! We are at the 12th hour; we are at the one-yard line, and He has chosen you to be alive during the most significant time in our history. No matter the cost, no matter the assaults, regardless of the global crises coming in wave after wave. Remember this—on a bad day, you are the best there is!

God is so smart, and He chose you to be present during this time. If you don't believe it, believe in the God who placed you on the planet. He believes in you and calls you to be the answer for this generation because Christ is in you, the hope of glory!

You're Made in His Image and Likeness

One of the greatest lies the devil told goes to the beginning when Satan spoke to Eve in the Garden. "For God knows that in the day you eat of it your eyes will be opened, and you will be like God" (Gen. 3:5). The devil attempted to persuade God's original children into believing a half-truth regarding their relationship with the Father and their identity. The devil's intent was to convince Adam and Eve that God was holding back something from them. The actual truth was they were already like God! "God said, 'Let us make man in Our image, according to Our likeness'" (Gen. 1:26). God's very first action toward mankind was to bless them. God's very first words were "be fruitful and multiply" (Gen. 1:28).

The devil's lies are the same lies today. He instills a sense that you don't deserve anything from God and that God is withholding something from you. This kind of thinking is a lie from hell! God's desire has always been that His kids occupy and take over the family business. God created it; He wants His family to run it all.

Your Presence Should Demand an Explanation

When walking in the midst of a dark and perverse generation, remember, you're different. The world is dead; you're alive. This means your presence should demand an explanation. Whenever you show up, Jesus just walked in, because He resides in you. It's your time for confidence—shake off the old grave clothes, be loosed of everything that so easily entangles you, and run with endurance the race that is set before you. Just like Jesus, the author and finisher of our faith, who for the joy set before Him endured the shame. You, my friend, were that joy set before Him!

It's Only Forever

A man of God named Dave Duell, whom I loved and ministered with, would often say, "Hey, it's only forever!" He graduated to heaven a few years ago. As I go through life and do everything possible to impact the world for Jesus, his words come back to me: "It's only forever." Knowing that you have an eternal destination is a comfort, but it also gives a sense of determination. Eternity is where we will receive the rewards or results of missed assignments. This personally gives me drive to live for significance. In eternity, you will not be floating on a cloud or in a nebulous state of consciousness, barely recognizing other saints who have gone before you. As I've referred to before, my wife, Heather, broke her neck and actually visited heaven for a time. She and I have spoken extensively about her encounter there. What we have to look forward to, even on the lowest level, is absolutely amazing. It is not an abstract experience; it's far more real than the "here and now." Eternity is a place of rewards and new assignments for the righteous.

Kings and Priests

And has made us kings and priests to His God and Father, to Him be glory and dominion forever and ever. Amen.

—Revelation 1:6

And He has on His robe and on His thigh a name written: KING OF KINGS AND LORD OF LORDS.

—Revelation 19:16

Jesus is the King of kings and the Lord of lords. Understanding the meaning behind this is a wonderful and sobering thought. Remember back to the part where we looked at the parable where we are called to rule and reign forever with Jesus. We are kings and lords. He is the King of the kings and Lord of the lords!

And as they heard these things, he added and spake a parable, because he was nigh to Jerusalem, and because they thought that the kingdom of God should immediately appear. He said therefore, A certain nobleman went into a far country to receive for himself a kingdom, and to return. And he called his ten servants, and delivered them ten pounds, and said unto them, Occupy till I come. But his citizens hated him, and sent a message after him, saying, We will not have this man to reign over us. And it came to pass, that when he was returned, having received the kingdom, then he commanded these servants to be called unto him, to whom he had given the money, that he might know how much every man had gained by trading. Then came the first, saying, Lord, thy pound hath gained ten pounds. And he said unto him, Well, thou good servant: because thou hast been faithful in a very little, have thou authority over ten cities. And the second came, saying, Lord, thy pound hath gained five pounds. And he said likewise to him, Be thou also over five cities. And another came, saying, Lord, behold, here is thy pound, which I have kept laid up in a napkin: for I feared thee, because thou art an austere man: thou takest up that thou layedst not down, and reapest that thou didst not sow. And he saith unto him, Out of thine own mouth will I judge thee, thou wicked servant. Thou knewest that I was an austere man, taking up that I laid not down, and reaping that I did not sow: wherefore then gavest not thou my money into the bank, that at my coming I might have required mine own with usury? And he said unto them that stood by, Take from him the pound, and give it to him that hath ten pounds. (And they said unto him, Lord, he hath ten pounds.) For I say unto you, That unto every one which hath shall be given; and from him that hath not, even that he hath shall be taken away from him. But those mine enemies, which would not that I should reign over them, bring hither, and slay them before me.

—Luke 19:11-27, KJV

He who is faithful in what is least is faithful also in much; and he who is unjust in what is least is unjust also in much. **Therefore if you have not been faithful in the unrighteous mammon, who will commit to your trust the true riches?** *And if you have not been faithful in what is another man's, who will give you what is your own? No servant can serve two masters; for either he will hate the one and love the other,* *or else he will be loyal to the one and despise the other. You cannot serve God and mammon.*

—Luke 16:10-13

REIGNING OVER TERRITORY IN ETERNITY

This parable in Luke 19, as well as Luke 16:11, has prophetic implications. Rewards for how stewardship is handled here on earth will play out in eternity. Notice that the types of rewards involve ruling over territory—cities, to be exact. Please understand, you were not created to live in heaven. Adam was created to rule the earth. In the end, there will be a new heaven and a new earth. The new earth is where we will reside and begin ruling. Much like the Garden of Eden, man was told to tend to it and take dominion over it. It is highly likely that had Adam not fallen, he and Eve would have continued expanding the Garden until the entire earth was under their dominion. It could be that they would have continued into the solar system until they even occupied other planets, causing them to flourish as well. It's only speculation, but ruling and reigning with Jesus for eternity, could mean we will be responsible for expanding God's kingdom to the ends of the universe. This might be how we would exercise our kingship and lordship. Who knows what He has in store for His sons and daughters after we get past this present age. The Book of Revelation states that we will reign forever and ever.

> *And there shall be no more curse, but the throne of God and of the Lamb shall be in it, and His servants shall serve Him. They shall see His face, and His name shall be on their foreheads. There shall be no night there: They need no lamp*

nor light of the sun, for the Lord God gives them light. And
they shall reign forever and ever.

—Revelation 22:3-5

What we do here and now is what will determine the level of reigning you will experience in eternity.

GOING RED

And they overcame him by the blood of the Lamb and by the
word of their testimony, and they did not love their lives to
the death.

—Revelation 12:11

Now is the time to stand up and enforce the covenant promises on this earth. You are called to rise in this time, overcoming by the blood of the Lamb and the word of your testimony, and not loving your life even unto death. This is the formula for overcoming. In reference to the Blood of Jesus, His covenant, and all that it provides, we use the phrase "going red." For many years, our ministry and audience have become known as the "Red Church." Not a denomination, not a doctrine, just a simple understanding that anyone, anywhere, who is washed in the Blood of Jesus will rise, regardless of doctrinal differences that are not heaven or hell issues.

If Jesus is your Lord and you're covered by His blood, then I consider you part of the Red Church. We are His blood-bought body. We know our covenant rights. "Going red" is a statement declaring Jesus is Lord, and we are covered in His blood. We're "going red" no matter what circumstances we face in our lives. This also carries the idea that we are to take the covenant of God to the ends of the earth by the preaching of the gospel. This is the highest responsibility a believer has. It is the number one way we break hell's economy and make God rich. You need to "go red" and take the message of Jesus to everyone you meet.

This is what God gets behind financially and in every other resource and way that He has made available to us. He who wins souls is wise, according to Proverbs. Why? Because lost souls are the only thing God does not have. *Going Red* means we take the gospel of Jesus to them, winning them to Christ and making disciples. A person being saved is the only true thing we can give to God. A person saved and matured in the things of God is more valuable to the Lord than finding a gold mine. To Him it would resemble receiving an inheritance of untold value. Psalm 116:15 gives us insight into the value God places on His mature saints.

> *Precious in the sight of the Lord is the death of His godly ones.*
>
> **—Psalm 116:15, NASB**

> *Precious (important and no light matter) in the sight of the Lord is the death of His saints (His loving ones).*
>
> **—Psalm 116:15, AMPC**

The word *precious* in this verse is the Hebrew word *yaqar,* which also means "costly." This verse could read: "Costly in the sight of the Lord is the death of His godly saints."

When God loses a mature believer to the grave, although He is thrilled to receive them in eternity, the cost is great on this earth. Why? Because of their experience and wisdom, the abilities they possessed from years of maturing their gifts and knowing Him at a high level, are no longer working on the earth. Within the global population, there are very few who know God through a disciplined life of surrender, prayer, and consecration. Few are tenured warriors, accurately tuned in to the Holy Spirit, having weaponized faith from years of practice. These rare ones are highly effective agents for the kingdom and are not easily replaced. The Lord of heaven only has so many of this caliber of believer in each generation.

Remember, there are two things that make God rich:

1. Lost souls getting saved. Converts who are transformed into mature believers through discipleship.
2. A tenured saint who lives a long life enforcing God's will on earth. These individuals are highly valuable to the Lord.

There are darker days coming than we ever imagined. The kind of darkness our society is facing must be met by supernatural, mature believers. If Jesus tarries, the body of Christ must step into its full potential as an unbeatable global superpower, highly capable of thwarting the powers of darkness. Together, we can effectively destroy the works of the devil; should the *catching away* of the saints happen sooner than later, the kingdom of darkness would breathe a sigh of relief!

A fire-baptized church, red with the blood of Jesus, releases a punishment against the darkness that it cannot tolerate. The current plans of evil cannot prevail with the church of Jesus Christ standing in the way.

Together we can break hell's economy, destroy strongholds over many lives, and ultimately change the world. It begins with you. You are the answer. My friend, I am so thankful you took this journey with me. I bless you in the Name of Jesus and declare that your best days are before you. That you will discover your place in the body of Christ.

I hope to see you out there on the battlefield. As a united front, we will push back the agenda of darkness. I believe you will rise to your divine occasion. God believes in you, and so do I. Don't shrink back—you are so valuable to all of us. As you continue to give your *yes* to the Lord, He will position you. It's your time to break hell's economy!

For Jesus,

Joseph Z

ABOUT JOSEPH Z

Joseph Z is a Bible teacher, author, broadcaster, and international prophetic voice. Before the age of nine, he began encountering the voice of God through dreams and visions. This resulted in a journey that has led him to dedicate his life to the preaching of the gospel and the teaching of the Bible, often followed by prophetic ministry.

For nearly three decades, Joseph planted churches, founded Bible schools, preached stadium events, and held schools of the prophets around the world. Joseph and his wife Heather ministered together for 15 years and made the decision in 2012 to start Z Ministries, a media and conference-based ministry. During this time, they traveled the United States, taking along with them a traveling studio team live broadcasting from a new location several times a week. A season came when Heather became very ill due to hereditary kidney failure. After three years of dialysis and several miracles, she received a miracle kidney transplant. Joseph and Heather decided to stop everything, they laid everything down and ministered to their family for nearly three years.

In 2017 Joseph had an encounter with the Lord and received the word to "go live every weekday morning"—Monday through Friday. What started with him, Heather, and a small group of viewers, has turned into a large and faithful online broadcast family. Today, his live broadcasts are reaching millions every month with the gospel and current events—which he has labeled "prophetic journalism." He additionally interviews some of the leading voices in the church, government, and the culture.

He and his wife, Heather have two adult children that faithfully work alongside them. Joseph's favorite saying when ending letters, books, or written articles is, "for Jesus." As, "for the testimony of Jesus is the spirit of prophecy." —Revelation 19:10

Joseph spends his time with his family, writing books, broadcasting, and training others in the Word of God.

For Further Information

If you would like prayer or for further information about Joseph Z Ministries, please call our offices at

(719) 257-8050
or visit **josephz.com/contact**

Visit JosephZ.Com for additional materials

School of the Prophets

School of the prophets is volume 1 of a growing prophetic master course. It includes 39 video sessions with a corresponding manual and audio files. The material inside was developed by Joseph Z from nearly three decades of training believers around the world at conferences and events. This course thoroughly covers the office of the prophet, how you are called to prophesy, dreams, visions, visitations, strange encounters, word of knowledge, predicting the future, deja vu, trances, what society calls empaths, and so much more! You will discover that the word of God is the final authority on growing your gift of prophecy. This course is not just for prophets but is designed specifically for everyone in the Body of Christ!

Demystifying the Prophetic

Throughout this powerful teaching Joseph Z brings clarity and understanding to things such as déjà vu, multidimensionalism, strange happenings and a variety of common prophetic encounters. Taking a realistic approach in explaining these unique experiences and breaking them down supernaturally as well as scientifically. In part two of this series Joseph Z talks about capacity, leadership, and how not to institutionalize a revelation. You will learn the difference between mature and immature believers function in the voice of God with this BIBLE LOADED teaching!

Archangels - Servants of Fire

Angels have a duty to minister to believers in Jesus, because God has given them charge over us. Your relationship with Angels is highly important as you relate to them through the activated Word of God. They witnessed the fall of Lucifer and know what is in store for mankind. According to the apostle Paul, believers will judge fallen angels. There are many powerful advantages to knowing more about angels. As you listen to this message, prepare to gain biblical knowledge about angels, and to unlock their full potential, for YOUR benefit today!

Surviving a Jacked-Up World

In this series Joseph Z teaches on how to survive and thrive in a world of darkness. He elaborates on how the systems and nations of the world continue to silence and put more demands on the body of Christ. Joseph also highlights historic events that took place when it came to standing for the truth no matter the cost. Explaining how the governing authorities have been sabotaged to fit into the demonic system to usher in the spirit of Antichrist. He expounds on how the Body of Christ has the power to thrive and survive by having Jesus as their Lord which gives them peace, authority, and power to overcome. At the end of this series you will realize that we are called to arise in the boldness and strength of Jesus within us. You will also discover the balance between doing what God wants us to do and obeying the governing authorities.

Anger of Satan

You are the reason Satan transitioned from being Lucifer (an Archangel of glory) into the Devil, History's most vile celestial villain. His hatred for mankind has led him on a strategic rage filled agenda to destroy mankind as the ultimate vengeance toward God for creating mankind. This Series will give you a great understanding of how valuable you are and also the strategy of the Devil to remove from us the understanding of the "COMPLETE GOSPEL". You will learn that the Gospel we have all heard preached is correct but it is not complete until it is working through you. In this series, you will not only learn about Satan and

his origin. You'll uncover the answers to some of the questions you've always had but never asked, and begin a journey of victory, Sonship, and taking your dominion as a free moral agent over the powers of darkness.

Secret To the Life of John

SECRET to the LIFE OF JOHN is a teaching series that will blow the lid off popular fatalist point of views regarding destiny and YOUR quality of life. There was a massive difference between John and all his peers. This difference made a life altering impact on his destiny. His SECRET is so powerful it is a MUST HAVE REVELATION for every believer. YOUR LIFE will be magnificently impacted by the truth found in this series. Get ready to have a paradigm shift in your faith!

Apologetics - Defending the Faith

In a world of uncertainty and many who base their reality on emotion, this series will offer you tools to stand up for what you believe. Apologetics is often misinterpreted to mean an apology. When in fact, the proper definition of apologetics means to have an answer for your faith. It is important to understand that we as believers in the Word of God can be empowered to give confident and reasonable answers to Biblical topics in Love. You will learn some basic thoughts and ideas that will strengthen your confidence in what you believe as well as influence the world around you with truth and power based on the world view of a thinking believer.

Spiritual Warfare

Since the fall of Adam, there has been an ongoing war between the forces of good and evil. Oftentimes, we see free moral agents (humans) being entangled with the agents of darkness and used for nefarious activities. When we hear the phrase 'spiritual warfare', a lot of us have misconceptions about it, fueled by our cultures and age old superstitions. We are all warriors in a war and Christ came to offer us redemption from Satan's captivity. He came to destroy the works of the devil and bring him to nothing. The devil has no power over you and he knows this. Prepare to be enlightened on the dynamics of spiritual warfare, to enable you to unlock some raw spiritual horsepower that is guaranteed to send Satan and his cronies running.

Wealth of Jesus

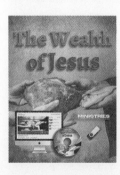

The world wants us to believe that Jesus operated in poverty and lack while on earth. Throughout His days on earth, Jesus was able to meet needs even before they became visible to those around him. All authority has been given to Jesus, both in heaven and on earth. Wealth has never been a concept Jesus operates in because He is above it. Jesus truly mastered wealth and as His representatives, He expects us to do the same. You'll come to learn through this series that Jesus has an endless supply of wealth, but having a knowledge of it is not enough, as God expects us to key into that covenant of wealth!

Stay Connected by Downloading the Joseph Z App

Search "Joseph Z" in your preferred app store.

Uncensored Truth

LIVE Chat

Prophetic Journalism

Real Time Prophetic Ministry

Interviews with Leading Voices

Video Archives

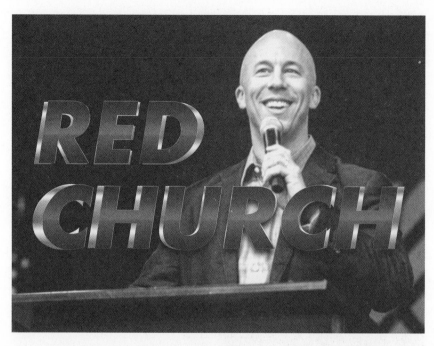

Red Church LIVE Weekly Broadcast!

Join Joseph LIVE Every Weekday Morning
Monday through Friday
on All Social Media Platforms!

Equipping Believers to Walk in the Abundant Life

John 10:10b

Connect with us for fresh content and news about forthcoming books from your favorite authors...

Facebook @ HarrisonHousePublishers

Instagram @ HarrisonHousePublishing

www.harrisonhouse.com